THE MG FILE

AN ERIC DYMOCK MOTOR BOOK

THE MG FILE

MODEL BY MODEL

AN ERIC DYMOCK MOTOR BOOK

DOVE PUBLISHING

First published in Great Britain in 2001

by

DOVE PUBLISHING
Old West Kirk Manse, 31 Argyle Terrace, Rothesay, Bute PA20 0BD

Text copyright © Eric Dymock 2001

Designed by Ruth Dymock
Jacket design Andrew Barron

ISBN 0 9534142 3 X

British Library Cataloguing-in-Publication Data A catalogue record
for this book is available from the British Library

Colour separation by Colourwise, Burgess Hill, West Sussex

Printed and bound in Singapore by Tien Wah Press

Contents

Introduction

It is possible to spend a lot of time and effort defining a brand, yet nothing identifies it more surely than its products. Drivers since the 1920s have known that MG means affordable active driving. The MG File shows how this reputation was and is being developed, paints a portrait of MG and its sporting achievements, drawing the threads of its history together model by model right up to the present.

This book contains details, diligently researched, of the MGs made since Cecil Kimber took his first tentative steps at The Morris Garages in the shadow of Oxford's old city walls. Heritage is important to MG and it is the brand values that defined the envelope within which MG Rover engineers have worked in creating a new generation of MGs. The inheritance of the best part of eighty years, making what the author of The MG File calls Britian's best-loved sports car, was in their minds throughout one of the most vigorous development cycles in motor industry history.

The MG File will be an important source of reference for the cars that established MG's heritage, and it also charts MG's history in motor sport. What other car could have captured hearts and minds in 1930s Italy, the spiritual home of motor racing, like MG did in the classic Mille Miglia. MG had a fine tradition of punching above its weight in long-distance racing at Brooklands and at Les Vingt-Quatre Heures du Mans.

The same goes for new MG Rover Group. It now has the resilience to be a long-distance runner and win against strong odds. I am delighted to welcome the MG File, first edition.

Kevin Howe
MG Rover Chief Executive

MGs exemplified the sports two-seater. Although seldom the fastest cars of the day or the most expensive, MGs became part of the British way of life, the stuff of summer weekends or romantic novels. An MG was a staple of children's die-cast miniatures, touching the emotions of the young and the young at heart alike. The MG Midget of 1929 lit a spark of enthusiasm that never went out, even in the 1980s when production of traditional open sports cars was suspended.

Even if the Bright Young Things of the 1930s did not have quite the glamour of the Bentley Boys, they had MGs. In the 1940s the archetypal RAF pilot climbed out of his MG into his Spitfire and in America, heartland of the large softly sprung gas-guzzler, an MG was a nimble precise sports car raced by amateurs. Professor Richard Knudson and his fellow

New England MG enthusiasts embraced its advertising slogan: "The Sports Car America Loved First". Some cars became classics because there were so few of them. MGs became classic because there were so many.

**Left: Longwall 1912.
Mr Morris's Oxford garage
selling wide range of cars.
Morris Oxford prototypes
were built here by city wall,
but only MG was Kimber's
14/40 Sports 2-seater
"Old Number One"
FC 7900 in 1924.**

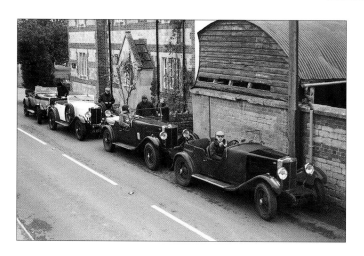

Top: the Early MG Society prepares for a strenuous weekend.

Far right: Syd Enever (in no 61) in relaxed mood after the 1931 Brooklands Double Twelve. Alec Hounslow is passenger in the car behind.

The creation of MG Cars was so curiously recondite that the opening years of the 1920s are littered with claimants to be the first MG. Some romantic histories by Alfred Edgar Frederick Higgs, or Barré Lyndon as he preferred to known, did little to disperse the mists obscuring the former livery stables in Longwall Street Oxford where the roots of the make were put down. MG evolved in a world in which expediency was more vital to survival than taking notes for posterity. Lyndon made his name as a Hollywood scriptwriter, and his books enshrined MG in dramatic folklore. He bequeathed a legacy of myth and legend that gave MG an epic quality beyond the realms of anything so prosaic as a car.

The creation of MG belongs to Cecil Kimber and William Morris, later Lord Nuffield, in the 1920s and 1930s. Wiry ambitious Morris was a bicycle racer before the turn of the century, selling bicycles from a shop in Queen Street, Oxford. He repaired them in premises in Longwall Street, graduating to selling cars with agencies for Arrol-Johnston, Humber, Belsize, Hupmobile, Singer, Standard and Wolseley. The workshop was known as The Oxford Garage, changed to The Morris Garage, then in 1913 to The Morris Garages or MG. Morris had been hiring out cars since 1905 and by 1912 he was making them.

There was nothing grandiose about the early years. Morris began assembling cars at a former military training college leased in nearby Cowley from parts made elsewhere, and in 1912 appointed Edward Armstead to run the sales department at Queen Street. In 1922 this expanded to a picturesque mews in Alfred Lane, later called Pusey Street, where selling twenty cars a week was brisk business.

The Morris Oxford of 1913 had a 1018cc T-head engine made by local firm White & Poppe, and by the end of 1914 over a thousand cars at £175 were sold. The larger 1,548cc Cowley with American Continental engine came just as war intervened. By the time the cars reappeared afterwards, wartime import duty had made their engines too pricey, so Hotchkiss in Coventry was making them instead. Morris made a virtue out of being essentially an assembler of cars rather than a manufacturer. His advertising boasted: "Each part is made by an expert". Nevertheless he also liked buying suppliers, to control every aspect of car manufacturing, and keep the profit from each. Hotchkiss became Morris Engines Branch.

However competition was keen and Morris had to slash prices to make good his orders for components. A Cowley 2 seater cost £495 in October 1920, £299.10s a year later, £225 by October 1922. His survival was a close-run thing, and although by 1925 he was outselling Austin and Ford, he was also delighted to find Morris Garages selling profitable premium-priced special editions of his cars. Following the price cuts, margins on the regular Cowley and Oxford were narrow.

Left: Support car for EX120 when it tackled the 100mph record. M-type Midget was up to carrying two spare wheels.

In 1922 Edward Armstead left The Morris Garages and committed suicide. Morris was buying up every supplier he could find and in the course of negotiating with E G Wrigley, which made axles, came across Cecil Kimber, a bright executive who was losing his savings as the firm failed. He saw the quality and ingenuity of a born salesman and made Kimber general manager at Morris Garages. Significantly Morris did not appoint Kimber to Morris Motors; the job he had in mind needed more specialised skill.

The MG story began in earnest when Kimber duly created a sideline. Besides selling, servicing, and repairing new and used cars, he was fitting them up with a variety of coachwork, just as bespoke carriage builders did for wealthy customers. Cars still featured a separate chassis and body, and although perhaps not especially inventive Kimber, like William Lyons in Blackpool and EC Gordon England in North London, had an eye for style. He pampered a middle-class clientele, allowing them to specify an individual design in the same way as their betters in the luxury market. Even though the chassis was made by the humble W R M Motors Ltd, the

Why MG?

Out of compliment to Sir William R. Morris, Bt., we named our production the M.G. Sports, the letters being the initials of his original business undertaking, "The Morris Garages," from which has sprung that vast group of separate enterprises including THE M.G. CAR COMPANY, Pavlova Works, Abingdon-on-Thames.

principle was the same and Kimber supplied them with special coachwork, made by Raworth of Oxford, or Carbodies of Coventry. Mr Morris may have disapproved of the interruption to the smooth flow of sales, but put up with it for the money.

Cecil Kimber carved out the octagonal initials and added pedigree to Morris's homely ingenuity. Born in Dulwich, London, of a scholarly family, Kimber's limp was a legacy of a youthful motorcycling accident, but he displayed a managerial tenacity that seemed to appeal to Morris. Kimber identified what the world's motor industry came to know as niche marketing. He was convinced there was a demand for a car costing 20 per cent extra, provided it was 10 per cent faster, but it was not an easy proposition to put to the parsimonious Morris in 1924.

The Morris Garages Cowley Chummy of 1924 turned out to be cheaper than Morris's, so Morris stopped making the plain Sports Cowley, a poor seller anyway, and the stage was set for a car that was not only stylish but also fast. Morris owners bought engine conversions such as Pope Ricardo aluminium cylinder heads at £8 15s 0d (£8.75), or

From Longwall to Longbridge

overhead valve sets from Chesterfield or Lap at around £25. But extra speed on its own was not enough; it did not show. The customers wanted a car with an appearance, name and reputation.

MG advertising was not noted for modesty and was not above pulling stunts such as demonstration runs up a Cornish trials hill. The Super Sports Morris it promised:
"Will climb the famous Porlock Hill at 24 miles an hour. The gradient for this noted acclivity is one in five and the Treasury Rating of the car is only 11.9hp. It will be seen therefore, that the inherent possibilities of the famous Morris engine can be brought out by those who know how. The result is an exceptionally fast touring motor car capable of 60 miles an hour on the flat, and wonderful acceleration. The modified steering and springing gives a glued-to-the-road effect producing finger-light steering at high road speeds. Mounted on this out-of-the-ordinary chassis is the most delightful two-seater body imaginable. Beautifully comfortable, with adjustable seat and single dickey, the finish is of the highest class and the style irreproachable. The 'tout ensemble' is one of the finest productions we have ever turned out from our famous Queen Street showrooms. For a car of such distinction the price, £350 is extraordinarily modest."

The significance of the announcement was that for the first time an MG octagon was superimposed on Super Sports Morris. The first MG car then? Not quite, although it can be argued that MG as a make dated from this May 1924 issue of The Morris Owner.

From Longwall to Longbridge

Far left: Syd Enever (on right) pushes the Earl of March's C-type to the start of the 1931 Brooklands 500 mile Handicap. His oily overalls contrast with the driver's immaculate whites; Enever was the practical machanic whose ingenuity would result in MG's most successful cars. His chassis design for the MGA with its splayed side members was a stroke of genius.

Left: octagons abounded at MG. They were embossed on the cars' upholstery, office typewriters had a special octagonal MG key, and here in the Abingdon test house the instrument boards are eight-sided.

From Longwall to Longbridge

Top: Nuvolari in K3
winning the 1933 TT.
His riding mechanic
Alec Hounslow (waving)
became MG development
engineer right up to the
advent of the MGB GT V8.

Before the first batch of Super Sports Morrises was finished, an order came in for a Morris Oxford with an aluminium four-seater body. Kimber liked it so much that he based a new model on that as well. Changes to the Oxford chassis, which was brought in complete then stripped and reassembled included flattened springs, lowered steering, raised axle ratio, and a tuned engine. Mudguards were painted smoke blue or claret, or a colour to match the upholstery, a matching hood and carpets enhanced the polished aluminium body. Both two and four-seat versions of the MG 14/28 were built in Pusey Street during 1924, with polished aluminium Ace discs on beaded-edge artillery wheels. The first MG at last? Again not quite, although the MG octagon featured on the car for the first time, on the step-plates in the door sills.

The 14/28, according to author of 'Early MG', Phil Jennings, 'offered 10 per cent better performance, 50 per cent better handling, and 80 per cent better appearance than the standard Morris Oxfords on which they were based.' Kimber's success lay in achieving the improvements at only a 20 per cent increase in price.

MGs were often road-going facsimiles of cars made for trials, the quaint British sport of driving up muddy hills, or rally cars. It was the 1930s before they began to look like racing cars. The 1930 MG Six Mark III Road Racing Model had only one type of body, an open four-seater made to international racing regulations. It had sketchy wings and small back seats, and was the last of the tall six-cylinder MGs made between 1928 and 1933, survivor from the Vintage years.

Sport became an essential ingredient of MG. The great Italian driver Tazio Nuvolari drove one to a memorable victory in the 1933 TT, a notable endorsement of MG's international standing. The following year MG won again over Bentley. MG K3 Magnettes won the team prize and the 1100cc class in the Mille Miglia, an away win against Italy on its home ground at a sport in which it excelled. MGs broke records, and EX127 the 'Magic Midget' was the first 750cc car to do 120mph. In 1939 Lt Col AT "Goldie" Gardner's EX135 made a deep impression in Germany when it exceeded 200mph on the autobahn with an engine of only 1100cc.

The only MG to be made at Morris Garages' workshop at Longwall Oxford was Kimber's Old Number One FC7900. It had simple machine tools but no space for production. In 1922 Kimber acquired premises in Alfred Lane to make the Chummy and the first 14/28s. More room was soon needed so

Below: Lt Col Alfred Thomas Goldie Gardner, inveterate record-breaker, was first and foremost a racing driver. Awarded an MC in 1916 he was badly wounded in the hip, and crashed his C-type in 1932 aggravating his injuries. Seen here at Brooklands with the ex-Horton K3 that led to EX 135.

TRIPLEX SAFETY GLASS
"FORT" DUNLOP TYRES

The M.G. MAGNA
'L' Type Salonette

£345 *ex Works*

This delightful Salonette on the M.G. Magna chassis combines luxurious coachwork with the well-known M.G. sporting performance. The sliding roof with its dainty windowlets gives a well-lighted effect to the interior. The leather-covered pneumatic upholstery, the deep pile carpets, the Purdah glass rear window, and the generously-equipped facia board, all combine to make this little Saloon the finest value obtainable in present-day sports cars. Luggage accommodation has not been overlooked, and the rear panel of the car folds outwards, making a neat luggage platform. The bodywork is obtainable in any of the M.G. two-tone colour finishes without additional charge.

in 1925 Kimber persuaded Morris to let him use space at Osberton, radiator suppliers in Bainton Road Oxford, which Morris had acquired, and was turning into Morris Radiators. MG occupied spare bays there until 1927 when it moved once again, to a factory specially built at a cost of £20,000 in Edmund Road, Cowley. There was no paint shop so MGs had to be sent for mudguard fitting and painting to Morris Garages coachwork repair shop in Leopold Street Oxford.

Finally in September 1929, such was the success of MG, production was moved to Abingdon-on-Thames to the Pavlova leather factory. Pavolva had built extensions to its factory to fulfil demand for belts, holsters, harnesses, and military equipment during the 1914-1918 war. It was now surplus to requirements and became MG's production home for fifty years and spiritual base afterwards for the MG Car Club.

Within a few years of the move to Abingdon, MG was imperishable. Kimber's legacy was a romantic vision of a sports car, made in the rural heart of Britain. He was fond of little homilies in MG advertisements and not above a certain amount of self-publicity. He drew an analogy with one of his other passions, sailing:

"Sometimes I steal away from Abingdon and go sailing at the week-end. To my mind there is something in common between sailing and motoring. One does not sail merely for speed's sake. What matters most is the way your craft handles, whether she's racing along with a stiff breeze abeam, or tacking against wind and tide. Now isn't that the secret of the charm of MG cars. They're fast, admittedly, but what matters most is the way they handle, whether you're dawdling along enjoying the spring sunshine, or shaking out a reef and making the knots along an empty arterial road."

As a result of Kimber's visionary marketing MG, as part of the Nuffield empire in the 1940s and 1950s then as a

Left: Chris and Noel Shorrock (left) of the supercharger company with Goldie Gardner in striped tie. John Thornley with his foot on the Y-type's running board stands with Syd Enever, John Crook, David McDonald (Dunlop Mac) and Reg Jackson. The occasion is Goodwood record attempt and the photograph is signed by Dick Benn (extreme right), owner of this Shorrock-supercharged 1¼ litre Y type.

component of the British Motor Corporation (BMC) and its successors, gained a strong following. Kimber had a feel for cars and a feel for customers, yet he was ill served for his efforts. On July 1 1935 Lord Nuffield sold MG and Wolseley to Morris Motors Ltd. Leonard Lord was its managing director and the

charmed life that Kimber had enjoyed under Nuffield was not to last. Lord first cancelled MG's racing programme but as the late Wilson McComb the notable MG historian wrote: "Lord has often been blamed for this step, but the decision was taken by Nuffield. For years he had allowed Cecil Kimber far more freedom than his other managers, but he believed that the first duty of his various organisations was to build cars for the public. There seems little doubt that the advent of the blatantly single-seater R-type was more than he was prepared to tolerate in the way of idealistic Kimberisms. Did he make the right decision? Almost certainly yes, for Kimber had so little restraint that he was quite capable of pouring money into racing as eventually to bankrupt MG."

Lord demoted Kimber from managing director to general manger and in 1941, following a disagreement over Abingdon's role in war work, Nuffield sacked him. Cecil Kimber remained in the motor industry but he was disillusioned and unhappy at losing any chance of taking part in the sports car revival after the war. In February 1945 he died in a railway accident outside King's Cross.

Cecil Kimber at MG and William Lyons at Jaguar had the same kind of vision, the same eye for detail and style. The

Right: 27 May 1971 George Turnbull, briefly managing director of Austin Morris Division of British Leyland poses with the quarter-millionth MGB off the line at Abingdon. Behind is Old Number One rolled out for the occasion. The left-hand-drive Blaze MGB GT was given away as a national sweepstake prize in the USA the following September.

Far left: Brands Hatch 1000-mile sports car event 22/23 May 1965. MGB 8DBL driven by Warwick Banks and John Rhodes, outright winner of the race at average of 75.23mph (121.07kph), finishing seven laps ahead of the next car. MGBs finished 1-2-3 in the 1600-2600cc class.

difference was that Lyons was able to keep control of Jaguar and lead it to achievement and ultimately prosperity. Kimber, subservient to his proprietor William Morris, could not. Yet like Lyons, Kimber demonstrated that a sports car brand could be built on the components and technical resources of a popular volume car range. MG's special Morrises in the 1920s were analogous to SS Jaguar's special sporting Austins.

In the 1930s Jaguar prospered with engines and chassis platforms made by the Standard Motor Company. MG's ambitions to develop its own cars in Kimber's time were thwarted. Beyond a handful designed from the ground up, its technical requirements were met by Morris throughout the years when Morris and MG, together with Wolseley and Riley, both snatched from financial oblivion by Nuffield, formed the Nuffield Organisation. In the 1950s with Austin this became the British Motor Corporation (BMC), then by processes of amalgamation and takeover, culminated in British Leyland (BL) and its successor companies. In due course all was dismantled again and became plain Rover. Yet MG never lost the commercial logic of the 1920s, refining, redesigning, and adding zest and excitement to volume produced cars, making MG the best-known sports car in history.

In 1953 John Thornley was appointed general manager, as dedicated to preserving the Kimber legacy as LP Lord was to erasing it. Lord would have liked to expunge Nuffield too, out of animosity following his dismissal after demanding a share of the business. However he was pragmatic enough to keep MG in business even though he had no time for Barré Lyndon-style romanticism. MG was always better being run by strong-minded individuals. Administration by committees or parsimonious accountants was invariably disappointing. Its success came through practicality, a talent for style, and good value products. Kimber's skill, which he wove into MG culture, lay in knowing his market and securing the means to meet it.

He was backed by a formidable array of engineers, notably Albert Sydney Enever, whose role in MG's survival has not gained the recognition it deserved. Between joining in 1930 until he retired in 1971 as chief engineer, Syd Enever's influence on MG cars was profound. His qualifications were more practical than formal, and he has been accorded less than his due by managements that regarded him more as a skilled artisan than a brilliantly intuitive engineer. EX135, the Gardner MG, and two of the most successful sports cars ever, the MGA and MGB, were the inspiration of Syd Enever.

From Longwall to Longbridge

A hundred thousand MGAs and half a million MGBs came out of the factory at Abingdon-on-Thames. MGs became cult cars, nothing else was ever so brim-full of nostalgia. Yet the celebrations surrounding the fiftieth year of production at Abingdon turned within weeks to dismay when Sir Michael Edwardes, BL chairman announced the factory's closure in 1980. BL claimed it was losing £900 on every MGB it made, but there was deep scepticism that this was an accountant's fiction, and MG simply did not fit in with Triumph-dominated BL's plans. It was scant reward for the 1100-strong workforce's exemplary industrial relations record, but Edwardes could see no future for the symbiotic relationship Kimber had forged between the sports car and the volume car.

Left: Enever's beautifully proportioned MGA blended the traditional MG grile with perfectly tailored lines.

A consortium led by Alan Curtis, chairman of Aston Martin, tried to mount a rescue. Curtis described an unlikely member of it, Lord George Brown Labour foreign secretary 1966-1968, as invaluable behind the scenes. Others included Peter Cadbury, chairman of Westward TV, Norwest Holst the construction group, and David Wickens of British Car Auctions but their bid was rejected and BL refused to relinquish the MG name. The last MGB came off the line at Abingdon on 23rd October 1980 after which the factory was closed, sold off, and redeveloped.

MG went into a sort of suspended animation, applied to sporting versions of BL cars, not all of them unworthily, until the mid 1980s when MG re-emerged under Rover stewardship in the 1980s. Its return from oblivion was actively pursued and the turning point was the MG EX-E of 1985.

This was a concept car designed to show that MG was on the way back, not as a resuscitated backward-looking relic, but as a modern make of car fit for the 1990s. In 1988 British Motor Heritage was created to make new bodies for classic MGs, and the RV8 introduced in October 1992, 30 years after the MGB.

Work had begun on the MGF in partnership with Mayflower Vehicle Systems, a consortium including Motor Panels, a long-established body-building business that made bodies for most Coventry car manufacturers including Jaguar. Ten years elapsed between the EX-E and the MGF during which BL had become Austin-Rover and been absorbed by British Aerospace. As Rover Group it had a partnership with Honda of Japan, then in 1994 was sold to BMW, which invested heavily in it until in May 2000 it was relinquished to the Phoenix Consortium under John Towers for £10.

Towers had moved, by motor industry standards, with the speed of light. An entirely new range of cars was planned as the company moved towards balancing the books. A new programme saw MG variants of Rovers introduced by Towers and his deputy chairman Nick Stephenson, former Rover chief engineer then a senior director of Huntingdon racing car manufacturer Lola. They had been clear about policy before

Left: MGFs in their 1997 colours on the hallowed Brooklands banking where their forebears made their name.

From Longwall to Longbridge

the ink was dry on the May 2000 agreement with BMW. By July they had recruited Peter Stevens, another former colleague at British Leyland, to oversee the design of new MGs. Stevens, whose design credentials include the Jaguar XJR 15, Lotus Elan, and the £650,000 McLaren F1, was soon at work on a series of MGs based on existing Rovers as well as a flagship supercar to compete in the 24 Hours Le Mans race.

Recalling the badge engineering from which British Leyland suffered, Towers was reassuring: "Forget the MG Maestro and MG Montego. These new cars will have different driving dynamics from Rovers and a degree of real performance. The whole experience of owning an MG will be special." He had not overlooked the historical precedent for MGs emerging as developments of an existing saloon and touring range. Cecil Kimber's principles for MG were merely being reapplied and all Rover's 300 British dealers were automatically offered the MG franchise.

Towers paid tribute to the quality and integrity of the cars the new group inherited. The engineering flexibility of the platforms enabled designers to create new cars of strong sporting character, and BMW's quality measurement system was superlative.

MG-Rover's fortunes depended on husbanding its cash-flow, and reorganising itself by concentrating its activities on one site, Longbridge Birmingham. Overheads under the old regime that had to bear the costs of engineers and executives commuting between Munich and Gaydon, the British technical centre, were eliminated.

Managing director then chief executive of Rover up to May 1996, Towers knew what he was getting into. He joined from Perkins as engineering director in 1988 and during his four-year tenure as MD Rover went from a loss of £49 million to an operating profit of £92 million. It was the culmination of a transformation started more than a decade earlier by Sir Michael Edwardes and Sir Graham Day.

MG accounts for a quarter of MG Rover's output. Its re-launch was a characteristic motor industry media extravaganza with loud music, dry ice, flashing lights, racy film and gleaming cars but no troupe of dancers. It was done in dour Longbridge, in the Exhibition Hall across Lowhill Lane from where Red Robbo used to hold massed meetings. Keynote speakers used the sort of hyperbole even politicians would shrink from; the expectation was that the new MGs would be received to warm praise, like the Rover BRM, a short production run of the 200 a couple of years before.

Work on the new cars started well before BMW sold Rover. According to Robe Oldaker, product development director, it was done clandestinely because the cars would have been BMW competitors. Now they could be legitimately regarded as bargain BMWs, appealing to keen drivers at prices starting in the UK under £10,000

By its eighth decade MG had at last achieved some sort of independence. It said a good deal for the deep foundations on which it was built that it had survived at all. It was a testimony to the integrity of the Kimbers and the Morrises and the Lords, Thornleys, Enevers and others that it had survived with its reputation so high.

Right: MGF Super Sports with the first production K3 Magnette under Starkey's Bridge, Donington Park, notorious bottleneck on the old circuit.

At the time of WRM Motors' voluntary liquidation in 1919 (to get rid of burdensome agency contracts) Cowleys and Oxfords both used the same 102in (259.1cm) frame, suspension, controls, 11.9hp Hotchkiss engine, carburettor, gearbox, clutch, transmission, axles, and steering. The two-seat Cowley was the cheaper by £50. Sales improved in 1921 following £100 price cuts, and the Morris Cowley Sports Model was a 2-seater with polished aluminium body, tapered tail, high axle ratio, and "specially tuned" engine. After the last one was produced in October 1922, the price was reduced to clear stock, but Kimber at Morris Garages still found them hard to sell. Accordingly he bought them in as bare chassis and equipped them with bodywork probably by Carbodies. This "Occasional Four", with two 14in (35.6cm) wide inward-facing additional seats demanded a certain "chumminess" between their occupants and those in the front. It was better than a dickey seat however since the hood enclosed all four. Morris Garages lowered the tail by repositioning the three-quarter elliptic rear spring, and orders for batch production were sought from Morris main dealers, Parkside of Coventry and GCR Buist of Newcastle upon Tyne. Upholstery was leather instead of the Cowley's customary Pegamoid.

BODY roadster, 2 doors, 4 seats; saloon, 2 doors, 4 seats.

ENGINE 4 cylinders, in-line; 11.9hp treasury rating; 69.5mm x 102mm, 1548cc; 26bhp (19.4kW) @ 2800rpm; 16.8bhp/L (12.5kW/L).

ENGINE STRUCTURE side valves in L-head, helical timing gears; cast iron block and upper part of crankcase; cast-iron pistons to 1924, then aluminium; 12volt Lucas Magdyno or BTH mag-generator ignition; magneto with self-starter; carburettor SU sloper G2; 3-bearing crankshaft.

TRANSMISSION rear wheel drive; two driven plate clutch with cork inserts running in oil; 3-speed non-synchromesh gearbox; enclosed torque tube; spiral bevel final drive 4.42:1.

CHASSIS DETAILS steel channel-section chassis; suspension, front half-elliptic leaf springs, rear three-quarter elliptic; Gabriel rebound snubbers optional £6.10s (£6.50); brakes on rear wheels only on some models with hand and foot brake operating separate shoes in 9in (22.9cm) drums; Four wheel brake models Elliott-type front axle with 9in (22.9cm) 2-shoe drums; worm and wheel steering; 700 x 80 Dunlop Cord beaded-edge tyres; 3-stud steel artillery wheels.

DIMENSIONS wheelbase 102in (259.1cm); track 48in (121.9cm).

PERFORMANCE maximum speed 56mph (90.1kph); 0-40mph (64.4kph) 30sec; fuel consumption 28-30mpg (9.4-10L/100km).

PRICE Morris Cowley Sports £398 10s (£398.50) reduced to £315.

PRODUCTION 109.

Top right: the Chummy came as either an open car or this rakish saloon de luxe, still essentially a Morris.

Far right: with body "of graceful proportions made of finest possible materials, with one door on near side".

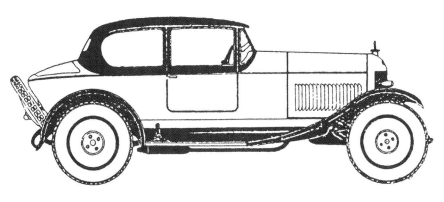

THE M.G. CHUMMY SALOON DE LUXE MORRIS

For the 1924 model year Morris Motors introduced an Occasional-4 that at £215 was a good deal cheaper than Morris Garages' Chummy. Accordingly Kimber brought in a rakish 2-seater with new bodywork by Charles Raworth of Oxford, one of Morris's original suppliers. Modifications to the Oxford chassis were scarcely more ambitious than with the Chummy, and the cars were still essentially specially bodied Morrises, with Morris identity plates and Morris guarantees. The sloping windscreen was flanked by glazed quarter-lights and there were two scuttle mounted marine-style ventilators.

The Raworths and their immediate successors were sold through Morris main dealers who bought the chassis, which was delivered to Morris Garages for modification, and then taken to the coachbuilders. The Morris Garages tested the finished cars before delivery although the firm's main job was still selling and servicing cars, Humbers, Sunbeams, Dodges, and Morrises, and motorcycles including Levis and Sunbeam. The specially-bodied embryo MGs were still a sideline and of the first 11.9hp Raworths only half a dozen were made between the middle of 1923 and 1924. Against the ordinary Cowley and 14/28 the Raworths were expensive and it took the best part of a year to find buyers for them.

BODY roadster, 2 doors, 2 seats.
ENGINE 4 cylinders, in-line; 69.5mm x 102mm, 1548cc.
ENGINE STRUCTURE side valves in L-head, helical timing gears; cast iron block and upper part of crankcase; cast-iron pistons to 1924, then aluminium; 12volt Lucas Magdyno or BTH mag-generator ignition; magneto with self-starter; carburettor SU sloper G2 or Smiths 5-jet; 3-bearing crankshaft.
TRANSMISSION rwd; wet cork clutch; 3-spd manual non-synchro gearbox; enclosed torque tube, spiral bevel final drive 4.42:1.
CHASSIS DETAILS steel channel-section chassis; suspension, front half-elliptic leaf springs, rear three-quarter elliptic; Gabriel rebound snubbers optional; brakes on rear wheels only on some models with hand and foot brake operating separate shoes in 9in (22.9cm) drums; four wheel brake models Elliott-type front axle with 9in (22.9cm) 2-shoe drums;

worm and wheel steering; 700 x 80 Dunlop Cord beaded-edge tyres; 3-stud steel artillery wheels.
DIMENSIONS wheelbase 102in (259.1cm); track 48in (121.9cm).
PERFORMANCE max 65mph (104.6kph); 0-50mph (80.5kph) 19sec; 19mpg (14.9L/100km).
PRICE £350.
PRODUCTION 6 Raworth.

Right: Alfred Lane, the Oxford street where Morris Garages began, forms a backdrop for a 1923/24 Raworth-bodied 2-seater on 11.9hp Cowley chassis.

This Super Sports Morris will climb the famous Porlock Hill at 25 miles per hour

The distinction between specially bodied Morris Oxfords sold through The Morris Garages, and the establishment of MG as a car manufacturer in its own right, is far from clear-cut. An advertisement in the June 1924 Morris Owner magazine used the MG octagon against a picture of a de luxe Landalette on the 14/28 Morris Oxford chassis. The following month there was an MG Sports Four Seater Morris Oxford in "burnished aluminium and smoke blue, or to choice" advertised with "The graceful lines of a yacht." Kimber's other preoccupation was sailing, and it was no surprise that this car too featured ship-style ventilator cowls. In 1925 there was an MG 14/28 Weymann saloon, "absolutely devoid of rattle", with four wheel brakes.

Yet it was not until mid-October 1927 that The Morris Garages registered cars with Oxford County Borough Council as anything other than Morris Oxford or Morris Cowley. One 14/28 was a well finished saloon advertised as "…on the famous 'Imshi' chassis", a reference to a six-month expedition by the Daily Mail's motoring correspondent through France, Italy, Morocco, Algeria, Tunisia, and Spain to prove the worth of the Morris Oxford. "Imshi" was Arabic for "Get a move on."

BODY saloon, 4 doors, 4 seats; coupe, 2 doors; 2 seats; weight 18cwt (914kg). Open 4-seater, 2 doors; weight 18.25cwt (927kg).
ENGINE 4 cylinders, in-line; 75mm x 102mm, 1802cc; compr 5.0:1; 35bhp (27kW) @ 4000rpm; 19.4bhp/L (15kW/L).
ENGINE STRUCTURE side camshaft; side valve; mushroom tappets; detachable cast iron cyl head and block; aluminium pistons; Smith, SU, or Solex carb; 3-bearing crank.
TRANSMISSION rear wheel drive; wet cork clutch; 3-speed non-synchromesh manual gearbox; enclosed torque tube; spiral bevel final drive 4.42:1.
CHASSIS steel channel-section chassis; ash-framed aluminium body; pressed steel scuttle; suspension, front half-elliptic leaf springs, rear three-quarter elliptic; Gabriel snuubers at front, Hartford shock absorbers at rear; Duplex Hartfords on salonette; Four wheel brakes, front patent Rubury, 12in (30.48cm) drums (with optional servo, £20, 1925-1926;

worm and wheel steering; 7 Imp gal (8.4 US gal, 31.8L) fuel tank; 700 x 80 Dunlop Cord beaded-edge tyres; 3-stud steel artillery wheels with Ace discs 1924-1925; bolt-on wire spoke 1925-1926. Saloon 28 x 4.95 Dunlop reinforced balloon tyres.
DIMENSIONS wheelbase 102in (259cm) and 108in (274cm); track 48in (121.9cm); length 152in (386.1cm); width 60in (152.4cm); height 65in (165.1cm) with hood up.
PERFORMANCE maximum speed 65mph (105kph); 19.4mph (31.2kph) @ 1000rpm; 0-50mph (80.5kph) 23.8sec; 26.1kg/bhp (33.8kg/kW) saloon, 26.5kg/bhp (34.3kg/kW) 4-seater; fuel consumption 19mpg (14.9L/100km).
PRICE open 4-seater £375; 2-seater £350; salonette £475; 4-seater salonette without tail compartment £495. Optional equipment included luggage carrier, a variety of mascots, rev counter, spot lights, and a monograme or crest on the door at £2.2s (£2.10).
PRODUCTION approx 400.

33

1926 14/40 and MkIV

In 1926 Morris replaced the bullnose radiator with a flat one that used less nickel but had more cooling capacity. Kimber enhanced it with an appliqué cutout MG octagon. Once again the distinction between models is imprecise and both bullnose and the heavier flat radiator 14/28s were essentially Morris Oxfords with MG Morris Garages bodies. The 14/40 was based on the Oxford, with flattened rear springs, remounted steering box, and raked column. It is more properly an MG and although the "40" represented, as Barraclough and Jennings put it, more of a target than an achievement Leystall tests on one 1927 car did produce 44.1bhp (32.9kW) at 4200rpm.

Kimber introduced Mark numbers because model year designations made selling last year's cars difficult and since he probably regarded the 1924 14/28s as Mark Is, the long-chassis 14/28s of 1925-1926 as Mark IIs, and the 1927 14/28 with flat radiator as Mark IIIs, he introduced Mark IV as the official name for the 1928 and 1929 14/40. MG octagonal motifs were added wherever possible. The model was guaranteed by MG, the chassis plate said MG, it was registered as an MG and in 1927 shown at Olympia on a Morris Garages, not a Morris stand.

BODY saloon, 4 seats; coupe, 4 seats; roadster, 2 seats; chassis weight 15.75cwt (800kg).
ENGINE 4 cylinders, in-line; 75mm x 102mm, 1802cc; cr 5.0:1; 35bhp (26.1kW) @ 4000rpm; 19.4bhp/L (14.5kW/L).
ENGINE STRUCTURE side cam; side valve; mushroom tappets; 2-bearing helical gear drive cam; cast iron cyl head and block; horizontal Solex 30mm carburettor; Lucas GA4 magneto with helical gear drive; 3-bearing crank; Cowley radiator shells on open cars, larger Oxford size on saloons.
TRANSMISSION rear wheel drive; wet cork 2-plate clutch; 3-speed non-synchromesh manual gearbox; enclosed torque tube; spiral bevel final drive 4.42:1.
CHASSIS DETAILS steel tapered channel-section chassis; cast aluminium scuttle; suspension, half-elliptic leaf springs (8-leaf front, 7 rear, 8 salonette), rear shackled half elliptic; Smith rebound shock absorbers at front; Hartford shock absorbers at rear; Four wheel brakes, 12in (30.48cm) drums with shrunk-on stiffeners (servo 1926-1927); Marles worm and wheel steering; 7 Imp gal (8.4 US gal, 31.8L) scuttle-mounted fuel tank; 1 gal (4.5litre) reserve; 700 x 80 Dunlop Cord beaded-edge tyres; 3-stud artillery steel wheels with Ace discs 1924-1925; bolt-on 5-stud wire spoke 1925-1926, 19in x 3.5in rims, 28in x 4.95in tyres.
DIMENSIONS wheelbase 106.5in (270.5cm); track 48in (121.9cm); turning circle 31ft (9.45metres); ground clearance 7.5in (19.1cm); length 150in (381cm); width 61in (154.9cm).
PERFORMANCE maximum speed 67mph (107.8kph); 19.4mph (31.2kph) @ 1000rpm; 22.9kg/bhp (30.7kg/kW); fuel consumption 28mpg (10.1L/100km).
PRICE 2-seater £340, 4-seater £350, salonette 2-seater £475, 4-seater £475; MkIV Sports Salonette £445.
PRODUCTION approx 900, 486 14/40s.

1925 14/40 Super Sports 2-seater "Old Number One"

The provenance of FC 7900 was never in doubt. A Morris Cowley modified in the spring of 1924 at Longwall Lane to Kimber's instructions, it had hand-forged side members curved over the rear axle, carrying out-rigged semi-elliptic springs. The engine was an overhead valve version of the 11.9hp prepared by Hotchkiss for the unsuccessful Glasgow-made Gilchrist.

Old Number One, as it came to be known, was completed with Morris Oxford brakes and its slim 2-seater body was made probably by Carbodies in the spring of 1925. Painted the anonymous shop grey of experimental models and prototypes, the car was registered FC 7900 on 27 March. The chassis frame broke during testing and the repair was discernible throughout its life. Kimber, with his friend Wilfred Matthews as passenger, won a gold medal on the Land's End Trial at Easter 1925.

Although Kimber referred to it as "my first MG," it was not quite, despite the efforts of various BMC and Leyland publicists. The engine was sleeved down to 69mm bore to bring it under 1500cc for the Land's End. It was sold to a friend of Kimber's for £300 and rescued from a Manchester scrapyard in 1932 for £15.

BODY roadster, no doors, 2 seats; weight 15cwt (762kg).
ENGINE 4 cylinders, in-line; 69mm x 100mm, 1496cc; compr 5.0:1; 38bhp (28.3kW) @ approx 3500rpm; 25.4bhp/L (18.9kW/L).
ENGINE STRUCTURE pushrod overhead valves; 2-bearing helical gear drive side camshaft; cast iron cross-flow cylinder head and block; Lucas GA4 magneto with helical gear drive; 3-bearing crankshaft; bronze SU carburettor, hand-pumped air pressure fuel feed; belt-driven dynastart disconnected, starting by handle.
TRANSMISSION rear wheel drive; wet cork single plate clutch; 3-speed non-synchromesh manual gearbox; hypoiz final drive 00.0:1.
CHASSIS DETAILS modified Cowley channel section steel; front suspension half-elliptic springs; rear half-elliptic springs and live axle; drum brakes, 12in Oxford at front, four shoes at rear operated by hand lever; PAS; 000L fuel tank; 710 x 90 tyres, bolt-on wire spoke wheels.
DIMENSIONS wheelbase 102in

(259.1cm); track 48in (121.9cm).
PERFORMANCE maximum speed 70mph (112.65kph); 20mph approx (32.2kph) @ 1000rpm; 0-60mph (96kph) 20sec; 20.1kg/bhp (26.9kg/kW).
PRICE £279 (Kimber's figure)
PRODUCTION 1.

It scarcely matters whether "Old Number One" was the first MG ever; it epitomises the early years of MG and remained a vigorous performer long after its allotted span.

Top left and right: "Old Number One" at Goodwood in 1999.

Cecil Kimber was adamant that his engine came within the 1500cc limit for the Land's End Trial. Details of how this was achieved were vouchsafed to Classic car founding editor Michael Bowler by Syd Beer the noted MG collector. Bowler re-enacts Kimber's exploits (below) and Eric Dymock drives the historic car at Gaydon (far right).

1927 14/40 Featherweight Fabric saloon ("Old Speckled Hen")

Like "Old Number One", claims to be an historic MG could be advanced on behalf of the surviving 14/40 Featherweight saloon. A quest for lighter bodywork was undertaken in reaction to the additional 1cwt (50.8kg) the Morris Oxford had put on in 1926 without a compensating increase in power. Cowley engineer Hubert Charles raised engine power by polishing combustion chambers and valve ports, and fitting stronger valve springs. This improved matters although probably not all engines were up to the 40bhp (29.8kW) the change in nomenclature implied. For 1928 a new 4-door body by Gordon England was introduced, with echoes of the 1926 Riley Nine Monaco.

Detective work by Jonathan Wood and Mike Allison on WL 3450 suggest Old Speckled Hen may have started life as a 14/28 on 9 May 1927, and after its bodywork was fitted was registered on 22 September. A factory demonstrator, it was sold in 1928, but seems to have been returned to be used as a works hack. Its unusual silver-flecked paintwork earned its nickname of "owd speckly un", later articulated as Old Speckled Hen the name adopted by Abingdon brewer Morland for a splendid strong pale ale.

BODY saloon, 4 doors, 4 seats; weight 20.5cwt (1041kg).
ENGINE 4 cylinders, in-line; 75mm x 102mm, 1802cc; cr 5.0:1; 35bhp (26.1kW) @ 4000rpm; 19.4bhp/L (14.5kW/L).
ENGINE STRUCTURE side cam; side valve; mushroom tappets; 2-bearing helical gear drive camshaft; cast iron cylinder head and block; horizontal Solex 30mm carburettor; Lucas GA4 magneto with helical gear drive; 3-bearing crankshaft; Lucas dynamotor starter and lighting set.
TRANSMISSION rear wheel drive; wet cork 2-plate clutch; 3-speed non-synchromesh manual gearbox; enclosed torque tube; spiral bevel final drive 4.42:1.
CHASSIS DETAILS steel tapered channel-section chassis; cast aluminium scuttle; suspension, half-elliptic leaf springs (8-leaf front, 7 rear, 8 salonette), rear shackled half elliptic; Smith rebound shock absorbers at front; Hartford shock absorbers at rear; Four wheel brakes, 12in (30.5cm) drums with shrunk-on stiffeners (servo 1926-1927); Marles worm and wheel steering; 7 Imp gal (8.4 US gal, 31.8L) scuttle-mounted fuel tank; 1gal (4.54L) reserve; 28 x 4.95 Dunlop Balloon tyres; bolt-on 5-stud wire spoke wheels 19in x 3.5in rims, 28in x 4.95in tyres.
DIMENSIONS wheelbase 106.5in (270.5cm); track 48in (121.9cm); ground clearance 7.5in (19.1cm); length 150in (381cm); width 59in (149.9cm).
PERFORMANCE maximum speed 65mph (105kph); 29.8kg/bhp (39.9kg/kW).
PRICE £445.
PRODUCTION 32 featherweight fabric saloons.

Nobody was better qualified to restore Old Speckled Hen than Fred Body. Here (right) the original negotiates a typical gravel surface of the 1920s while a marshal looks for the next competitor.

Introducing the Midget and the 18/80 at the 1928 motor show was a turning point for MG. Production had begun at Edmund Road, and the firm orders at Olympia on which Kimber insisted before committing to a new car, were encouraging. The 18/80 was the first MG to use the distinctive MG radiator, even though it continued with Morris components, and was also the first 6-cylinder MG. Morris engines tended to be basic and side-valve but during Morris's acquisition of Wolseley, with Frank Woollard a former colleague of Kimber's as works manager, it embarked on more adventurous designs with an overhead camshaft. William Morris disapproved of the expense and the engine was unsuccessful in Morrises. The 18/80 was treasury rated at 17.9hp (9 or 17.7) but never attained anything like the implied 80bhp. About 60bhp was the best ever.

Advertisements claimed it had the sports performance and luxurious ease of a two thousand guinea creation, and it was truly a competitor for the contemporary Alvis and Lagonda, remaining a notable MG of the Vintage period. MG designed the chassis, with 6in (15.2cm) deep channel section side members and box-section cross-bracing, and also the axles, although the torque tube transmission was pure Morris.

BODY saloon, 4 doors, 4 seats; sports, 2 doors, 2 seats; salonette, 2 doors, 4 seats; open tourer, 4 doors, 4 seats; chassis weight 19cwt (965kg), 2-seater 23cwt (1168kg), saloon 25.75cwt (1308kg).
ENGINE 6 cylinders, in-line; 69mm x 110mm, 2468cc; cr 5.75:1; 60bhp (44.7kW) @ 3200rpm; 24.3bhp/L (18.1kW/L).
ENGINE STRUCTURE Duplex gear and chain-driven overhead camshaft; cast iron block, detachable cylinder head with pent-roof machined combustion chambers; 2 horizontal SU carburettors; chain drive to distributor, water pump, and dynamo, skew drive to oil pump and distributor; coil ignition; 4-bearing counterbalanced crankshaft.
TRANSMISSION rear wheel drive; five-plate cork insert clutch; 3-speed non-synchromesh manual gearbox; torque tube drive; spiral bevel final drive 4.25:1.

CHASSIS DETAILS steel channel-section cross-braced chassis upswept front and rear; upward-inclined half-elliptic leaf springs front-shackled 34in front and 50in rear; single arm Hartford Duplex shock absorbers; Perrot-shaft 12in finned drum brakes on early cars, later cable brakes, some with servos; Marles steering; 10 Imp gal (12 US gal, 45.5L) fuel tank; 2 gal (9.1L) reserve; 19 x 5 Dunlop Fort tyres; Rudge-Whitworth centre lock wire wheels.
DIMENSIONS wheelbase 114in (289.5cm); track 48in (122cm); turning circle 43ft (13m); gr clearance 8in (20.3cm); length 156in (396cm); width 60in (152cm); ht 67in (170cm) saloon, 62.5in (159cm) 2-seater.
PERFORMANCE maximum speed 80mph (129kph); 20.5mph (33kph) @ 1000rpm; 0-60mph (96kph) 30sec; 19.5kg/bhp (26.1kg/kW) 2-seater; fuel consumption 18mpg (15.7kph).
PRICE chassis only £420, 2-seater £480, Tourer £485, Salonette £545, Saloon £555.
PRODUCTION 500.

Left: 18/80 Curiosity: the moulded MG on the bulkhead upright was neither octagonal, nor could it ever be seen except when the bodywork was entirely removed.

The MG Sports

The M.G. Car Company
Pavlova Works
Abingdon-on-Thames

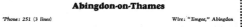

'Phone: 251 (3 lines)   Wire: "Emgee," Abingdon

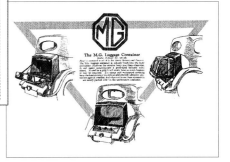

A wider track and a 4-speed gearbox alone would not have justified the substantial prices of the Mark II 18/80. Detailing was careful, aluminium components were polished, engines carefully balanced, and the three-ringed aluminium pistons ground and lapped. An automatic Tecalemit chassis lubrication system actuated by the car's movement extended servicing intervals to 3000miles (4828km).

The Mark II did not replace the Mark I but sold alongside it. Mark I Speed Models meanwhile gained a Brooklands 80mph (128.7kph) certificate for 12 guineas a time, cynics suggesting this was to cover a mechanic's time at the Surrey track making sure it would actually manage it. Triplex safety glass and a Dewandre vacuum brake servo were added but there was a certain amount of equivocation over the additional gear. It was described as a "silent third", a fashionable reassurance in an era of loudly whining gears or "twin top", an admission that there was perhaps not much difference between ratios of 1:1 and 1.306:1. Extra equipment and a more substantial chassis carried a weight penalty of some 3cwt (152kg). Mark I production petered out in July 1931, Mark IIs in summer 1933 but, eclipsed by the success of small MGs, some 18/80s were not sold until 1934.

BODY saloon, 4 doors, 4 seats; sports, 2 doors, 2 seats; salonette, 2 doors, 4 seats; open tourer, 4 doors, 4 seats; chassis 22cwt (1118kg), tourer 27cwt (1372kg), saloon 29.3cwt (1486kg). Speed Model, 2 staggered doors, left front passenger and right rear 25.8cwt (1311kg).
ENGINE 6 cyl, in line; 69mm x 110mm, 2468cc; compr 5.75:1; 60bhp (44.7kW) @ 3200rpm; 24.3bhp/L (18.1kW/L).
ENGINE STRUCTURE Duplex gear and chain-driven overhead cam; cast iron block, detachable cylinder head with pent-roof machined combustion chambers; 2 horizontal double float SU carbs; chain drive to distributor, water pump and dynamo, skew drive to oil pump and distributor; coil ign; 4-bearing counterbalanced crank.
TRANSMISSION rear wheel drive; five-plate cork insert clutch; 4-speed non-synchromesh manual gearbox with remote control; torque tube drive; spiral bevel final drive 4.27:1.
CHASSIS steel channel-section cross-braced chassis upswept front and rear; upward-inclined half-elliptic leaf springs front-shackled 39in (99cm) front and 50in (127cm) rear; rear springs shackled both ends and carried outside the frame; Silentbloc shackle bearings; single arm Hartford Duplex shock absorbers; 14in finned cable-operated drum brakes; Marles steering; 12 Imp gal (14.4 US gal, 54.6L) fuel tank; 2 gal (9.1L) reserve; 19 x 5 Dunlop Fort tyres; Rudge-Whitworth centre lock wire wheels.
DIMENSIONS wheelbase 114in (290cm); track 52in (132cm); turning circle 37ft 6in (11.4m); ground clearance 8in (20.3cm); lgth 156in (396cm); wd 64in (163cm); ht 64.5in (164cm) tourer, 67in (170cm) saloon.
PERFORMANCE maximum speed 80mph (128.7kph); 20.5mph (33kph) @ 1000rpm; 24.8kg/bhp (33.2kg/kW) saloon; 18mpg (15.7L/100km).
PRICE chassis only £550, 2-seater £625, Tourer £630, Salonette £655 (fabric body and Triplex glass), Saloon £670 (coachbuilt).
PRODUCTION 236.

The new four-speed gear box fitted to the M.G. Six Sports
Mark II chassis, showing helical constant mesh gears.
The third is particularly silent and the top is a direct drive.

Primary and secondary shafts are each carried in three ball
bearings, and, which ever gear is engaged, the load is taken
close up against the bearings, thus reducing to a minimum
the possibility of shaft distortion, which is mostly responsible for gear noises.

Top: four-speed
gearbox fitted to
Mk II chassis,
showing helical
constant mesh gears.

The Mark II Speed Model was a slow seller. It cost £100 more than a Mark I and although on the face of it a bargain, it was still a heavy car. Its tall radiator had vertical slats with adjustment by thermostatic control. Figures published in *The Motor* showed that a supercharged 2.0-litre Lagonda could do 90mph (144.8kph), a Delage Sports Eight 85.7mph (137.9kph), an Invicta saloon 81.08mph (130.48kph), and an Aston Martin 11.9hp 81mph (130.35kph). Top speed of a Mark I 18/80 Speed Model was 80.36mph (129.32kph). A Mark II 2-seater could only manage 78.26mph (125.94kph) and its acceleration was also slower. A Mark I would reach 60mph in about 30sec whereas a Mark II took 40sec.

The Mark II began a new chassis numbering scheme that survived to the 1950s. This replaced straightforward numbers with a letter prefix, in this case A. Motor industry tradition avoided commencing a series with 0001, and MG chose 0251, which was the factory telephone number. The Mark II 18/80 inaugurated true non-Morris derived MGs even though the engine came from Morris Motors Engine Branch. Conceived by Kimber, and connived at by his old colleague at EG Wrigley, Frank Woollard, as an MG more than a Morris, its pedigree was secure.

BODY sports, 2 doors, 4 seats; weight 22.75cwt (1156kg).
ENGINE 6 cylinders, in-line; 69mm x 110mm, 2468cc; compression 5.75:1; 60bhp (44.7kW) @ 3200rpm; 24.3bhp/L (18.1bhp/L).
ENGINE STRUCTURE Duplex gear and chain-driven overhead camshaft; cast iron block, detachable cylinder head with pent-roof machined combustion chambers; two horizontal double float SU carburettors; chain drive to water pump, and dynamo; skew gear to distributor and oil pump; coil ignition; 4-bearing counterbalanced crank.
TRANSMISSION rear wheel drive; five-plate cork insert clutch; 4-speed non-synchromesh manual gearbox; torque tube drive; spiral bevel final

drive 4.27:1.
CHASSIS DETAILS steel channel-section cross-braced chassis upswept front and rear; upward-inclined half-elliptic leaf springs front-shackled 39in front and 50in rear; Silentbloc shackle bearings; two Hartford Duplex shock absorbers at front; 14in (36cm) finned cable-operated drum brakes; Marles steering; 12 Imp gal (14.4 US gal, 54.6L) fuel tank; 2 gal (9.1L) reserve; 19 x 5 Dunlop Fort tyres; Rudge-Whitworth centre lock wire wheels.
DIMENSIONS wheelbase 114in (290cm); track 52in (132cm); turning circle 37ft 6in (11.4m); ground clearance 8in (20.3cm); length 156in (396cm); width 64in (163cm); height 64.5in (164cm) tourer, 67in (170.2cm) saloon.
PERFORMANCE maximum speed 78.3mph (125.9kph); 20.5mph (33kph) @1000rpm; 0-60mph (96kph) 40sec; 19.3kg/bhp (25.9kg/kW); 18mpg (15.7L/100km).
PRICE £630.
PRODUCTION 5.

1930-1931 18/100 Mk III Tigress

One of the rarest and greatest MGs, the 18/100 Mk III, acquired the Tigress appellation unofficially and retrospectively. A catalogued racing model, the dry-sump engine had a twin spark plug crossflow cylinder head. On Marks I and II 18/80s the carburettors were underneath the exhaust manifold. Now the ports and the combustion chambers were machined and polished, the compression ratio was raised, new SU carburettors with egg-shaped dashpots introduced, and the camshaft reprofiled to provide more valve overlap. Power output of 18/80s went up to around 83bhp (61.9kW) for the Tigress, more in a high state of tune, but it was still generally disappointing and the car failed in the 1930 Brooklands Double Twelve, allegedly when a carburettor butterfly was drawn into the engine. The explanation was regarded sceptically as concealing a more profound failure. By 1930 the Tigress was obsolescent, heavy, too slow to compete with the Aston Martins and Alfa Romeos let alone the Bentleys that were leaders in the field. To make things worse M-type Midgets not only stayed the Double Twelve course but also won the team prize. The Tigress had a formidable performance, and although only 5 of the planned 25 were made it went down in MG folklore as the one car capable of challenging the great Vintage makes.

BODY sports, 2 doors, 4 seats; weight 26.25cwt (1333.5kg).
ENGINE 6 cylinders, in-line; 69mm x 110mm, 2468cc; compr 6.9:1; 83bhp (61.9kW) , 96bhp (71.6kW) racing spec; 33.6bhp/L (25.1kW/L), 38.9bhp/L (29kW/L) racing spec.
ENGINE STRUCTURE dry-sump; chain and spur gear-driven overhead camshaft; cast iron block, detachable cyl head with pent-roof machined combustion chambers; twin spark plugs; double valve springs; dual ignition; two downdraught SU carbs; chain drive to water pump, and dynamo; skew drive to oil pump and distributor; dual coil ignition; 4-bearing counterbalanced crankshaft.
TRANSMISSION rear wheel drive; single-plate cork insert clutch; compressed graphite thrust race; 4-speed non-synchromesh remote control manual gearbox; torque tube drive; spiral bevel final drive 4.27:1.
CHASSIS DETAILS steel channel-section cross-braced chassis upswept front and rear; upward-inclined half-elliptic leaf springs front-shackled 39in (99cm) front, 50in (127cm)rear; Silentbloc shackle bearings; 2 Hartford Duplex shock absorbers at front, 4 at rear; 14in finned cable-operated drum brakes; Marles steering; 28 Imp gal (33.6 US gal, 127L) tank; two fillers; two Autopulse electric pumps; 28x4.75 tyres; Rudge-Whitworth centre lock wire wheels.
DIMENSIONS wheelbase 114in (289.6cm); track 52in (132cm); turning circle 37ft 6in (11.4m); ground clearance 8in (20.3cm); length 156in (396cm); width 64in (163cm); height 64.5in (164cm).
PERFORMANCE max 100mph (161kph);16.1kg/bhp (21.5kg/kW), 13.9kg/bhp (18.6kg/kW) racing spec; fuel con 18mpg (15.7L/100km).
PRICE £895.
PRODUCTION 5.

Top: Geoff Radford with Rothschild Tigress at Goodwood.

Far left: Tigress tie-bar mascot of leaping felines was by artist F Gordon Crosby after a panther by French sculptor G Brau. It reappeared when Crosby was invited to submit a design for a Jaguar in 1938.

Left: cream with brown wings, the 1930 Double 12 Tigress with regulation Brooklands silencer.

Introducing a prototype at a motor show, and waiting for orders before starting to make any, was by no means uncommon in 1928. The new Morris Minor's overhead camshaft engine, conceived by Wolseley, which had been making ohc engines since its WW1 Hispano-Suiza aircraft days, suited perfectly. Morris had 40 per cent of the market but a small car to meet the competition from the Austin Seven was vital. Its aim was "...a car that can be housed in the average tool shed or motorcycle shelter at the side of a suburban villa." It was an idyllic picture to which a smart 2-seater MG was a sure addition.

The M-type was intended to be complementary to the 18/80, which Kimber probably saw as MG's destiny, but in the event it was the smaller car that became the greater. Within a few years big MGs were all but forgotten, but MG Midgets, of which the M-type was the precursor, would be the archetypal small sports car. Austin had broken the ground with the Cozette supercharged Seven Sports at £225, and MG's reply was a car not yet fully developed and scarcely different from the Morris Minor launched at the same Olympia show. Yet the Minor was such an ideal basis for a small sports car that *The Autocar* was moved to predict: "The MG Midget will make small sports car history."

BODY roadster, 2 doors, 2 seats; weight 10cwt (508kg); coupe, 2 doors, 2 seats, 11.5cwt (584kg); metal-panelled bodies approx 1cwt (51kg) extra.

ENGINE 4 cylinders, in-line; front; 57mm x 83mm, 847cc; compr 5.4:1; 20bhp (14.9kW) @ 4500rpm, later 27bhp (20.1kW); 23.6bhp/L (17.6kW/L), later 31.9bhp/L (23.7kW/L).

ENGINE STRUCTURE overhead camshaft; vertical camshaft drive; cast iron block, detachable head; Rotax or Lucas 6v coil ignition; 1.25in SU carburettor with gravity feed from scuttle tank and mixture control on dash; 2-bearing crankshaft.

TRANSMISSION rear wheel drive; single plate dry clutch; 3-speed non-synchromesh manual gearbox (4-speed optional); open propellor shaft with fabric disc universal joints; spiral bevel final drive 4.89:1.

CHASSIS DETAILS steel channel section, tapered, upswept fore and aft, with six cross members; semi-elliptic leaf springs pivoted at front, shackled at rear; Hartford friction dampers; rod and cable 8in drum brakes; worm and wheel steering; 4.5 Imp gal (5.4 US gal, 20.5L) fuel tank, 2 gal reserve; bolt-on wire wheels 19in; 27in x 4in Dunlop balloon tyres.

DIMENSIONS wheelbase 66in (167.6cm); track 42in (106.7cm); ground clearance 9in (22.9cm); length 110.25in (280cm); width 50in (127cm).

PERFORMANCE maximum speed 60mph (96kph); 16.4mph (26.4kph) @ 1000rpm; 0-50mph (80.5kph) 25sec, 0-60mph (96kph) 45sec; coupe 29.2kg/bhp (39.2kg/kW), later 21.6kg/bhp (29.1kg/kW); fuel consumption 40mpg (7.1L/100km).

PRICE 2-seater £185, Sportsman's Coupe £245.

PRODUCTION 3,235 (2,329 open 2-seaters, 273 metal-panelled, 493 fabric-bodied Salonettes, 37 metal-panelled coupes, 21 racers and Double-12 replicas, 82 chassis supplied to coachbuilders).

The 8/33 M.G. Midget Mk. I Sportsman's Coupé

This is a new model introduced for those who prefer closed car comfort combined with that wonderful liveliness and ease of control for which this car has already won fame. The coachwork is of the very highest class procurable, and, except for size, is definitely produced to rank with the most expensive cars built. A sliding roof enables one to take full advantage of the sunshine and fresh air.

The 8/33 M.G. Midget Sportsman's Coupé £245 0 0
             (with Chromium Plating and Triplex Glass)

1930 M-type 8/45 Midget Double Twelve

Within a month or two of production getting under way in the spring of 1929, M-types appeared at Brooklands. Five took part in a JCC Member's Day and all gained gold medals, an achievement repeated at a similar event run by the MCC Trials. The peculiarly British sport of climbing muddy hills brought more successes, and in the January 1930 Monte Carlo Rally Mont des Mules hill-climb, F M Montgomery not only won the 1100cc class but beat the winners of the next three classes up.

More power was found when H N Charles arrived at Abingdon as chief designer and found that the standard valve timing included a 2 degree period when both valves were shut. He designed a new camshaft that provided more speed for a stirring performance in the JCC Double-Twelve Hour race at Brooklands. Midgets finished 3rd, 4th, 5th, 6th, and 7th in their class behind two Riley Nines and came 14th, 17th, 18th, 19th and 20th overall, winning the team prize.

Production Midgets also benefited from the new valve timing and replicas of the Brooklands cars went on sale optimistically termed 8/45s. Treasury-rated at 8hp was true enough but the 45 was nothing to do with the real power output, but finished with brown bodywork and cream wings it was well worth £60 more than the standard car.

BODY racing car, 2 doors, 2 seats; weight 10cwt (508kg).
ENGINE 4 cylinders, in-line; front; 57mm x 83mm, 847cc; compr 5.4:1; 27bhp (20.1kW); 31.9bhp/L (23.8kW/L).
ENGINE STRUCTURE overhead camshaft; vertical camshaft drive; cast iron block, detachable head; Rotax or Lucas 6v coil ignition; 1.25in SU carburettor with gravity feed from scuttle tank and mixture control on dash; 2-bearing crankshaft.
TRANSMISSION rear wheel drive; single plate dry clutch; 3-speed non-synchromesh manual gearbox (4-speed optional); open propellor shaft with fabric disc universal joints; spiral bevel final drive 4.89:1.
CHASSIS DETAILS steel channel section, tapered, upswept fore and aft, with six cross members; semi-elliptic leaf springs pivoted at front, shackled at rear; Hartford friction dampers; rod and cable 8in drum brakes; worm and wheel steering; 4 Imp gal (4.8 US gal, 18.2L) fuel tank, 2 gal reserve; [Le Mans cars had a 18 Imp gal (21.6 US gal, 81.8L) tank in the tail]; bolt-on wire wheels 19in; 27in x 4in Dunlop balloon tyres.
DIMENSIONS wheelbase 66in (167.6cm); track 42in (106.7cm); ground clearance 9in (22.9cm); length 110.25in (280cm); width 50in (127cm).
PERFORMANCE maximum speed 60mph (96kph); 16.4mph (26.4kph) @ 1000rpm; 0-50mph (80.5kph) 25sec, 0-60mph (96kph) 45sec; 18.8kg/bhp (25.3kg/kW); fuel consumption 40mpg (7.1L/100km).
PRICE £245.
PRODUCTION 18.

A record-breaking car built for George Eyston MC, former Royal Artillery captain and racing driver, pioneered an enduring feature of MG Midget design. MG tagged experimental designs with an EX number and this was the 120th. The chassis was a prototype and instead of the frame being upswept over the back axle, it went flat underneath, giving the car (and all subsequent Midgets) a suitably low build. The M-type engine stroke was reduced by 29mm to bring it within the 750cc class, it had roller bearings in the valve gear, JAP motorcycle valves, and a specially counterbalanced crankshaft. Brooklands was under repair at the time so EX120 was taken to Montlhéry south of Paris.

Kimber gave Eyston every encouragement and, determined that an MG would beat Austin and be the first 750cc car to reach 100 mph, authorised the deployment of Eyston's Powerplus supercharger. Although it achieved its objective in breaking 750cc records, it took three attempts in February 1931 before attaining 103.13mph (165.97kph). In December Eyston took the car to France in an attempt to improve on this, but it caught fire and was badly damaged, the driver receiving severe burns. The car's remains were taken back to Abingdon and destroyed.

BODY single seat racer.
ENGINE 4 cylinders, in-line; front; 54mm x 81mm, 742cc.
ENGINE STRUCTURE overhead camshaft; vertical camshaft drive; cast iron block, detachable head; Rotax or Lucas 6v coil ignition; Powerplus supercharger; SU carburettor; 2-bearing counterbalanced crankshaft.
TRANSMISSION rear wheel drive; single plate dry clutch; 4-speed non-synchromesh manual gearbox; open propellor shaft with fabric disc universal joints; spiral bevel final drive.
CHASSIS DETAILS steel channel section, tapered, upswept in front, underslung at rear, with tubular cross members; semi-elliptic leaf springs pivoted at front, shackled at rear; Hartford friction dampers; rod and cable 8in drum brakes; worm and wheel steering; centre-lock wire wheels.
DIMENSIONS wheelbase 69in (175.3cm).
PERFORMANCE maximum speed 103.13mph (165.97kph).
PRODUCTION 1.

Top and right: Eyston in record attempt at Brooklands March 1931.

1931-1932 C-type Montlhéry Midget

At Eyston's celebration lunch, Kimber showed a prototype chassis of a new production racing model, the Montlhéry Midget. Fourteen were laid down for the 1931 Brooklands Double Twelve barely eight weeks away, a far taller order than a one-off record car. The engine had not been designed and hardly any components made. Everybody in the factory was pressed into service, making a thoroughbred with cowled air intake and boat tail, enclosing such a big tank for long-distance racing that the rear dampers were adjustable by the driver to allow for lightening as fuel was consumed. Twin wind deflectors, a feature of MG sports cars for years, made their debut on the C-type.

Almost the entire Abingdon workforce turned up to see their team win the Double Twelve outright, at an average of 65.62mph (105.6kph), and take the first five places beating an 1100cc Brooklands Riley as well as keen rivals Austin on handicap. To prevent such a clean sweep in the 500 Mile race, Brooklands handicappers set small cars an impossible 93.97mph (151.22kph), but E R Hall averaged 92.17mph (148.33kph) to finish third. Success came in the Ulster TT and R T Horton fitted his with an offset single-seat body to lap Brooklands at 115.29mph (185.54kph).

BODY open, 2 seats, cutaway doors, 2 seats.

ENGINE 4 cylinders, in-line; front; 57mm x 73mm, 746cc; cr 8.5:1, 5.8:1; 37.5bhp (27.96kW) @ 6000rpm unsupercharged, 52.5bhp (39.15kW) @ 6500rpm s/c; 50.3bhp/L (37.5kW/L) unsupercharged; 70.5bhp/L (52.6kW/L) s/c.

ENGINE STRUCTURE overhead camshaft; vertical camshaft drive; cast iron block, detachable head; downdraught SU carb; optional s/charger; 2-bearing counterbalanced crankshaft; scuttle oil tank.

TRANSMISSION rear wheel drive; twin-plate clutch; ENV 4-speed non-synchromesh manual gearbox with central remote control; spiral bevel final drive 5.37:1 or 5.5:1.

CHASSIS straight and parallel channel section side members underslung at the rear, tubular cross-bracing; semi-elliptic springs front and rear with shackles and bronze trunnions; Andre Hartford dampers with rear adjustment from cockpit; cable-operated 8in drum brakes later 10in, fly-off handbrake on all four wheels; Marles steering; 15 Imp gal (18 US gal, 68.2L) fuel tank; centre lock wire wheels, 27 x 4 tyres.

DIMENSIONS wheelbase 69in (175.3cm); track 42in (106.7cm).

PERFORMANCE maximum speed 85-90mph (137-145kph) contemporary tests. PRICE £295 unsupercharged, £345 supercharged, quickly revised to £490 and £575. PRODUCTION 44.

Left: cars on their way to
Irish GP 1931 at Phoenix
Park. H D Parker drove
8621, R Watney 8622, and N
Black 8623. In the picture,
Parker is in the driving seat
with Cecil Cousins perched
behind. Enever and
Taylor sit in 8623.

Top: start of the 1931
Ulster TT

It would be nice to think that MG prospered following the successes on the track but alas it did not. Although production doubled in 1930, the workforce had to be cut by a third, and staff agreed to a 10 per cent wage cut until profitability returned. The Depression of the 1930s took its toll and in 1931 sales fell by a quarter. The introduction of the D-type would not help matters much. In effect an M-type with a 3in (7.6cm) stretch and open or closed 4-seat bodywork, it was heavy and, although some of the C-type's chassis improvements such as the underslung frame were included, the good proportions and racy lines were gone.

Sales brochures called it the 8/33 MG Midget Occasional Four or Foursome Coupe (long chassis) and the first 100 D-type 4-seaters had the same body as the 6-cylinder F-type made at the same time. After this the wheelbase was increased by 2in (5.1cm) and the chassis side rail section made deeper. The D signified a settling-down of MG chassis design, and the placing of the cross-tubes remained much the same for subsequent J, F, and L-types. Only the dimensions of the engine compartment varied. Standard D-types had close-fitting cycle-type front wings, and brakes were operated by Bowden cables from a single cross shaft.

BODY roadster/coupe, 2 doors, 4 seats; weight 13cwt approx (660kg).
ENGINE 4 cylinders, in-line; front; 57mm x 83mm, 847cc; compr 5.4:1; 27bhp (20.1kW) @ 4500rpm; 31.9bhp/L (23.8kW/L).
ENGINE STRUCTURE overhead camshaft; vertical camshaft drive; cast iron block, detachable head; coil ignition; SU HV2 carburettor with electric SU pump; 2-bearing crankshaft.
TRANSMISSION rear wheel drive; single plate dry clutch; 3-speed non-synchromesh manual gearbox with central remote control (4-speed optional); open propellor shaft with fabric disc universal joints; spiral bevel final drive 5.37:1.
CHASSIS DETAILS straight and parallel channel section side members underslung at the rear, rivetted steel, with tubular cross members; semi-elliptic leaf springs shackled and trunnioned; Hartford friction dampers; cable operated 8in drum brakes; Adamant worm drive steering; 8 Imp gal (9.6 US gal, 36.4L)

fuel tank; centre lock wire wheels 19in x 4in Dunlop balloon tyres.
DIMENSIONS wheelbase 84in (213.4cm) early cars, later 86in (218.4cm); track 42in (106.7cm); length 132in (335cm); width 50in (127cm).
PERFORMANCE maximum speed approx 65mph (105kph); 24.4kg/bhp (32.8kg/kW); fuel consumption 35-38mpg (7.4-8.1L/100km).
PRICE open 4-seater £210, Salonette £250.
PRODUCTION 208 open 4-seater, 37 salonette, 5 chassis.

1931-1932 F1 12/70 Magna

Introduced in time for the 1931 London Motor Show, the Magna represented a further development of the underslung parallel-frame chassis first seen on the C-type. It had the characteristic tubular brazed cross-members that also served as suspension pick-up points and was suitably lengthened to accommodate the 6-cylinder engine. The nascent Nuffield Organisation pioneered the exchange of componentry among its brands, Morris, Wolseley, MG, and later Riley to great effect. The principle was re-invented many times. This MG borrowed the engine of the contemporary Wolseley Hornet and, although it was not one of MG's most inspired cars, the acquisition of a small 6-cylinder engine was extremely serviceable even though great lengths were gone to conceal it. Steel plates on the crankcase effected a disguise and the giveaway cylinder dimensions were faked in publicity brochures. Advertising was shrill: "No chains are used for the camshaft drive of the Magna engine. The enormous centrifugal forces generated are too great to expect even the best of chains to withstand. MG engineers chose shaft and a silent spiral bevel drive, which they knew from their experience with the MG Midget, to be capable of withstanding speeds in excess of 8000 rpm", twice as fast as any Magna engine would ever reach.

BODY salonette, 2 doors, 4 seats; open tourer, 2 doors, 4 seats; weight 19.25cwt (979kg), chassis weight 9.5cwt (483kg).
ENGINE 6 cylinders, in-line; front; 57mm x 83mm, 1271cc; compr 5.0:1; 37.2bhp (27.7kW) @ 4100rpm; 29.3bhp/L (21.8kW/L).
ENGINE STRUCTURE overhead camshaft; spiral bevel gear vertical camshaft drive; cast iron block, detachable head; coil ignition; two SU horizontal carburettors; 4-bearing crankshaft.
TRANSMISSION rear wheel drive; single dry plate clutch; 4-speed ENV non-synchromesh gearbox with central remote control; spiral bevel final drive 4.89:1.
CHASSIS DETAILS straight and parallel channel section side members underslung at the rear, rivetted steel, with tubular cross members; semi-elliptic springs front and rear with shackles and bronze trunnions; Hartford friction dampers; shaft and cable operated 8in ribbed drum brakes; Marles steering; 6 Imp gal (7.2

US gal, 27.3L) fuel tank, 2 gal (2.4 US gal, 9.1L) reserve; Rudge-Whitworth centre lock wire wheels 27in x 4in tyres 19in rims.
DIMENSIONS wheelbase 94in (239cm); track 42in (106.7cm); length 124.5in (316.2cm); width 50in (127cm); height 53in (134.6cm);
PERFORMANCE maximum speed 72.5mph (116.7kph); xxmph (kph) @ 1000rpm; 0-60mph (96kph) 25sec; 26.3kg/bhp (35.3kg/kW); fuel consumption 26mpg (10.9L/100km).
PRICE Occasional Four £250, Foursome Salonette £289.
PRODUCTION 1250.

1932 12/70 F2 F3 Magna

A 2-seater, the F2, accompanied second thoughts on the Magna that included bigger brakes, more power, and better cooling to avert the overheating caused by the Wolseley Hornet engine block disguise. Small cars were perfectly acceptable if they could rid themselves of some of a small car's disadvantages such as a noisy engine. The Magna's compact 6-cylinder with its inherent smooth running was highly agreeable for drivers familiar with something bigger. Owners enjoyed the flexibility and refinement to which they were accustomed yet had the economy and low road tax associated with an engine of 1ˇ litres. Pulling power at low speeds was good and the gear ratios were chosen for touring rather than sporting driving. The performance of four-seat Magnas suffered with a full load of occupants and some cars were further handicapped by unsuitably heavy bodywork.

The salonette was well appointed, very fully equipped with an embryo luggage boot, although when its lid was laid flat doing service as a luggage carrier the effect on handling was startling. The sliding roof had distinctive windows to lighten the rather gloomy interior. Bodywork for the F2 was essentially borrowed from the J2 Midget with cycle-type wings and crowded instrument panel. The F3 designation was applied to 4-seaters.

BODY salonette, 2 doors, 4 seats; open tourer, 2 doors, 4 seats; weight 19.25cwt (978kg), chassis weight 9.5cwt (483kg).
ENGINE 6 cylinders, in-line; front; 57mm x 83mm, 1271cc; compr 5.0:1; 37.2bhp (27.7kW) @ 4100rpm, or 47bhp (35kW); 29.3bhp/L (21.8kW/L) OR 37bhp/L (27.5kW/L).
ENGINE STRUCTURE overhead camshaft; spiral bevel gear vertical camshaft drive; cast iron block, detachable head; coil ignition; two SU horizontal carburettors; OR one 1∫ SU; 4-bearing crankshaft.
TRANSMISSION rear wheel drive; single dry plate clutch; 4-speed ENV non-synchromesh gearbox with central remote control; spiral bevel final drive 4.89:1.
CHASSIS DETAILS straight and parallel channel section side members underslung at the rear, rivetted steel, with tubular cross members; semi-elliptic springs front and rear with shackles and bronze trunnions; Hartford friction dampers; shaft and cable operated 12in ribbed drum brakes; Marles steering; 6 Imp gal (7.2 US gal, 27.3L) fuel tank, 2 Imp gal (2.4 US gal, 9.1L) reserve; Rudge-Whitworth centre lock wire wheels 27in x 4in tyres ZZ rims.
DIMENSIONS wheelbase 94in (238.8cm); track 42in (106.7cm); turning circle xx; ground clearance xx; length 124.5in (316cm); width 50in (127cm); height 53in (135cm).
PERFORMANCE maximum speed 72.5mph (116.7kph); 0-60mph (96kph) 25sec; 26.3kg/bhp (35.3kg/kW) OR 20.8kg/bhp (27.9kg/kW); fuel consumption 26mpg (10.9L/100km).
PRICE Occasional Four £250, Foursome Salonette £289.
PRODUCTION 1250 all Magnas.

The J-type Midgets, of which there were four sorts between 1932 and 1934, were essentially developments of the M-type with the 847cc 4-cylinder overhead camshaft engine. The J1 and J2 had twin SUs, gave 36bhp (26.8kW) and were built in substantial numbers, while the J3 and J4 were 746cc supercharged and made in much smaller numbers. The J1 four-seater introduced at the beginning of August 1932 before the autumn motor show exploited the fine reputation MG was creating in motor racing with cutaway doors, cycle-type wings, and fold-flat windscreen.

The characteristic double-humped scuttle cowl, inspired by Eyston's Montlhéry record-breaker, came with J2 but the J-type image was reflected in every open MG until the middle 1950s. The slab fuel tank with external spare wheel was a legacy of trials, where competitors liked twin spares accessible for muddy hills and extra rearwards weight.

A feature of MG design was mounting the radiator not on the chassis, but on an extension to the front engine mounting so that there was no relative movement between them. The experience of designer H N Charles, with highly flexible fighter aircraft airframes and mountings, led to his memorable remark that, "The heavy things must stand still."

BODY roadster, 2 doors, 4 seats; salonette, 2 doors, 4 seats; chassis weight 9.75cwt (495kg).
ENGINE 4 cylinders, in-line; front; 57mm x 83mm, 847cc; 36bhp (26.8kW) @ 5500rpm; 42.5bhp/L (31.6kW/L).
ENGINE STRUCTURE overhead camshaft; vertical camshaft drive; cast iron block, Elektron sump; detachable cross-flow AB head; coil ignition; 2 semi-downdraught SU carburettors with Petrolift or electric SU pump; 2-bearing crankshaft; 12volt Rotax starting and lighting.
TRANSMISSION rear wheel drive; single dry plate clutch; 4-speed non-synchromesh manual gearbox; spiral bevel final drive 5.37:1 or 5.87:1.

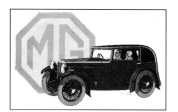

CHASSIS DETAILS straight and parallel channel section side members underslung at the rear, rivetted steel, with tubular cross members; semi-elliptic springs front and rear with shackles and bronze trunnions; Hartford friction dampers; 8in drum brakes; Marles steering; 12 Imp gal (14.4 US gal, 54.6L) fuel tank, salonette 6 Imp gal (7.2 US gal, 27.3L); Rudge-Whitworth detachable wire wheels; 27 x 4.00 tyres 19in rims.
DIMENSIONS wheelbase 86in (218cm); track 42in (107cm); turning circle 34ft (10.4m); length 130in (330cm) 4-seater, 124.5in (316cm) salonette; width 52in (132cm) both 4-seater and salonette; height 52.4in (133cm).
PERFORMANCE maximum speed 70mph (113kph) approx; 0-60mph (96kph) 25sec; 13.8kg/bhp (18.5kg/kW).
PRICE chassis only £175; 4-seater £199.10s (£199.50), de luxe equipment £12.12s (£12.60), salonette £255.
PRODUCTION 380.

1932-1934 J2 Midget

Late in 1933, as the J1, J3 and J4 were discontinued and the cycle-winged J2 re-equipped with swept wings and running boards, the style and specification of the classic MG two-seater was nearly complete. It was not the only feature that provided the J2 with its own distinctive personality; close-ratio gearbox, centre-lock wire wheels, and a large-diameter octagon-backed dial served as both speedometer and tachometer with engine revs marked off for third and top gears. The 12 guineas-worth of de luxe equipment included an electric clock, Ashby steering wheel, stone guards on the headlamps (de rigeur for racing), oil thermometer, bonnet strap, cam-and-lever-type fuel fillers (presumably to speed up pit stops), stop tail and reverse lamp, and water temperature gauge. Leather upholstery and pneumatic cushions were standard, although *The Autocar's* claim that thanks to the cutaway doors both driver and passenger have unlimited freedom of movement was hopeful.

The 1932 motor show J2 was shown in two-tone red along with a two-tone blue J1 salonette with matching blue leather upholstery. The J2's top speed was a bone of some contention. *The Autocar's* road test of RX9980 at 80.35mph (129.3kph), even with the windscreen folded flat, was regarded with scepticism by many J2 owners.

BODY roadster, 2 doors, 2 seats; weight 11.25cwt (571.5kg).
ENGINE 4 cylinders, in-line; front; 57mm x 83mm, 847cc; 36bhp (26.8kW) @ 5500rpm; 42.5bhp/L (31.7kW/L).
ENGINE STRUCTURE overhead camshaft; vertical camshaft drive; cast iron block, Elektron sump; detachable cross-flow AB head; coil ignition; 2 semi-downdraught SU carburettors with Petrolift or electric SU pump; 2-bearing crankshaft; 12volt Rotax starting and lighting.
TRANSMISSION rear wheel drive; single dry plate clutch; 4-speed non synchromesh manual gearbox with central remote control; spiral bevel final drive 5.37:1 or 5.87:1.
CHASSIS straight and parallel channel section side members underslung at the rear, rivetted steel, with tubular cross members; semi-elliptic springs front and rear with shackles and bronze trunnions; Hartford friction dampers; cable operated 8in ribbed drum brakes; fly-off handbrake; Marles steering; 12

Imp gal (14.4 US gal, 54.6L) tank; Rudge-Whitworth detachable wire wheels; 27 x 4.00 tyres 19in rims.
DIMENSIONS wheelbase 86in (218cm); track 42in (107cm); turning circle 34ft (10.4m); length 124in (315cm); width 51.5in (131cm); height 52.4in (133cm).
PERFORMANCE maximum speed 80mph (129kph) contemporary test; 14.7mph (23.7kph) @ 1000rpm; 0-60mph (96kph) 25sec;15.9kg/bhp (21.3kg/kW).
PRICE chassis only £175; £199.10s (£199.50), de luxe equipment £12.12s (£12.60), salonette £255.
PRODUCTION 2983.

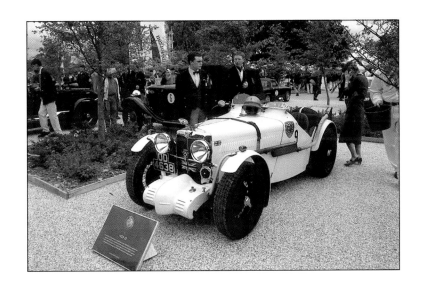

Following the J1 and J2 by some nine months and superseding M, C, and D-type Midgets, the J3 was outwardly indistinguishable from the J2 except for a Powerplus supercharger, driven off the front of the crankshaft and concealed under the apron between the front dumb-irons. The J3 engine was brought within the 750cc racing class by means of a shorter-throw crankshaft and owing to the supercharger at the front could not be fitted with a starting handle. Based on the C-type engine, but without a counterbalanced crankshaft, it normally ran on 50% Ethyl and 50% Benzol and would trickle along at 500rpm in top gear without oiling up the 14mm KLG 718 plugs. The supercharger bearings were lubricated from the sump and upper cylinder lubricant was recommended to lubricate the blades. Chassis lubrication for J-types was by means of a Tecalemit system that piped grease from a group of nipples conveniently situated under the bonnet, an arrangement used by MG for many years which worked well when the car was new but tended to clog up with age.

George Eyston, Tommy Wisdom, and Albert Denly set international Class H records at Montlhéry with a J3 in 1933 including 1 hour to 24 hours at 70.1mph (112.8kph) and W E Belgrave won his class with one in the Alpine Trial.

BODY roadster, 2 doors, 2 seats; weight 11.25cwt (571.5kg).
ENGINE 4 cylinders, in-line; front; 57mm x 75mm, 746cc; 45bhp (33.6kW) @ 6000rpm; 60.3bhp/L (50kW/L).
ENGINE STRUCTURE overhead camshaft; vertical camshaft drive; cast iron block, Elektron sump; detachable cross-flow AB head; coil ignition; SU carburettor with Autopulse pump; 2-bearing crankshaft; 12volt Rotax starting and lighting; 6a Powerplus supercharger on 5lb (0.3bar boost).
TRANSMISSION rear wheel drive; single dry plate; 4-speed non synchromesh manual gearbox with central remote control; spiral bevel final drive 4.89:1.
CHASSIS DETAILS straight and parallel channel section side members underslung at the rear, rivetted steel, with tubular cross members; semi-elliptic springs front and rear with shackles and bronze trunnions; Hartford friction dampers; cable operated 8in ribbed drum brakes; fly-off handbrake; Marles steering; 11 Imp gal (13.2 US gal, 50L) fuel tank; Rudge-Whitworth detachable wire wheels; 27 x 4.00 tyres 19in rims.
DIMENSIONS wheelbase 86in (218cm); track 42in (107cm); turning circle 34ft (10.4m); length 124in (315cm); width 51.5in (131cm); height 52.4in (133cm).
PERFORMANCE maximum speed 93mph (149.7kph); 0-60mph (96kph) 17sec; 12.7kg/bhp (17kg/kW).
PRICE £299.10s (£299.50), chassis only s/c £275.
PRODUCTION 22.

The last of the J quartet was a ready-made sports-racing car. The J4 had a higher-pressure supercharger than the J3, close-ratio gearbox, outside exhaust, 12in brakes from the new L-type Magna, and to emphasise its competition nature, no doors. The fastest J-type, it did several Brooklands laps at over 100mph, no mean feat on a bumpy track for a lightweight car. Its centrally split track rod was designed to control strong reactions through the steering, and was adopted on subsequent racing MGs, including the celebrated K-series.

Lap record for the twisty Ards circuit in Northern Ireland was set by Hugh Hamilton in a J4 at 77.2mph (124.24kph) in 1933; a formidable display of driving prowess. Hamilton was a notable driver who finished second to Tazio Nuvolari in the 1933 RAC International Tourist Trophy, and won the 800cc class of a race at the Nürburgring by 25 minutes. At the 1933 Le Mans 24 hours race, Ludovic Ford and M H Baumer entered a J4 and not only finished a creditable sixth overall, but came second (to a Riley) in the imortant Index of Performance. This was decided by a formula taking account of engine capacity against distance covered and was highly regarded by the organisers since it usually offered the best chance of a French win. An unsupercharged J5 was listed but none was ever made.

BODY roadster, 2 doors, 2 seats; weight 11.25cwt (571.5kg).

ENGINE 4 cylinders, in-line; front; 57mm x 75mm, 746cc; 72bhp (53.7kW) @ 6000rpm; 96.5bhp/L (72kg/L).

ENGINE STRUCTURE overhead camshaft; vertical camshaft drive; cast iron block, Elektron sump; detachable cross-flow AB head; coil ignition; 2 semi-downdraught SU carburettors with Petrolift or electric SU pump; 2-bearing crankshaft; 12 volt Rotax starting and lighting; No or No9 Powerplus supercharger.

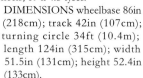

TRANSMISSION rear wheel drive; 2-plate dry clutch; 4-speed ENV non-synchromesh manual gearbox with central remote control; spiral bevel final drive 5.37:1.

CHASSIS DETAILS straight and parallel channel section side members underslung at the rear, rivetted steel, with tubular cross members; semi-elliptic springs front and rear with shackles and bronze trunnions; Hartford friction dampers; cable operated brakes, 12in drums; Marles steering with track-rod divided in the middle; Rudge-Whitworth wire wheels; 19 x 4.5 tyres.

DIMENSIONS wheelbase 86in (218cm); track 42in (107cm); turning circle 34ft (10.4m); length 124in (315cm); width 51.5in (131cm); height 52.4in (133cm).

PERFORMANCE maximum speed 100mph (160.9kph); 0-60mph (96kph) 16sec approx; 7.9kg/bhp (10.6kg/kW). PRICE £495.

PRODUCTION 9.

1932 EX 127 Magic Midget

Conceived in 1931, Eyston's second 750cc record-breaker had a long and successful career. The driveline was offset and the back axle made asymmetrically to lower the driving position. Reg Jackson at Abingdon designed a single-seater body that tapered to a pointed tail and fitted snugly with a small windscreen round the driver. Aerodynamics was already a well-developed science in aircraft, and Jackson pioneered its application to cars, testing a quarter scale model of EX 127 in the Vickers wind-tunnel at Brooklands.

Eyston was still recovering from his injuries when EX 120 caught fire, so Ernest Eldridge took EX127 to Montlhéry and did 5 kilometres at 110.28mph (177.47kph). Just before Christmas 1931, in bitterly cold weather and wearing special asbestos overalls after his experience in EX 120 the previous September, Eyston took four records of up to 10miles (16.1km) at 114.77mph (184.69kph). He failed to claim 120mph on the wet sands at Pendine in South Wales during February 1932 following difficulties with timing equipment. Unofficially he managed 122mph (196.33kph), but the official RAC timing equipment was found to be out of ink, so the record was never confirmed. He eventually managed it back at Montlhéry in December.

BODY single-seat record breaker.
ENGINE 4 cylinders, in-line; front; 57mm x 73mm, 745cc; compr xx.x:1; 52.5bhp (39.2kW) supercharged @ 0000rpm; 70.5bhp/L (52.6kW/L).
ENGINE STRUCTURE overhead camshaft; vertical camshaft drive; cast iron block, detachable head; downdraught SU carburettor; s/c; 2-bearing counterbalanced crankshaft; scuttle oil tank.
TRANSMISSION offset to left. Rear wheel drive; twin-plate clutch; ENV 4-speed non-synchromesh manual gearbox with central remote control; spiral bevel final drive 5.37:1 or 5.5:1
CHASSIS DETAILS straight and parallel channel section side members underslung at the rear, tubular cross-bracing; semi-elliptic springs front and rear with shackles and bronze trunnions; Andre Hartford dampers with rear adjustment from cockpit; cable-operated 8in drum brakes later 10in, fly-off handbrake on all four wheels; Marles steering; centre lock wire wheels with Ace discs, 27 x 4 tyres.

DIMENSIONS wheelbase 69in (175cm); track 42in (107cm).
PERFORMANCE maximum speed 128.62mph (206.47kph).
PRODUCTION 1.

Modifications in 1933 resulted in the cockpit being too tight a fit for the robust Eyston so the rather smaller Albert Denly was deputed to take the entire catalogue of Class H records at 128.62mph (206.47kph).

Right: the car as it went to Kohlrausch. Syd Enever sits in car, Artur Baldt (Kohlrausch's mechanic) on right.

Far right: on the back straight at Brooklands 16 Sep 1933.

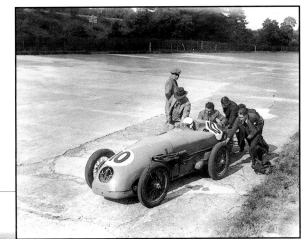

Road-going K-series cars had two wheelbase lengths, K1 of 9ft and K2 of 7ft 10³/₁₆th in, and three engines of 1087cc with three carburettor KA and twin carburettor KB, and twin carburettor 1271cc KD. K1s with the KA engine were usually saloons, K1s with the KB engine were more often 4-seater tourers.

MG chassis design was by now well established and the Wolseley-derived crossflow engines followed MG convention with the 57mm bore that lasted from the C-type Montlhéry Midget to the PA, Q and even the racing R-type of the middle 1930s. The stroke was shorter than the Wolseley; 71mm instead of 83mm, as a demonstration of Abingdon independence. Innovations on the K1 included a pillarless four-door body (right) known as the KN, and either a 4-speed non-synchromesh gearbox or a Wilson preselective. The invention of Major W G Wilson and made by ENV, this was an epicyclic gearbox with a selector lever (in the MG in place of the normal gear lever), and a gearshift pedal instead of the conventional clutch. For 1934 a single-plate Don-Flex clutch was interposed so that the first movement of the pedal worked the clutch, then the preselector, to make gearchanges smoother and quieten the mechanism when idling.

BODY saloon, 4 doors, 4 seats; weight 21cwt (1067kg).
ENGINE KA, 6 cylinders, in-line; front; 57mm x 71mm, 1087cc; 39bhp (29.1kW) @ 5500rpm; 35.9bhp/L (26.8kW/L). KB, 41bhp (30.6kW) @ 5500rpm. KD, 57mm x 83mm; 1271cc; 48.5bhp (36.2kW) @ 5500rpm.
ENGINE STRUCTURE overhead camshaft; vertical camshaft drive; cast iron block; detachable head; Elektron sump; BTH Polar inductor magneto; KA and KB 3 SU OM carburettors and fuel system; KD 2 SU HV2 carburettors; 4-bearing crankshaft.
TRANSMISSION rear wheel drive; single dry plate clutch; KA and KD 4-speed preselector KB 4 speed non-synchromesh manual gearbox; spiral bevel final drive 5.78:1.
CHASSIS DETAILS straight and parallel channel section side members underslung at the rear, rivetted steel, with tubular cross members; semi-elliptic springs front and rear with shackles and phosphor-bronze trunnions; Hartford friction dampers; cable operated brakes with 13in Elektron and cast-iron drums; Marles-Weller steering with divided track-rod; 11 Imp gal (13.2 US gal, 50L) fuel tank, plus 2 gal reserve; 19 x 4.75 Dunlop Fort tyres; Rudge-Whitworth centre lock wire wheels.
DIMENSIONS wheelbase 108in (274cm); track 48in (122cm); length 150in (381cm); width 58in (147cm).
PERFORMANCE maximum speed 70mph (112.7kph); 0-50mph (80.5kph) 28sec; KA 27.4kg/bhp (36.7kg/kW).
PRICE KN saloon £445 with Wilson; Tourer £385 Wilson £25 extra; chassis £315.
PRODUCTION 71 including KA and KB. Engines, 80 with KD.

Bodywork on the K-type featured a return to the flowing wings and relatively spacious interiors not seen since its spiritual predecessor the 18/80.

1932-1935 Magnette K2 (KB and KD engines)

MG averred that, since what they liked to call their Light Six engines were designed for supercharging, they had a big margin of safety unblown. Anxious to dispel the notion that Magnettes were "hotted-up," Abingdon preferred to describe them as more in the nature of de-tuned racing cars.

The K2 2-seater had cutaway doors like the Magna, cowled scuttle, fold-flat windscreen, and strongly made sidescreens but it was more touring than sporting. Open K2s had a 2-plate large-diameter clutch, and a four-speed close-ratio gearbox and spiral-bevel final drive; racing K2s had straight-bevel final drive gears. Customers for the handsome upright closed body could choose between mounting the spare wheel outside, on the lid of the shallow luggage boot or inside, when the boot lid could be used as a luggage platform (see far right). The MG octagon was pressed into service as a brake light between the arrow direction indicators on the back. By 1934 Triplex glass was standard on all MGs.

Road testers found the engine unwilling to run much under 20mph in top gear (flexibility was treasured in the days of difficult gearchanging), and recommended engine speeds of over 2000rpm for the best results. At 5000rpm in third gear the Magnette would reach over 50mph (80.5kph).

BODY saloon, 4 doors, 4 seats; sports, 2 seats.
ENGINE KB, 6 cylinders, in-line; front; 57mm x 71mm, 1087cc; compr 6.4:1; 41bhp (30.6kW) @ 5500rpm; 37.7bhp/L (28.2kW/L). KD, 57mm x 83mm; 1271cc; 48.5bhp (36.2kW) @ 5500rpm.
ENGINE STRUCTURE overhead camshaft; vertical camshaft drive; cast iron block; detachable head; Elektron sump; BTH Polar inductor magneto; KD two SU HV2 carburettors and fuel system; 4-bearing crankshaft.
TRANSMISSION rear wheel drive; single dry plate clutch; KA and KD 4-speed preselector KB 4 speed non-synchromesh manual gearbox; spiral bevel final drive 5.78:1.
CHASSIS DETAILS straight and parallel channel section side members underslung at the rear, rivetted steel, with tubular cross members; semi-elliptic springs front and rear with shackles and phosphor-bronze trunnions; Hartford friction dampers; cable operated brakes with 13in Elektron and cast-iron drums;

Marles-Weller steering with divided track-rod; 11 Imp gal (13.2 US gal, 50L) fuel tank, plus 2 gal reserve; 19 x 4.40 Dunlop Fort tyres; Rudge-Whitworth centre lock wire wheels.
DIMENSIONS wheelbase 94.2in (239cm); track 48in (122cm); width 58in (147cm).
PERFORMANCE maximum speed 70mph (113kph); 0-50mph (80.5kph) 28sec.
PRICE K2 chassis £315; 2-seater £360.
PRODUCTION 15 possibly with KA or more likely KB engines, 5 with KD.

The quadrant control for preselecting gears had notches to help the driver choose the nest ratio without looking, rather like the gate pattern of a conventional transmission.

1933-1934 Magnette K3

The K3 may not, after all, go down in history as the greatest MG, but it can perhaps lay claim to having been the most charismatic. Its influence on a motor racing world dominated by Continental European manufacturers was significant. The Midget was already well established in British motor sport at club and national level, MG had made its mark in Class H record-breaking, but contemplating anything in top-flight international racing seemed beyond hope. In the Mille Miglia or at Le Mans, MG seemed out of its class.

The moving force in changing things was Lord Howe, experienced at the wheel of a Bugatti, but who patriotically wanted to compete in a British car. He encouraged Sir William Morris to sanction MG's participation, promising to bear the cost of taking a team of cars to the Mille Miglia. They stopped off with a prototype at the Bugatti factory where the Earl was a valued customer. "The front axle is not strong enough," was Ettore Bugatti's verdict and new stronger ones were ordered at once from the factory. A year later Ronnie Horton's unmodified axle duly broke.

The Mille Miglia recce in 1933 under the auspices of the great Anglophile Count Johnny

BODY racing, 2 seats, no doors; chassis weight 13.5cwt (686kg), complete 18.25cwt (927kg).
ENGINE 6 cylinders, in-line; front; 57mm x 71mm, 1087cc; compr 6.2:1; 120bhp (89.5kW) @ 6500rpm; 110.4bhp/L (82.3kW/L).
ENGINE STRUCTURE overhead cam, vertical cam drive; triple valve springs; cast iron block; detachable cross-flow head; finned Elektron sump; lubrication from scuttle-mounted 20 gal (90.9L) oil tank; ign by polar induction magneto; $1^{7/8}$in SU carburettor and twin fuel systems; 4-bearing crank; Powerplus No 9 eccentric vane supercharger driven off front of crank at ∫ engine speed, later Marshall; BTH Polar inductor magneto.
TRANSMISSION rear wheel drive; Wilson 4-speed preselector gearbox; straight-cut bevel final drive 4.9, 4.3, or 5.7:1.
CHASSIS DETAILS straight and parallel channel section side members underslung at the rear, rivetted steel, with tubular cross members; semi-elliptic springs front and rear with shackles and phosphor-bronze trunnions; Hartford friction dampers, two longitudinally at front, four transversely at rear; cable operated brakes with 13in Elektron and cast-iron drums; fly-off handbrake on all four, cockpit adjuster; Marles-Weller steering with divided track-rod, later Bishop Cam; 27.5 Imp gal (33 US gal, 125L) fuel tank; 19 x 4.75 tyres Rudge-Whitworth centre lock wire wheels.
DIMENSIONS wheelbase 94.2in (239cm); track 48in (122cm).
PERFORMANCE maximum speed 106mph (170.6kph); 20.04mph (32.3kph) @ 1000rpm on 4.33 final drive; 7.7kg/bhp (10.4kg/kW).
PRICE chassis £675, complete car £795.
PRODUCTION 33 including prototypes and Ex135.

The M.G. Magnette K3 Racing Model. Unsupercharged £595. Supercharged £695
With Pre-selector Gearbox.

Lurani, included an introduction to Enzo Ferrari whose Scuderia Ferrari was in effect the rival Alfa Romeo team, and Tazio Nuvolari perhaps the greatest driver in the history of motor racing. The Mille Miglia drivers were to be Sir Henry "Tim" Birkin whose tragic death took place not long afterwards, with Bernard Rubin, rich industrialist and former owner of the Bentley team, Lord Howe, Hugh Hamilton a salesman for University Motors the leading MG dealer in London, and Lurani and Eyston.

The job of the Birkin/Rubin car was to go fast enough to break the opposing Maseratis. Over the first 129miles (207.6km) from the start at Bologna it averaged 87.95mph (141.54kph), overtook 35 competitors, and broke the class record by 13min. Across the mountains to Florence it kept the lead but at Siena after 228.5miles (367.7km) the car went out with a broken valve. The nearest Maserati was an hour behind.

At Rome Eyston and Lurani were leading the class comfortably, beating the 1100cc record by nearly half an hour, with Howe and Hamilton close behind. They suffered from plug trouble and punctures but still finished ahead and won the team prize, the important Gran Premio Brescia, never before won by a foreign team in this compelling event run in the heartland of motor racing.

Further accomplishments followed at Brooklands, when Whitney Straight, then a student at Cambridge, scored another notable victory in the Coppa Acerbo at Pescara, once again at Maserati's expense, then Nuvolari agreed to drive a K3 in the Ulster Tourist Trophy. Victory in the TT, followed by further triumphs at Brooklands and the Class G outer circuit speed record. In the 1934 Le Mans a K3 was in second place when it was forced off the road but in 1935 it won the 2.0-litre class. A K3 won the 1100cc championship of Italy and the brilliant pair of Richard Seaman and Hugh Hamilton, both sadly to die racing, scored notable successes in continental events.

The record of the K3 was one of astonishing achievement that continued throughout the 1930s. Some of the British pre-eminence in motor racing from the 1960s onwards might be traced to the pioneering endeavours of the K3 in the 1930s.

Right: the competitions shop at Abingdon in late 1933 houses Nuvolari's TT car No 17, E R Hall's Brooklands 500 mile race No22 with optional head fairing, and the Magic Midget.

Left: the 1933 Mille Miglia team after its arrival in Italy. Tall figure in middle is Bernard Rubin standing behind JB1474 that he shared with Sir Henry 'Tim' Burkin. On left, Count Giovanni (Johnny) Lurani in JB1475 who drove with George Eyston. Lord Howe's and Hugh Hamilton's car JB1472 is on the right.

1933 K3 Magnette Ulster TT Nuvolari car

Tazio Nuvolari raced motorcycles before moving on to cars, gaining victories with Bugatti, Alfa Romeo, and Maserati. Small, wiry, with trademark yellow jersey and leather waistcoat, his driving style was spectacular. Nuvolari raced bandaged after injuries, he broke bones, pulled faces, and was so animated behind the wheel that he seemed to be leaping about the cockpit. He took corners like a slalom skier, sliding the car sideways and seldom using the brakes; "Brakes only slow you up." He triumphed in grand prix racing, and in sports car races such as the punishing Targa Florio and Mille Miglia, showing enormous courage with difficult cars such as the Alfa Romeo Bimotore.

When he wanted to drive a K3 in the Tourist Trophy, Kimber was delighted to offer one with Alec Hounslow as riding mechanic. Nuvolari's method was to drive over the limit in practice, then ease back. The first time he saw the car was on first morning's practice, and the workings of the preselector gearbox were explained without the benefit of an interpreter. The car furthermore was wearing number 17, unlucky at the time in Italy, where only even numbers were being used on racing cars. On his first lap he lost control at least three times and within eight had worn out a complete set of tyres. He won just the same, breaking the 1100cc lap record seven times.

BODY racing, 2 seats, no doors; chassis weight 13.5cwt (686kg), lightweight racing body.
ENGINE 6 cylinders, in-line; front; 57mm x 71mm, 1087cc; compr 6.2:1; 120bhp (89.5kW) @ 6500rpm; 110.4bhp/L (82.3kW/L).
ENGINE STRUCTURE ohc, vertical cam drive; triple valve springs; cast iron block; detachable cross-flow head; finned Elektron sump; lubrication from scuttle-mounted 20 gal (90.9L) oil tank; ignition by polar induction magneto; $1^{7/8}$in SU carb and twin fuel systems; 4-bearing crank; Powerplus No 9 eccentric vane s/charger driven off front of crank at ∫ engine speed, later Marshall; BTH Polar inductor magneto.
TRANSMISSION rwd; Wilson 4-speed preselector gearbox; straight-cut bevel final drive 4.9, 4.3, or 5.7:1.
CHASSIS DETAILS straight and parallel channel section side members underslung at the rear, rivetted steel, with tubular cross members; semi-elliptic springs front and rear with shackles and phosphor-bronze trunnions; Hartford friction dampers, two longitudinally at front, four transversely at rear; cable operated brakes with 13in Elektron and cast-iron drums; fly-off handbrake on all four, cockpit adjuster; Marles-Weller steering with divided track-rod; 27.5 Imp gal (33 US gal, 125L) fuel tank; 19 x 4.75 tyres Rudge-Whitworth centre lock wire wheels.
DIMENSIONS wheelbase 94.2in (239.3cm); track 48in (121.9cm).
PERFORMANCE maximum speed 106mph (170.6kph); 20.04mph (32.3kph) @ 1000rpm on 4.33 final drive.

1933 Ulster TT: Nuvolari
masters the Wilson box
(above) and (left) refuels
in the pits.

1933 K3 Magnette single seater

After finishing 4th in the Ulster TT, Eddie Hall rebodied his K3 as a single seater for the Brooklands 500 miles race a fortnight later. With a high axle ratio it did 118mph (nearly 190kph) on the outer circuit, winning at 106.53mph (171.44kph). Ronnie Horton built an offset body along the lines of his curious C-type, completing an hour at 117.03mph (188.34kph), a Class G record. This car and Eyston's EX135 combined to make the Gardner-MG.

Hugh Hamilton's offset single-seater won the 1934 Coppa Acerbo Junior and was timed on a flying kilometre at 122.25mph (196.74kph). Reg Parnell later converted it to independent front suspension. Norman Black in a stripped and long-tailed two-seater K3 K3024 won the 1934 Mannin Beg. H S Linfield tested a K3 for *The Autocar* in April 1934 with the Marshall Roots-type supercharger "driven at engine speed with a pressure of 10psi (.689bar) to12psi (.827bar)".

Among notable racing K3s was K3011, bought by Whitney Straight who commissioned beautifully proportioned two-seater bodywork by Thomson and Taylor. Dick Seaman, one of Britain's most distinguished drivers of the 1930s, began his career with K3011 winning his class and setting a new sports car record at Mont Ventoux.

K3011:
BODY racing, 2 seats, no doors; chassis weight 13.5cwt (686kg) complete approx 17cwt (867kg).
ENGINE 6 cylinders, in-line; front; 57mm x 71mm, 1087cc; compr 6.2:1; 120bhp (89.5kW) @ 6500rpm; 110.4bhp/L (82.3kW/L).
ENGINE STRUCTURE overhead camshaft; vertical camshaft drive; triple valve springs; cast iron block; detachable cross-flow head; finned Elektron sump; lubrication from scuttle-mounted 20 gal (90.92L) oil tank; ignition by polar induction magneto; one 1⅞in SU carb and twin fuel systems; 4-bearing crankshaft; Powerplus No 9 eccentric vane supercharger driven off front of crankshaft at ∫ engine speed, later Marshall; BTH Polar inductor magneto.
TRANSMISSION rwd; Wilson 4-speed preselector gearbox; straight-cut bevel final drive 4.9, 4.3, or 5.7:1.
CHASSIS DETAILS straight and parallel channel section side members underslung at the rear, rivetted steel, with tubular cross members; semi-elliptic springs front and rear with shackles and phosphor-bronze trunnions; Hartford friction dampers, two longitudinally at front, four transversely at rear; cable operated brakes with 13in Elektron and cast-iron drums; fly-off handbrake on all four, cockpit adjuster; Marles-Weller steering with divided track-rod; 27.5 Imp gal (33 US gal, 125L) fuel tank; 19 x 4.75 tyres Rudge-Whitworth centre lock wire wheels.
DIMENSIONS wheelbase 94.2in (239cm); track 48in (122cm); length 145in (368.3cm).
PERFORMANCE maximum speed approx 110mph (177kph); 17.85mph (29kph) @ 1000rpm on 4.89 final drive; 7.2kg/bhp (9.7kg/kW).
PRICE chassis £675, complete car £795.

After winning the 1933 Coppa Acerbo Junior, Italian rivals dismantled the K3's engine to check the dimensions.

Left: R T Horton with
the Jensen-bodied K30007
attempting Class G records
at Brooklands on 13 April
1934. He took the records
the following month.

Developed from the F-type, the L-type Magna had the more powerful but smaller KC engine, but never sold as well. There were not many external changes for 1934, bigger headlamps and more flowing wings did not upset the good proportions of the body with its stylishly tilted radiator. There were separate windows at the rear and Abbey Coachworks instead of Carbodies made the Salonette.

More important was the introduction of the Continental Coupe, a 2-door 4-seater with a substantial luggage trunk at the back, in reality mostly filled with petrol tank. "Very individual … striking-looking" was how *The Autocar* guardedly described it. "Somehow it is natural to think of MGs as open cars but there must be a considerable number of owners who require the advantages of a closed body and … appreciate … a sports engine and chassis." The interior was furnished in fine style, the sliding roof provided with "windowlets" to give an airy appearance, and the paintwork on offer included a tasteful but scarcely understated black and yellow. It took more than a year to dispose of the last of the Continental Coupes. Overconfidence in ordering bodies was not infrequent at Abingdon. The 4-seat L-types were known as L1, the 2-seater with a J2 Midget style body as L2.

BODY sports, 2 seats, 15.25cwt (775kg); tourer, 2 doors, 4 seats, 16.5cwt (838kg), chassis 12.75cwt (648kg); salonette/Continental Coupe, 2 doors, 4 seats, 17.25cwt (876kg)/17cwt (864kg); sports chassis chassis 12.25cwt (622kg), other chassis 12.75cwt (648kg).
ENGINE 6 cylinders, in-line; front; 57mm x 71mm, 1087cc; 41bhp (30.6kW) @ 5500rpm; 37.7bhp/L (28.1kW/L).
ENGINE STRUCTURE overhead camshaft; spiral bevel gear vertical cam drive; cast iron block, detachable head; Elektron sump; coil ignition; 2 SU horizontal carbs; 4-bearing crank.
TRANSMISSION rear wheel drive; twin plate clutch; 4-speed ENV non-synchromesh gearbox with central remote control; spiral bevel final drive 5.37 or 5.87:1.
CHASSIS DETAILS straight and parallel channel section side members underslung at the rear, rivetted steel, with tubular cross members; semi-elliptic springs front and rear with shackles and bronze trunnions; Hartford friction dampers; shaft and cable operated 12in ribbed drum brakes; Marles-Weller steering; 12 Imp gal (14.4 US gal, 54.6L) fuel tank (2-seater); Rudge-Whitworth centre lock wire wheels 19in x 4.5in tyres.
DIMENSIONS wheelbase 94.2in (239cm); track 42in (107cm); turning circle 36ft (11m); ground clearance 6in (15.2cm); length 124.5in (316cm); wd 51.5in (131cm); ht 50in (127cm).
PERFORMANCE maximum speed 75mph (120.7kph); 0-60mph (96kph) 24sec; 23.9kg/bhp (32kg/kW) tourer; 22-24mpg (11.8-12.8L/100km).
PRICE chassis £245; 2-seater £285; 4-seater £299; salonette £345, Cont Coupe £350.
PRODUCTION 576.
PRICE chassis £235; open 2-seater £285; open 4-seater £299; salonette £345.

Right: The L-type had a long rearward extension for the remote control for the gearbox, bringing the lever close to the driver's head.

The next stage in the evolution of the Midget had bigger brakes, a 3-bearing crankshaft and a stronger chassis, but it was 2cwt (101.6kg) heavier than the J-type, production of which ended in January 1934. The new car's chassis was based on the J-type, lengthened at the back to carry the heavy slab fuel tank and the spare wheel mounting, mindful of the vogue for carrying twin spare wheels on trials. The crankshaft not only had the advantage of a steadying centre bearing, it also was increased in diameter and better lubricated. A touch of luxury was supplied by the facia, wood veneered like expensive cars, chrome-bordered, and supplied with two downward facing lights. Sporting owners were offered a supercharger for £27. They could obtain a Zoller blower with a complete kit of parts for fitting it, approved by the factory, together with a different set of spark plugs suitable for the inevitably hotter combustion chambers. The P-type (the 'A' designation was applied later) Airline coupe was more of a styling success than the Magna Continental. Its smart leather trim and wood veneer facia were perfectly in tune with contemporary coachbuilt cars as well as other relative newcomers such as SS, later Jaguar. It even had some luggage space behind the seats in response to a growing demand for cars with touring as well as sporting attributes.

BODY sports, 2 seats, weight 14cwt (711kg); Airline Coupe open, 4 seats.
ENGINE 4 cylinders, in-line; front; 57mm x 83mm, 847cc; compr 6.4:1; 36bhp (26.8kW) @ 5500rpm; 42.5bhp/L (31.7kW/L).
ENGINE STRUCTURE overhead camshaft; spiral bevel gear vertical camshaft drive; cast iron block, detachable cross-flow head; coil ignition; 2 SU horizontal carburettors; 3-bearing crankshaft.
TRANSMISSION rear wheel drive; single dry plate clutch; 4-speed non synchromesh manual gearbox; spiral bevel final drive 5.375, 5.875, 5.125:1.
CHASSIS DETAILS straight and parallel channel section side members underslung at the rear, rivetted steel, with tubular cross members; semi-elliptic springs front and rear with shackles and bronze trunnions; Hartford friction dampers front, Luvax hydraulic rear; shaft and cable operated 12in ribbed drum brakes; Marles-Weller, later Bishop cam steering; 12 Imp gal (14.4 US gal, 54.6L) fuel tank, 10 Imp gal (12US gal, 45.5L) 4-seater; 19 x 4 tyres; Rudge-Whitworth centre lock wire wheels.
DIMENSIONS wheelbase 87.65in (222.6cm); track 42in (106.7cm); length 135in (342.9cm); width 51in (129.5cm); height 52in (132.1cm) with hood up.
PERFORMANCE maximum speed 72mph (116kph); 14.7mph (23.7kph) @ 1000rpm; 19.8kg/bhp (26.5kg/kW).
PRICE 2-seater £220, later £222, 4-seater £240.
PRODUCTION 1396 2-seaters; 498 4-seaters; 28 Airline Coupes, 53 chassis for coachbuilders, 27 converted to PBs.

The car driven by George Eyston into third place in the 1934 Mannin Beg race in the Isle of Man was made of K3 components, with an offset transmission so that it could be equipped with a sports racing or track body. Known as the Magic Magnette, or Humbug, Brooklands' whimsy for its brown and cream striped track body, EX135 was its official works experimental number.

Its first racing victory came in the 1934 British Empire Trophy and Eyston took 11 Class G speed records. In 1937 the car came into the hands of Lt Col ATG Gardner who fitted Ron Horton's K3 engine that had had first a Zoller, then a Centric supercharger. Gardner took records with it at Frankfurt in 1937 then, reputedly with encouragement from Eberan von Eberhorst the Auto Union designer, had an elegant streamlined body created by Reid Railton to make one of the best-known record cars ever.

BODY streamlined single-seater; chassis weight 13.5cwt (686kg).
ENGINE see text.
TRANSMISSION rear wheel drive; Wilson 4-speed preselector gearbox; straight-cut bevel final drive.
CHASSIS DETAILS straight and parallel channel section side members underslung at the rear, rivetted steel, with tubular cross members; semi-elliptic springs front and rear with shackles and phosphor-bronze trunnions; Hartford friction dampers, two longitudinally at front, four transversely at rear; cable operated brakes with 13in Elektron and cast-iron drums; fly-off handbrake on all four; Marles-Weller steering with divided track-rod.
DIMENSIONS wheelbase 94.2in (239.3cm); track 48in (121.9cm).
PERFORMANCE see text.

Left: Reg Jackson tuning the EX135 engine on MG's dynamometer.

Right: from (l) to (r) A Bicknell, J Kesterton, Count Johnny Lurani, Reg Jackson, Syd Enever, a Dunlop rep, Count Ottolini, John Dugdale, Chris Shorrock and G Tuck. Dedication reads: "To Sid *(sic)* – with all the best. ATG Gardner Dessau 1939".

The career of EX 135 as the Gardner-MG got under way in 1937, with Class G records on the Frankfurt-Darmstadt autobahn. In November 1938 it did 186.6mph (300.3kph). In May 1939 within only a few months of the outbreak of war Gardner persuaded the Reich authorities to close the Dessau autobahn and reached an astonishing 203.5mph (327.5kph), and a few days later with the 1087cc engine bored out to 1105cc to qualify for Class F he astonished the assembled dignitaries with 204.3mph (328.8kph).

In 1946, barely eighteen months after the war, Gardner took the car to the unfinished Belgian motorway at Jabbeke. Its speed of 159.2mph (256.2kph) broke the Magic Midget's Class H record that had stood for 10 years. In 1948 the little green car was in action again although it no longer carried the MG symbol on the nose. Gardner was after a parcel of Class E records with a prototype

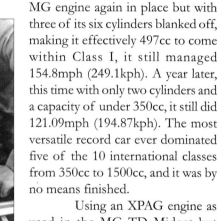

Jaguar XK twin overhead cam 2.0-litre 4-cylinder engine (the XK 120 engine less two cylinders) in the K3 chassis at a speed of 176.69mph (284.35kph). On September 15 1949 with the MG engine again in place but with three of its six cylinders blanked off, making it effectively 497cc to come within Class I, it still managed 154.8mph (249.1kph). A year later, this time with only two cylinders and a capacity of under 350cc, it still did 121.09mph (194.87kph). The most versatile record car ever dominated five of the 10 international classes from 350cc to 1500cc, and it was by no means finished.

Using an XPAG engine as used in the MG TD Midget but Shorrock-supercharged to 213bhp (158.8kW), it was taken to Bonneville and attained 202.02mph (325.11kph). The car was then honourably retired to the British Motor Industry heritage collection at Gaydon, England.

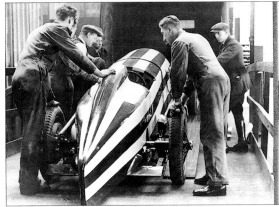

Top: Pure humbug. One
of two EX135 bodies
supplied to Eyston and
used for record breaking.

Left: Goldie Gardner in
car, and Syd Enever (r).

Ringing the changes with standard components in much the same way as it produced sports cars, a supercharged P-type engine in a chassis and body similar to the K3 created a production racing car. It was offered to aspiring competition drivers to enhance MG's reputation on the track, but even though it was 8in (20.3cm) longer and had a track 3in (7.6cm) wider than a racing J4, it was difficult to handle given its generous horsepower. It was only made between May and October 1934 but its shortcomings prompted work to start on the R-type racing car.

The high pressure Zoller supercharger designed by Laurence Pomeroy Jnr and Col W A McEvoy in consultation with H N Charles ran at 2.5 atmospheres boost, and its production output of 113bhp (84.3kW) was developed by 1936 to 146.2bhp (109kW) at 7500rpm. This enormous surge of power prompted the incorporation of a special clutch in the preselector gearbox that was designed to slip as soon as a certain torque figure was exceeded in order to protect the transmission from disintegrating.

In 1937 a single-seater Q-type driven by George Harvey-Noble set the 750cc Class H Outer Circuit record at Brooklands at 122.4mph (197kph).

BODY racing, 2 seats; weight 13cwt (660kg).
ENGINE 4 cylinders, in-line; front; 57mm x 73mm, 746cc; compr 6.25:1; 113bhp (84.3kW) @ 7200rpm; 151.5bhp/L (112.9kW/L).
ENGINE STRUCTURE overhead camshaft; spiral bevel gear vertical camshaft drive; cast iron block, detachable cross-flow head; Elektron sump; coil ignition; Zoller supercharger driven from front of crankshaft, SU carburettor; 3-bearing crankshaft.
TRANSMISSION rear wheel drive; Wilson 4-speed preselector gearbox; straight-cut bevel final drive 4.5, 4.87, or 4.125:1.
CHASSIS DETAILS straight and parallel channel section side members underslung at the rear, rivetted steel, with tubular cross members; semi-elliptic springs front and rear with shackles and bronze trunnions; Hartford friction dampers at front Luvax hydraulic at rear; cable operated 12in ribbed drum brakes; Marles-Weller steering; divided track rod; 19 Imp gal (22.8 US gal, 86.4L) fuel tank; aluminium undershield; Rudge-Whitworth centre lock wire wheels; 18 x 4.75 tyres.
DIMENSIONS wheelbase 94.3in (239.5cm); track 45in (114.3cm); length 127in (322.6cm).
PERFORMANCE maximum speed 122mph (196.3kph); 5.8kg/bhp (7.8kg/kW); fuel consumption 8mpg (35.3L/100km).
PRICE £550.
PRODUCTION 8.

The Q-type's firm springing demanded not so much a high level of skill as a degree of bravura beyond that which could reasonably be expected of even the most gallant driver.

1934-1936 N-type Magnette

In September 1933 the motoring magazines cheerfully carried news of the 1934 Magnette. "Capacity increased to 1286cc," said *The Light Car*. *The Autocar* reassured readers that, "The new engine has the same horsepower rating and pays the same tax as the old one, but its dimensions are 57mm x 84mm; (1286cc)." So did *The Motor*.

Alas the press was being misled. The engine was 57mm x 83mm, the same as the old one, so it was 1271cc as before. Abingdon's spin doctors were less successful with *Motor Sport* in April 1934. It got the cylinder dimensions right but rounded off the capacity of "a cheaper MG Magnette" to 1250cc, in effect replacing the Magna range including the ill-starred Continental Coupe, a stock of which lingered on for some years after production stopped. The NA had rear-hinged doors and plain radiator; the NB from 1935 front-hinged doors and slatted radiator, and there was a racing version, the NE. The demands of trials and rally competitors were met too. They wanted less rear overhang than the regular gracefully swept-tail N-type, together with a slab-type fuel tank where they could hang their heavy spare wheels. The response was to mount a K2 body on a small number of N-types. They were known at the factory as KN, later ND.

BODY saloon/roadster, 2 doors, 4 seats; Airline Coupe, Allingham Coupe, 2 doors, 2 seats.
ENGINE 6 cylinders, in-line; front; 57mm x 83mm, 1271cc; 56bhp (41.8kW) @ 5500rpm; 44.1bhp/L (32.9kW bhp/L).
ENGINE STRUCTURE overhead camshaft; spiral bevel gear vertical camshaft drive; double valve springs; cast iron block, detachable cross-flow head; Rotax battery, coil ignition; two SU 1.25in carburettors; SU electric fuel pump; 4-bearing crankshaft.
TRANSMISSION rear wheel drive; 8.25in single dry plate clutch; 4-speed non synchromesh gearbox; spiral bevel final drive 5.12, 5.37 or 5.87:1.
CHASSIS DETAILS channel-section non-parallel steel frame deeper in the middle, upswept over front axle, underslung at rear; large diameter tubular cross members riveted and brazed in cast brackets; Silentbloc rubber-bushed body mountings; half-elliptic springs bushed at front, sliding trunnions at rear; Andre-Hartford dampers at front, Luvax rotary hydraulic at rear; Alford & Alder 12in cable-operated drum brakes; Bishop cam steering; 10 Imp gal (12 US gal, 45.5L) fuel tank, 11 Imp gal (13.2 US gal, 50L) on saloon; 18 x 4.75 tyres; 19in rims on saloon.
DIMENSIONS wheelbase 94.3in (239.5cm) or 108in (274.3cm); track 45in (114.3cm) or 48 in (122cm); turning circle 30ft (9.1m).
PERFORMANCE maximum speed 80mph (128.7kph); 15.5mph (25kph) @ 1000rpm; fuel consumption 25mpg (11.3L/100km).
PRICE 2-seater £390; 4-seater 399; pillarless 4-door £445; chassis £340.
PRODUCTION 780 NA/NB/KN, 24 ND.

Right: Early Airflow. Chrysler influence on streamlining, at least at the back, in 1935 Magnette Airline with windowlets in the roof.

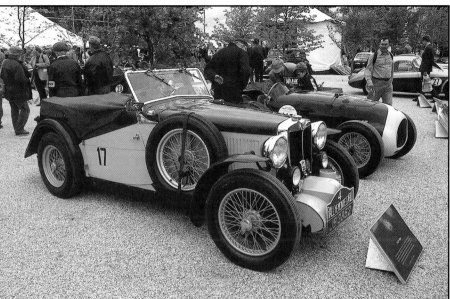

95

Almost unheard-of compression ratios with high-crown pistons, and a new camshaft with a lot of overlap, were among the ingredients of the small number of NEs made in August and September 1934. When the regulations were issued for the RAC TT race over the 13.6mile (21.9km) Ards circuit in Northern Ireland, an important event on the UK calendar, supercharged cars were prohibited and plans to enter a team of K3s had to be abandoned. Instead it was decided that Magnettes would stand a good chance, and after a swift development programme the NE was created. Narrow lightweight aluminium bodies were made, expediency gave way to style, and the engines were tuned.

As a rehearsal a team of three, with open racing bodywork, driven by Doreen Evans, Margaret Allen, and Irene Schwedler came third in the LCC Relay race at Brooklands. Encouraged, seven cars were built and six entered for the TT, three painted a distinctive cream and brown under George Eyston (no 25), three by the factory.

Eyston's drivers apart from himself were former motorcycle racers Wally Handley (no 26) and Charlie Dodson (no 27). Norman Black drove no 28. MG's second consecutive TT victory was won by a narrow margin (right). The winning speed was 74.65mph (120.13kph).

BODY racer, 2 seats; weight 16cwt (813kg).
ENGINE 6 cylinders, in-line; front; 57mm x 83mm, 1271cc; compr 9.8:1; 74.3bhp (55.4kW) @ 5500rpm; 58.5bhp/L (43.6kW/L).
ENGINE STRUCTURE overhead camshaft; spiral bevel gear vertical camshaft drive; triple valve springs; cast iron block, detachable cross-flow head; Rotax battery, coil ignition; two semi downdraught SU 1.375in carburettors; SU electric fuel pump; 4-bearing crankshaft.
TRANSMISSION rear wheel drive; 8.25in two plate clutch; 4-speed non synchromesh gearbox; spiral bevel final drive 4.875, 4.5, 4.125:1.
CHASSIS DETAILS channel-section non-parallel steel frame deeper in the middle, upswept over front axle, underslung at rear; large diameter tubular cross members riveted and brazed in cast brackets; Silentbloc rubber-bushed body mountings; half-elliptic springs bushed at front, sliding trunnions at rear; Andre-Hartford dampers at front, Luvax rotary hydraulic at rear; Alford & Alder 12in cable-operated drum brakes; Bishop cam steering; 10 Imp gal (12 US gal, 45.5L) fuel tank; 18 x 4.75 tyres.
DIMENSIONS wheelbase 96in (243.8cm); track 45in (114.3cm); turning circle 30ft (9.1metres); length 151in (383.5cm).
PERFORMANCE maximum speed 90mph (144.8kph); 10.9kg/bhp (14.7kg/kW).
PRODUCTION 7.

Right: After six hours and 465 miles (748.3kms) of racing, a bare 17sec separates C Dodson's supercharged NE from Eddie Hall's handicapped 3669cc Bentley as he wins the 1934 Ulster TT. His winning speed was within 3mph of Nuvolari's K3 of 1933.

1935 NE Magnette Musketeer

Since the specially-built TT cars were unsuitable for much else, it seemed appropriate to rebody three with P-type Midget slab tanks and rudimentary wings, to take part in trials. Following its victory in the TT Margaret Allen, one of the successful drivers in the LCC Relay race at Brooklands, drove JB4750 in the Wye Cup Trial of March 1935, and the refurbished team won first class awards in the Lands End and Edinburgh trials. They entered the Abingdon and Rushmere trials and the Welsh Rally, which they won outright and captured the team award. The NE's trials career was short-lived, the TT racing bodies were refitted and the cars were sold to the Evans's Bellvue Garage to race in the 1935TT. Later they reverted to being trials cars, one driven by Ernie Herrald.

In the course of several successful seasons the Musketeers' mounts became the works-built Magnette/Magna Specials (1936-37), with engines bored out and supercharged with Marshal IZ87 and Centric 260s. Kimber favoured Roots-type superchargers, so the Marshal unit was fitted to all three cars for the Exeter Trial of 1936. Experiments with tyres and lead weights in the back to improve traction were continually carried out. The cars retained their brown and cream paintwork, and the team was known as The Musketeers.

BODY sports, 2 seats; weight 16.3cwt (828kg).
ENGINE 6 cylinders, in-line; front; 57mm x 83mm, 1271cc, later 60mm x 83mm, 1408cc; compr 9.8:1; 68bhp (50.7kW) @ 5500rpm; 53.5bhp/L (39.9kW/L), later 48.3bhp/L (36kW/L).
ENGINE STRUCTURE overhead camshaft; spiral bevel gear vertical camshaft drive; triple valve springs; cast iron block, detachable cross-flow head; Rotax battery, coil ignition; two semi downdraught SU 1.375in carburettors; SU electric fuel pump; 4-bearing crankshaft.
TRANSMISSION rear wheel drive; 8.25in two plate clutch; 4-speed non synchromesh gearbox; spiral bevel final drive 4.875:1.
CHASSIS DETAILS channel-section non-parallel steel frame deeper in the middle, upswept over front axle, underslung at rear; large diameter tubular cross members riveted and brazed in cast brackets; Silentbloc rubber-bushed body mountings; half-elliptic springs bushed at front, sliding trunnions at rear; Andre-Hartford dampers at front, Luvax rotary hydraulic at rear; Alford & Alder 12in cable-operated drum brakes; 8:1 Bishop cam steering; 10 Imp gal (12 US gal, 45.5L) fuel tank; 19 x 4.0 tyres front, 18 x 4.75 rear.
DIMENSIONS wheelbase 96in (243.8cm); track 45in (114.3cm); turning circle 30ft (9.1m); length 151in (383.5cm).
PERFORMANCE maximum speed 90mph (144.8kph); 16mph (25.8kph) @ 1000rpm; 12.2kg/bhp (16.3kg/kW); fuel consumption 20mpg (14.1L/100km).
PRODUCTION 7.

Each Musketeer was duly named on the bonnet side Athos, Aramis, and Porthos. In 1937 the Musketeer names were continued on a team of red-painted TAs.

1934 EX 154

The Magic Midget EX 127 was sold to German MG enthusiast Bobby Kohlrausch for the Eifelrennen, but the cockpit was too cramped for racing on the Nürburgring and it was returned to the factory for rebuilding. This was so extensive that it was done under a new number EX 154 with a P-type chassis and axles, a Zoller-supercharged Q-type engine, Q-type brake drums, J4 torque reaction cables, and straight-cut gears in the final drive. The works specification for EX 154 included a J4 body, petrol tank, spare wheel carrier, and J2 cycle-type wings, and in this form Kohlrausch scored a number of successes on Continental hill-climbs, which tended to be longer and much higher than the domestic sort at Prescott or Shelsley Walsh. He made 4th fastest time of the day on the Grossglockner in 1935 against bigger-engined Bugattis, Maseratis, and Alfa Romeos. The smaller car's agility proved an advantage on the hairpin bends. However EX 127's record-breaking days were not over and with an all-enveloping streamlined teardrop body with exposed wheels he raised the 750cc record to 130.41mph (209.87kph). Kohlrausch had a bronze cylinder head made locally, sent the engine back to Abingdon for further development, and at Frankfurt in 1936 set a new record at 140.6mph (226.27kph), which remained unbeaten for the next ten years.

BODY sports, 2 doors, 2 seats; record-breaker single-seat.
ENGINE 4 cylinders, in-line; front; 57mm x 73mm, 746cc; 113bhp (84.3kW)@ 7200rpm; 151.5bhp/L (113kW/L).
ENGINE STRUCTURE overhead camshaft; spiral bevel gear vertical camshaft drive; cast iron block, detachable cross-flow head; Elektron sump; coil ignition; Zoller supercharger driven from front of crankshaft, SU carburettor; 3-bearing crankshaft.
TRANSMISSION rear wheel drive; prop shaft balanced to 8000rpm; Wilson 4-speed preselector gearbox; straight-cut bevel final drive 4.5, 4.87, or 4.125:1; rear axle nose-piece through-bolted.
CHASSIS straight and parallel channel section side members underslung at the rear, rivetted steel, with tubular cross members; semi-elliptic springs front and rear with shackles and bronze trunnions; Hartford friction dampers; shaft and cable operated 12in ribbed drum brakes; Bishop cam steering; 12 Imp gal (14.4 US gal, 54.6L) fuel tank; 19 x 4 tyres; centre lock wire wheels, Ace discs on rear.
DIMENSIONS wheelbase 87.7in (222.6cm); track 42in (106.7cm).
PERFORMANCE maximum speed 140.6mph (226.3kph).
PRODUCTION 1.

Top: Bobby Kohlrausch's record car, the much-modified Magic Midget, with his badge on the bonnet.

Right: Kohlrausch on the Reichs-autobahn at Frankfurt.

The last overhead camshaft Midget, the PB was bored out from 57mm to 60mm, providing a useful increase in power. The PA remained on sale and with Britain at last emerging for the Depression the price was reduced to £199.10s. The ruse did not work however, the remaining PAs did not sell well, and 27 were converted to PB specification. The PB was introduced in response to the MG Midget's first real competition. The Singer 9 also had an overhead camshaft engine, was gaining a useful reputation in motor sport, and the 1936 Le Mans had the obligatory slab fuel tank and cowled scuttle.

MG PB production began in June 1935 and ran for 9 months. Improvements included four closer-ratio gears and vertical slats instead of plain honeycomb in the MG radiator. The new facia (burr walnut replacing the forbidden American Sequoia redwood veneer) had a novel feature, in view of the 1934 Road Traffic Act that introduced Belisha Beacons and speed limits. A warning light was arranged to illuminate at 20mph, and go out again at 30mph, letting drivers know they were in a built-up area. Airline bodies on P-types were the work of H W Allingham, a freelance designer who had worked in the coachbuilding industry and drew up cars for Vauxhall, Ford, Austin, and Wolseley.

BODY sports, 2 seats, weight 15.5cwt (787kg); open, 4 seats, Airline Coupe.
ENGINE 4 cylinders, in-line; front; 60mm x 83mm, 939cc; compr 6.7:1; 43bhp (32.1kW) @ 5500rpm; 45.8bhp/L (34.2kW/L).
ENGINE STRUCTURE overhead camshaft; spiral bevel gear vertical camshaft drive; cast iron block, detachable cross-flow head; coil ignition; two SU horizontal carburettors; 3-bearing crankshaft.
TRANSMISSION rear wheel drive; single dry plate clutch; 4-speed non synchromesh manual gearbox; spiral bevel final drive 5.375, 5.875, 5.125:1.
CHASSIS DETAILS straight and parallel channel section side members underslung at the rear, rivetted steel, with tubular cross members; semi-elliptic springs front and rear with shackles and bronze trunnions; Hartford friction dampers front, Luvax hydraulic rear; shaft and cable operated 12in ribbed drum brakes; Bishop cam steering; 12 Imp gal (14.4 US gal, 54.6L) fuel tank; 10 gal (45.5L) 4-seater; 19x4 tyres; Rudge-Whitworth centre lock wire wheels; 4 x 19in.
DIMENSIONS wheelbase 87.3in (221.7cm); track 42in (106.7cm); turning circle 34ft (10.4m); ground clearance 6in (15.2cm); length 135in (343cm); width 51in (129.5cm); height 52in (132cm) with hood up.
PERFORMANCE maximum speed 75mph (120.7kph); 14.7mph (23.7kph) @ 1000rpm; 0-60mph (96kph) 27.4sec; 18.3kg/bhp (24.5kg/kW);fuel consumption 35mpg (8.1L/100km).
PRICE 2-seater £222; 4-seater £240; Airline £290.
PRODUCTION 408 2-seaters; 99 4-seaters; 14 Airline Coupes; 4 chassis for coachbuilders.

Carbodies of Coventry made the MG NA, PA, and PB Allingham Airline Coupes.

1935 P-type Midget Le Mans team car

MG's best performance at Le Mans came in 1934 when a K3 Magnette driven by Charlie Martin and Roy Eccles finished fourth behind a 2.3-litre Alfa Romeo and two 1.5 Rileys. It won the class at 68.9mph (110.9kph) against the Alfa's 74.4mph (119.7kph) and, enhancing MG's growing reputation, a PA Midget finished 17th. In June 1935 seven MGs were entered at Le Mans, three of them K3 Magnettes and four Midgets. One K3 Magnette (No. 39) entered by Maurice Baumer and John Ludovic Ford retired together with an orange one (No. 41, chassis K303 1) of Dutchman Eddie Hertzburger after 92 laps with supercharger problems. The K3 (No. 42), of P Maillard-Brune and Druck, entered on behalf of the famous chocolatier and MG-fancier Jacques Menier, finished ninth overall, won the 1100cc class and came second on the Index of performance. The Viale/Debille Midget (No.58), entered by P Maillard-Brune retired after 98 laps, also suffering with supercharger tribulations. The remaining three Midgets were PAs entered by the works as something of a publicity stunt. Under George Eyston's direction they were driven by women, and finished 24th, 25th, and 26th It was by no means a discreditable performance, and although they were well behind the rival Singer team, they were ahead of the even more rival Austin Sevens.

BODY sports, 2 seats, weight 15.5cwt (787kg).
ENGINE 4 cylinders, in-line; front; 60mm x 83mm, 939cc; compr 6.7:1; 43bhp (32.1kW) @ 5500rpm; 45.8bhp/L (34.1kW/L).
ENGINE STRUCTURE overhead camshaft; spiral bevel gear vertical camshaft drive; cast iron block, detachable cross-flow head; coil ignition; two SU horizontal carburettors; 3-bearing crankshaft.
TRANSMISSION rear wheel drive; single dry plate clutch; 4-speed non synchromesh manual gearbox; spiral bevel final drive with differential lock, 5.875:1, Vibrac axle shafts.
CHASSIS straight and parallel channel section side members underslung at the rear, rivetted steel, with tubular cross members; semi-elliptic springs front and rear with shackles and bronze trunnions; Hartford friction dampers front, Luvax hydraulic rear; shaft and cable operated 12in ribbed drum brakes; Bishop cam steering; 12 Imp gal (14.4 US gal, 54.6L) fuel tank, 10 gal 4-seater; 19 x 4 tyres; Rudge-Whitworth centre lock wire wheels; 4 x 19in; twin spare wheels.
DIMENSIONS wheelbase 87.3in (221.7cm); track 42in (106.7cm); turning circle 34ft (10.4m); ground clearance 6in (15.2cm); length 135in (342.9cm); width 51in (129.5cm); height 52in (132.1cm) with hood up.
PERFORMANCE maximum speed 75mph (120.7kph); 14.7mph (23.7kph) @ 1000rpm; 0-60mph (96kph) 27.4sec; 18.3kg/bhp (24.6kg/kW); 35mpg (8.1kg/kW).
PRODUCTION 3.

Right: Eyston's team of (l to r) Doreen Evans and Barbara Skinner, Mrs Simpson and Joan Richmond, and Colleen Eaton and Margaret Allen went down in MG folklore as the "Dancing Daughters", driving nos 55, 56 and 57.
The cars were afterwards converted to PB specification, the blocks bored out to 60mm and fitted with new pistons supplied by Wolseley. With differential locks, and standard instead of mesh windscreens they took part as "Musketeers" in the Torquay Rally a month after 1935 Le Mans.

1935 R-type single seater

Throughout the 1930s Continental factories dominated motor racing. The R-type was probably the best hope for a major British manufacturer to join in with any chance of success. MG had shown with the K3, the record cars, and the exploits of private owners that it had the talent and initiative to meet the challenge of single seater racing if only the necessary investment was forthcoming. For a time it was, until Leonard Lord, newly appointed by Lord Nuffield, came into the competition department at Abingdon and said, "Well that lot can go for a start." It was the pronouncement of the sort of myopic manager who was to preside over the dismantling of the British motor industry. He was later elevated to the peerage as Lord Lambury. The R-type had a backbone chassis, independent suspension along lines that Colin Chapman of Lotus might have recognised three decades hence, and won its class in the 1935 French Grand Prix. It was greeted with enormous enthusiasm but it needed development to make it competitive. It rolled too much on corners, a characteristic taken quickly into account by H N Charles, that the Mark II, alas stillborn, would have put right. It was not the end of Cowley's interference. Syd Enever drew up a production car with all independent suspension that might have seen it well ahead of the opposition, but to no avail.

BODY racing, single-seat.
ENGINE 4 cylinders, in-line; front; 57mm x 73mm, 746cc; compr 6.25:1; 113bhp (84.3kW) @ 7200rpm; 151.5bhp/L (113kW/L).
ENGINE STRUCTURE ohc; spiral bevel gear vertical camshaft drive through dummy dynamo; cast iron block, detachable cross-flow head; Elektron sump; coil ignition; Zoller supercharger driven from front of crankshaft, SU carb; 3-bearing crank.
TRANSMISSION rear wheel drive; Wilson 4-speed preselector gearbox with overload clutch; straight-cut bevel final drive 4.5, 4.87, or 4.125:1.
CHASSIS backbone steel girder chassis, divided to carry engine; independent suspension by torsion bars and double wishbones front and rear; centre-lock wire wheels; 18 x 4.75 tyres.
DIMENSIONS wheelbase 90.5in (229.9cm); track front 46.4in (117.9cm), rear 45.5in (115.6cm).
PRODUCTION 10.

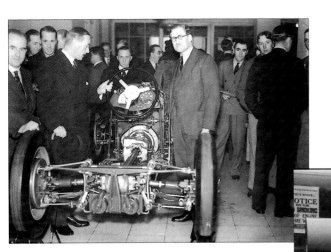

Left: G Eyston at
Brooklands May 1935.
Top: (l to r) C Kimber,
M Campbell and G Eyston
stand by the R-type's
rear suspension.

1936-1939 SA 2.0 litre saloon

Cecil Kimber invited James Wignall, of the coachbuilder Mulliner, to design a luxury saloon codenamed MH that became the SA. Although now only general manager of MG under Leonard Lord, Kimber was a director of Morris Motors, and still had a free hand in MG design even though most of the design department at Abingdon had gone to Cowley. Wignall was following the same trends, well observed and carefully executed, that William Lyons was following for his new SS Jaguar.

The SA was a superlative touring car with the advantage over the SS of a secure racing pedigree. MG had been deeply involved in motor sport for more than a decade in trials, rallies, the Mille Miglia, the TT, the Mannin Beg, Le Mans, the Coppa Acerbo, Brooklands, and record-breaking; SS Jaguar had yet to score any such success. Accordingly the SA could be seen as a car in impeccable taste when some of its rivals were regarded, perhaps in some cases unfairly, as more suitable for the promenade than serious motoring. There may have been nothing especially adventurous about the engineering, but the SA was astonishing value. Flowing wings, spacious boot, ample accommodation, leather upholstery and a burr walnut facia with dull gold dials made it every inch a grand tourer.

BODY saloon drophead coupe; 2 doors, 4 seats.
ENGINE 6 cylinders, in-line; front; 69mm x 102mm, 2288 or 69.5 x 102, 2322cc; compr 6.5:1; 78.5bhp (58.5kW) @ 4200rpm; 34.3bhp/L (25.6kW/L) or 33.8bhp/L (25.2kW/L).
ENGINE STRUCTURE pushrod overhead valve; cast-iron block and head; 2 downdraught SU carbs; twin SU fuel pumps; cooling by pump, fan, and thermostat; 4-bearing crankshaft; rubber mounted at four points.
TRANSMISSION rear wheel drive; cork-faced oil-filled clutch; 4-speed manual gearbox synchromesh on top and third (except early cars); Hardy Spicer needle roller-bearing propeller shaft; spiral bevel final drive 4.75:1.
CHASSIS DETAILS steel box-section frame with tubular cross-bracing; channel-section stiffeners forward; shackled half-elliptic springs all round; Luvax hydraulic dampers; Lockheed hydraulic brakes; 12in diameter drums; Bishop cam and lever steering; 12.5 Imp gal (15 US gal, 56.8L) fuel tank; Dunlop Magnum wire wheels 5.50 tyres 18in rims; Jackall hydraulic jacking system.
DIMENSIONS wheelbase 123in (312.4cm); track 53.4in (135.6cm); turning circle 40ft (12.2m); length 193in (488cm); width 66.5in (169cm); height 60in (152cm).
PERFORMANCE maximum speed 70mph (113kph) approx; fuel consumption 19mpg (14.9L/100km).
PRICE £375.
PRODUCTION 2738 includes saloon, open tourer and Tickfords.

By the time the SA reached production it had knock-on centre-lock wire wheels, the larger-bore engine, and a close-ratio gearbox.

The MG Two-Litre £375

Ex works

1936-1939 SA Tickford Coupe

Charlesworth Motor Bodies of Coventry was founded in 1907 and built bespoke coachwork for distinguished customers before going into the contract business with Morris in 1925. This meant making specialist styles in some quantity. It went through a reconstruction in 1931 and by the middle of the decade was making bodywork for Alvis, Lanchester, Daimler, and MG. Alvis was the biggest, taking four out of every five open four-seater tourers Charlesworth made, so it was unsurprising that those for MG in the SA and WA series were not altogether dissimilar. Charlesworth's economies of scale probably helped to keep the Coupe's price the same as the saloon. The drop-head Tickford coupe by Salmons of Newport Pagnell had a front extension that rolled back, then the entire top was wound down into a compartment in the shapely tail. The Tickford outside hood irons were as much a feature of the drophead coupe of the period as the so-called de ville position, in which the front part of the top furled to give the occupants the airiness of an open car without the draughts. The two big doors had frameless Triplex glass, and chassis lubrication was made easy (but perhaps not for a car's lifetime) by grouped nipples. Once again Kimber had recognized with great accuracy exactly what his valuable middle-class clientele aspired to.

BODY drophead coupe; 2 doors, 4 seats.
ENGINE 6 cylinders, in-line; front; 69mm x 102mm, 2288 or 69.5 x 102, 2322cc; compr 6.5:1; 78.5bhp (58.5kW) @ 4200rpm; 34.3bhp/L (25.6kW/L) or 33.8bhp/L (25.2kW/L).
ENGINE STRUCTURE pushrod overhead valve; cast-iron block and head; 2 downdraught SU carbs; twin SU fuel pumps; cooling by pump, fan, and thermostat; 4-bearing crankshaft; rubber mounted at four points.
TRANSMISSION rear wheel drive; cork-faced oil-filled clutch; 4-speed manual gearbox synchromesh on top and third (except early cars); Hardy Spicer needle roller-bearing propeller shaft; spiral bevel final drive 4.75:1.
CHASSIS DETAILS steel box-section frame with tubular cross-bracing; channel-section stiffeners forward; shackled half-elliptic springs all round; Luvax hydraulic dampers; Lockheed hydraulic brakes; 12in diameter drums; Bishop cam and lever steering; 12.5 Imp gal (15 US gal, 56.8L) fuel tank; Dunlop Magnum wire wheels 5.50 tyres 18in rims; Jackall hydraulic jacking system.
DIMENSIONS wheelbase 123in (312.4cm); track 53.4in (135.6cm); turning circle 40ft (12.2m).
PERFORMANCE maximum speed 80mph (129kph) approx; 20mpg (14.1L/100km).
PRICE Tickford Coupe £398.
PRODUCTION 700 approx.

Far right: Mrs Goldie Gardner "Una" with A T G Gardner.

THE M.G. TWO-LITRE
"Tickford" Folding Head Foursome

Drop-head Coupe. Coachwork by
Salmons & Sons

£398 (ex works)

1936-1939 TA Midget

Pushrod engines and Cecil Kimber's demotion were symptoms of change at MG. The challenge was to sustain a reputation, built on overhead cam engines and sporting achievement, with a prosaic pushrod which, although dignified with the works designation MPJG, was essentially the MSJM of the Series II Morris Ten. There was not much alternative. MG was predicated on Morris components and if the overhead camshaft engine was at the end of its useful volume production life, Abingdon had to make the best of it.

There was some advantage in the up-market SA having a pushrod engine; if it was good enough for the grand tourer it was good enough for the bargain sports car. Compensation came with hydraulic brakes and extra elbowroom. It was moreover faster although not by much. Top gear performance CE improved and the bigger engine just about counterbalanced the additional weight. The chassis was still the traditional MG pattern in 10gauge open channel-section steel with a boxed-in section alongside the engine. The foremost of the five tubular cross-members joined the front dumb-irons, the next carried the radiator, engine ties, and front engine mounting, number three the rear engine mount and gearbox, and four and five the rear spring pick-ups.

BODY sports; 2 doors, 2 seats; weight 15.75cwt (800kg).
ENGINE 4 cylinders, in-line; front; 63.5mm x 102mm, 1292cc; compr 6.5:1; 50bhp (37.3kW) @ 4500rpm; 38.7bhp/L (28.8kW/L).
ENGINE STRUCTURE duplex roller chain-driven camshaft; pushrod overhead valve; cast iron block and top half of crankcase; aluminium ribbed sump; cast iron head; coil ignition; two semi-downdraught SU carburettors; 3-bearing crankshaft; cooling by pump, fan, and thermostat.
TRANSMISSION rear wheel drive; single wet plate clutch; 4-speed manual gearbox; synchromesh on third and top (except on early cars); spiral bevel final drive 4.87:1.
CHASSIS DETAILS parallel steel channel-section frame, underslung at rear, with four tubular cross-bracing and boxed-in round engine and gearbox; semi-elliptic springs front and rear with Silentbloc bushes and sliding trunnions; Luvax hydraulic dampers; Lockheed hydraulic brakes

with 9in drums; cam gear steering; 15 Imp gal (18 US gal, 68.2L), later 13.5 Imp gal (16.2 gal, 61.4L) fuel tank; 4.50 x 19 tyres centre-lock wire wheels.
DIMENSIONS wheelbase 94in (238.8cm); track 45in (114.3cm); turning circle 37ft (11.3m); length 139.5in (354.3cm); width 53in (135cm); height 53.5in (136cm).
PERFORMANCE maximum speed 80.4mph (129.3kph); 16kg/bhp (21.5kg/kW); 28mpg (10.1L/100km).
PRICE sports 2-seater £222, Tickford 2-seater £269 10s.
PRODUCTION 3003.

The Light Car's **praise was faint: "An owner of a PA or PB Midget accustomed to cruising at 60mph would probably find himself in a TA holding the needle at 65".**

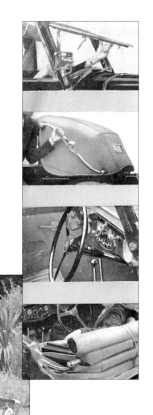

1936-1939 VA 1½ litre

The replacement of the 6-cylinder Magnette with the 4-cylinder VA was a further sign of Nuffield management rationality. The branding of Morris (low-priced), Wolseley (luxury middle class), and MG (sporting) was now well under way and the rationale remained to use as many common components as possible. The principle was already well established in America by General Motors, Nuffield was a pioneer practitioner of it in Europe, and it would become an industry-wide custom for the remainder of the century. Made from May 1937 to the outbreak of war, the VA shared its platform with the SA but the engine and axles came from the collective parts bin of the Wolseley 12 and Morris 12. *The Motor* could not bring itself to describe even the 4-seat open tourer, made not by Tickford or Charlesworth but by Morris Bodies Branch, as a sports car: "If one wanted to, then it would have to be classed with the new regime of silent sports motoring which is becoming so popular," was a flattering reference to Bentley, The Silent Sports Car of the 1930s. The VA managed 77mph (124kph) with the screen up when the testers took it to Brooklands and over 80mph (128.7kph) with it down, which was highly satisfactory for the time, and swifter than the contemporary SS Jaguar. It also suffered more than its share of production changes to engine and body.

BODY saloon, 4 doors, 4 seats; tourer, 2 doors, 4 seats; weight 21.25cwt (1079.5kg).
ENGINE 4 cylinders, in-line; front; 69.5mm x 102mm, 1548cc; compr 6.5:1; 55bhp (41kW)@ 4400rpm; 35.5bhp/L (26.5kW/L).
ENGINE STRUCTURE duplex roller chain-driven camshaft; pushrod overhead valve; cast iron block and top half of crankcase; aluminium ribbed sump; cast iron head; two semi-downdraught SU carburettors; coil ignition; 3-bearing crank; cooling by pump, fan, and thermostat; four rubber engine mountings.
TRANSMISSION rear wheel drive; single-plate wet clutch, later dry plate; 4-speed manual gearbox, synchro on third and top; needle roller bearing prop shaft; spiral bevel final drive 5.22:1.
CHASSIS DETAILS steel box-section frame with tubular cross-bracing; channel-section stiffeners forward; shackled half-elliptic springs all round; Luvax hydraulic dampers; Lockheed hydraulic brakes; 10in diameter drums; Bishop cam and lever steering; 12.5 Imp gal (15 US gal, 56.8L) fuel tank; centre-lock wire wheels 5 x 19 tyres; optional Jackall hydraulic jacking system.
DIMENSIONS wheelbase 108in (274cm); track 50in (127cm); turning circle 38ft (11.6m) left, 42ft (12.8m) right; ground clearance 7in (17.8cm); length 157.5in (400cm); width 61.5in (156.2cm).
PERFORMANCE, VA Tourer maximum speed 76.3mph (122.7kph) see text; 0-50mph (80.5kph) 15.8sec; 19.6kg/bhp (26.3kg/kW); 25-26mpg (10.7-11.3L/100km).
PRICE saloon £280, tourer £325, chassis £215.
PRODUCTION 2407.

Sporting trials were a well-publicised form of motor sport, attracting large crowds and gaining extensive press coverage. When L P Lord closed Abingdon's competition department, covert support was given to private owners who were doing well with their own MGs in trials. Whimsical names for cars abounded and in the light of their brown and cream paintwork, like that on well-known biscuit tins, the Cream Crackers kept MG in the limelight for the remainder of the decade. The team's first cars were alloy-bodied PBs, then for the 1937 season mildly tuned TAs scored a number of successes. The cars were entered in races from time to time, and for the 1938 season three more TAs were prepared, winning the Motor Cycling Club Championship. Developments were tried out when the drivers reported back on the cars' performance. Musketeers and Cream Crackers cars were both TAs in 1937, the Musketeers painted red to win the team prize in a 12-hour race at Donington. The last Crackers, BBL 78, 79, 80, and 81 were TAs with VA engines bored out to 1708cc and fitted with 73mm WA pistons. Being a works driver was no sinecure. The 1938 cars were supplied at a "special price" of £210 with a buy-back proviso at the end of the season for £170 subject to condition. Expenses were £4 per trial for maintenance and £5 for out-of-pocket payments.

BODY sports, 2 doors, 2 seats; weight 15.75cwt (800kg).
ENGINE 4 cylinders, in-line; front; 69.5mm x 102mm, 1548cc; compr 6.5:1; 55bhp (41kW) @ 4400rpm; 35.5bhp/L (26.5kW/L).
ENGINE STRUCTURE duplex roller chain-driven camshaft; pushrod overhead valve; cast iron block and top half of crankcase; aluminium ribbed sump; cast iron head; two semi-downdraught SU carburettors; coil ignition; 3-bearing crankshaft; cooling by pump, fan, and thermostat.
TRANSMISSION rear wheel drive; single wet plate clutch; 4-speed

manual gearbox; synchromesh on third and top; spiral bevel final drive 4.87:1.
CHASSIS DETAILS parallel steel channel-section frame, underslung at rear, with four tubular cross-bracing and boxed-in round engine and gearbox; semi-elliptic springs front and rear with Silentbloc bushes and sliding trunnions; Luvax hydraulic dampers; Lockheed hydraulic brakes with 9in drums; cam gear steering; 9 Imp gal (10.8 US gal, 40.9L) fuel tank.
DIMENSIONS wheelbase 94in (238.8cm); track 45in (114.3cm); turning circle 37ft (11.3m); length 139.5in (354.2cm); width 56in (142.2cm).
PERFORMANCE maximum speed 80.4mph (129.3kph); 14.5kg/bhp (19.5mpg); fuel consumption 28mpg (10.1L/100km).
PRICE sports 2-seater £222, Tickford 2-seater £269 10s, see text for Cream Cracker price.
PRODUCTION 3003.

1939 WA 2.6 litre

The last big MG of the 1930s was a development of the SA with wider body, as a saloon, Tickford drophead coupe, or Charlesworth tourer, of which only nine were made. The engine block dated back to the side-valve Morris Oxford Six of 1935, although with two carburettors' inlet tracts heavily embossed with the MG octagon and heavily finned manifolds like a racing Alfa Romeo, nobody would have known. It was equipped with Aerolite pistons, steel connecting rods, and since the new cylinder head had a compression ratio of 7.25:1 the factory recommended alcohol or leaded fuel of 82 octane. It was the first production MG to have a fully counterbalanced crankshaft and an oil cooler. A dual master cylinder assuaged Kimber's distrust of hydraulic brakes. The wide rear track was intended to help stability and provide more elbow room. Road tests of the WA were curtailed, because although quite fast in top speed terms, acceleration was leisurely. Rising costs at the onset of the war increased saloon prices to £450 and Coupe to £575 in May 1939. A side-mount spare wheel, fitted toolkit in the lid of the luggage locker, a double bulkhead rubber-sealed to insulate the occupants from engine noise, Jackall jacking system, and a beautifully furnished wood facia with Jaeger instruments, put the WA amongst the outstanding touring cars of the day.

BODY saloon/roadster/coupe; weight 24.25cwt (1232kg).
ENGINE 6 cylinders, in-line; front; 73mm x 102mm, 2561cc; compr 7.25:1; 95.5bhp (71.2kW) @ 4400rpm; 37.3bhp/L (27.8kW/L).
ENGINE STRUCTURE pushrod overhead valve; cast-iron block and head; two inclined SU carburettors; twin SU fuel pumps; cooling by pump, fan, and thermostat; 4-bearing crankshaft; rubber mounted at four points.
TRANSMISSION rear wheel drive; Borg & Beck single dry plate clutch; 4-speed manual gearbox synchro on second, third, and top; Hardy Spicer needle roller-bearing divided propeller shaft; spiral bevel final drive 4.8:1.
CHASSIS DETAILS steel box-section frame with tubular cross-bracing; channel-section stiffeners forward; shackled half-elliptic springs all round, Silentbloc bushes at rear; Luvax hydraulic dampers; Lockheed hydraulic brakes; 14in diameter drums; Bishop cam gear steering; 16

Imp gal (19.2 US gal, 72.7L) fuel tank; balanced centre-lock wire wheels 5.50 tyres 18in rims; Jackall hydraulic jacking system standard.
DIMENSIONS wheelbase 123in (312.4cm); track 53.4in (135.6cm) front, 56.5in (143.5cm) rear; turning circle 40ft (12.2m); length 191in (485.1cm).
PERFORMANCE 12.9kg/bhp (17.3kg/kW); fuel consumption 24.4mpg (11.6L/100km).
PRICE saloon £442; drophead coupe £468; Charlesworth tourer £450.
PRODUCTION 369.

The metamorphosis from TA to TB was overtaken by other momentous events in the last months of 1939. The biggest change to the car in April 1939 was the new XPAG engine, indeed not much else changed except for a dry clutch, close-ratio gears from the VA, a lower axle ratio, and a wider body. The snug Tickford with its de luxe interior was also continued although its extra 1.75cwt (88.9kg) affected performance. Winding windows and doors up to shoulder height enhanced practicality. Although the engine size went down from 1292cc to 1250cc, its Treasury-rated horse power went up from 10hp to 11hp owing to the increase in cylinder bore. T-series cars were equipped with the new engine before it was officially announced, the reluctance to make the change public perhaps influenced by the higher taxation bracket into which the TB now fell, even though the difference was only between £7.10s (£7,50) and £8.5s (£8.25). The corollary of the larger cylinder bore was a shorter stroke, 90mm instead of 102mm, so hitherto forbidden engine revs could be safely used. The counterbalanced crankshaft was a further inducement to employ the full rev range. The TB was not only the last MG introduced before the war, for Kimber stopped production as soon as the conflict began, but it was also the last MG made under his jurisdiction.

BODY sports; 2 doors, 2 seats; weight 15.5cwt (787kg).
ENGINE 4 cylinders, in-line; front; 66.5mm x 90mm, 1250cc; compr 7.25:1; 54.4bhp (40.6kW) @ 5200rpm; 43.5bhp/L (32.4kW/L).
ENGINE STRUCTURE duplex roller chain-driven camshaft; pushrod overhead valve; cast iron block and top half of crankcase; aluminium ribbed sump; cast iron head; coil ignition; two semi-downdraught SU carburettors; 3-bearing crankshaft; cooling by pump, fan, and thermostat.
TRANSMISSION rear wheel drive; Borg & Beck single dry plate clutch; 4-speed manual gearbox; synchro on second, third, and top; spiral bevel final drive 5.125:1.
CHASSIS DETAILS parallel steel channel-section frame, underslung at rear, with four tubular cross-bracing and boxed-in round engine and gearbox; semi-elliptic springs front and rear with Silentbloc bushes and sliding trunnions; Luvax hydraulic dampers; Lockheed hydraulic brakes with 9in drums; Bishop cam gear steering; 13.5 Imp gal (16.2 gal, 61.4L) fuel tank; 4.50 x 19.0 tyres; centre-lock wire wheels.
DIMENSIONS wheelbase 94in (238.8cm); track 45in (114.3cm); turning circle 37ft (11.3m); ground clearance 6in (15.2cm); length 139.5in (354.3cm); width 56in (142.2cm); height 53in (134.6cm).
PERFORMANCE maximum speed 75mph (120.7kph); 15.9mph (25.6kph) @ 1000rpm; 0-60mph (96kph) 22.7sec; 14.5kg/bhp (19.4kg/kW); fuel consumption 28mpg (10.1L/100km).
PRICE sports 2-seater £225, Tickford 2-seater £270.
PRODUCTION 379.

121

1945-1949 TC Midget

As soon as war work was ended, with Kimber gone and commercial and industrial recovery a long way off, there was enormous pressure on MG to get production under way as quickly as possible. There was certainly no time to develop a new model, and the SA, VA, and WA had to be abandoned. The T-series was simplified as a matter of expediency so the sliding trunnions, a cherished feature of Midgets from the time of the Montlhéry C-type of 1931, were sacrificed. The body was made 4in (10.2cm) wider, and in October 1945 production of the TC had started. By the end of the year 81 had been made, the following year 1,675.

It was a seller's market both in Britain and overseas, to which MG was being exhorted, indeed compelled, by government diktat to export. Notwithstanding that, the car's success was astonishing, despite its singular disdain of what were regarded as essential attributes in markets such as the United States. The TC had no heater, it was obtainable only in right hand drive, and the ride was distinctly firm. There was only 4in (10.2cm) of seat cushion adjustment less for the backrests although the steering column had a telescopic arrangement to alter the reach. Yet by 1949 MG had made and sold 10,000, more than three times the total of any MG hitherto.

BODY sports, 2 doors, 2 seats; weight 1735lb (787kg).
ENGINE 4 cylinders, in-line; front; 66.5mm x 90mm, 1250cc; cr 7.25:1; 54.4bhp (40.6kW) @ 5200rpm; 43.5bhp/L (32.4kW/L); 63.5lbft (85Nm) @ 2600rpm.
ENGINE STRUCTURE duplex roller chain-driven camshaft; pushrod overhead valve; cast iron block and top half of crankcase; aluminium ribbed sump; cast iron head; coil ignition; two semi-downdraught SU carburettors; 3-bearing crank; cooling by pump, fan, and thermostat.
TRANSMISSION rear wheel drive; Borg & Beck single dry plate clutch; 4-speed manual gearbox; synchro on second, third, and top; spiral bevel final drive 5.125:1.
CHASSIS DETAILS parallel steel channel-section frame, underslung at rear, with four tubular cross-bracing and boxed-in round engine and gearbox; semi-elliptic springs front and rear with shackles; Luvax lever arm hydraulic dampers; Lockheed hydraulic brakes with 9in drums; Bishop cam gear steering; 13.5 Imp gal (16.2 US gal, 61.4L) fuel tank; 4.50 x 19.0 tyres; centre-lock wire wheels.
DIMENSIONS wheelbase 94in (238.8cm); track 45in (114.3cm); turning circle 37ft (11.3m); ground clearance 6in (15.2cm); length 139.5in (354.3cm); width 56in (142.2cm); height 53in (134.6cm).
PERFORMANCE maximum speed 75mph (120.7kph); 15.9mph (25.6kph) @ 1000rpm; 0-60mph (96kph) 22.7sec; 14.5kg/bhp (19.4kg/kW); fuel consumption 28mpg (10.1L/100km).
PRICE sports 2-seater £527.16s 8d (£527.83) including purchase tax.
PRODUCTION last car 10 November 1949 serial number 10,001, chassis 10,251.

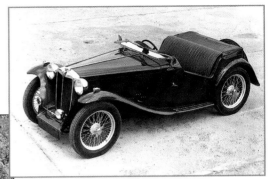

Independent front suspension, rack and pinion steering, the XPAG engine, and part-monocoque body construction; the ingredients of the post-war MG were coming together. The coil spring and wishbone ifs remained on MGs for half a century. Alec Issigonis as a young designer drew it up for a Morris Ten in the 1930s, but the management chose something cheaper. The Y-type was based on Morris Series E and Wolseley 8 press-work, although subtly done so that it could almost go unnoticed. An MG Ten planned for 1940 was postponed. The Y-type was not swift but handled well, fulfilling a requirement during severe petrol rationing for a small economical luxury saloon. MG had acquired a nostalgic prestige in wartime, encouraged by advertisements with servicemen beside motor launches or aircraft remarking, "It reminds me of my MG." Y-types backed up the sports cars in rallies, which were supplanting trials as the leading variety of club motor sport. Geoff Holt won the first Daily Express 1000 mile rally in 1950 driving a TD, and Len Shaw came third in a YA, both winning their class. Production of the YA began in April 1947 until superseded by the YB. A few chassis were sold to Swiss coachbuilders, and a series of special-bodied cars was planned for Roger Barlow of Los Angeles, one of MG's flourishing export markets.

BODY saloon; 4 doors, 4 seats; weight 21cwt (1067kg).
ENGINE 4 cylinders, in-line; front; 66.5mm x 90mm, 1250cc; compr 7.25:1; 46bhp (34.3kW) @ 4800rpm; 36.8bhp/L (27.4kW/L); 59lbft (79Nm) @ 2400rpm.
ENGINE STRUCTURE duplex roller chain-driven camshaft; pushrod ohv; cast iron block and top half of crankcase; aluminium ribbed sump; cast iron head; coil ignition; SU 1¼in carburettor; 3-bearing crank; cooling by pump, fan, and thermostat.
TRANSMISSION rear wheel drive; 7¼in Borg & Beck sdp; 4-speed manual gearbox; synchromesh on second, third, and top; Hardy Spicer needle roller bearing prop shaft; spiral bevel final drive 5.142:1.
CHASSIS DETAILS steel welded box-section side rails and tubular cross members, underslung at rear; ifs by coil spring and wishbone, live rear axle with shackled semi-elliptic leaf springs and Panhard rod; Luvax-Girling lever arm hydraulic dampers; Lockheed hydraulic brakes with 9in drums; rack and pinion steering; 13.5 Imp gal (16.2 US gal, 62L) fuel tank; 5.25 x 16 tyres; bolt-on steel disc wheels, Jackall hydraulic jacking system.
DIMENSIONS wheelbase 99in (251.5cm); track 47.4in (120.4cm) front, 50in (127cm) rear; length 161in (409cm); width 59in (149cm); height 58in (147cm).
PERFORMANCE maximum speed 71mph (114.3kph); 0-60mph (96kph) 28.2sec; 23.2kg/bhp (31.1kg/kW); fuel con 27mpg (10.5L/100km).
PRICE £671.11s 8d (£671 58) including purchase tax.
PRODUCTION 6158.

Top: pre-war MG Ten
mock-up of what was
later to become the
Y type 1¼ litre saloon.

1948-1950 YT 1¼ litre open 4-seater

Introduced at the first post-war motor show at Earls Court, the YT looked more sporting than the Y-type saloon, with small cowls on the scuttle and a TC-style fabric-covered instrument panel instead of the saloon's veneered wood. There were some detail differences between the chassis of the saloon and tourer; on account of its lighter weight the rear springs were dissimilar and there were alterations to the steering rack and column. The two doors were deeply cut away to emphasise the sporting nature but this meant sidescreens, not the winding windows of its pre-war coupe forebears. Hood and frame were stored in a compartment that reduced space in the back seat. Under pressure to export, the tourer was available with left hand drive, and even had flashing direction indicators instead of the saloon's semaphore trafficators.

Since only a few were expected to be sold in Britain (the bulk of production to America and Australia) it was priced the same as the saloon on the home market. The YTs did not benefit from the modifications carried out on the Y-series at the end of 1951 coinciding with the introduction of the TD. Even with the TC's twin carburettor engine, the YT was not a success. The world had moved on from the leisured, unhurried era of the VA tourer.

BODY open tourer, 2 doors, 4 seats; weight 2184lb (991kg).
ENGINE 4 cylinders, in-line; front; 66.5mm x 90mm, 1250cc; compr 7.25:1; 54bhp (40.3kW) @ 5200rpm; 43.2bhp/L (32.2kW/L); 63.8lbft (92Nm) @ 2600rpm.
ENGINE STRUCTURE duplex roller chain-driven camshaft; pushrod overhead valve; cast iron block and top half of crankcase; aluminium ribbed sump; cast iron head; coil ignition; two SU 1ˉin H2 carburettors; 3-bearing crankshaft; cooling by pump, fan, and thermostat.
TRANSMISSION rear wheel drive; 7ˉin Borg & Beck single dry plate clutch; 4-speed manual gearbox; synchromesh on second, third, and top; Hardy Spicer needle roller bearing prop shaft; spiral bevel final drive 5.142:1.
CHASSIS DETAILS steel welded box-section side rails and tubular cross members, underslung at rear; independent front suspension by coil spring and wishbone, live rear axle with shackled semi-elliptic leaf springs and Panhard rod; Luvax-Girling lever arm hydraulic dampers; Lockheed hydraulic brakes with 9in drums; rack and pinion steering; 13.5 Imp gal (16.2 US gal, 61.4L) fuel tank; 5.25 x 16 tyres; bolt-on steel disc wheels, Jackall hydraulic jacking system.
DIMENSIONS wheelbase 99in (251.5cm); track front 47.4in (120.4cm), rear 50in (127cm); length 161in (408.9cm); width 59in (149cm); height 58in (147cm) approx.
PERFORMANCE maximum speed 76mph (122.3kph); 0-60mph (96kph) 28.2sec;18.3kg/bhp (24.6kg/kW); fuel consumption 27mpg (10.5L/100km).
PRICE £671.11s 8d (£671 58) including purchase tax.
PRODUCTION 877.

1947 Coachbuilt Y-types

MGs had been popular with coachbuilders in the 1930s. Cecil Kimber had a striking looking supercharged K1 with bodywork by Corsica (it took its name from the street in Kings Cross, not the Mediterranean), specialists in rakish coupes. Magnas bodies were made by Swiss coachbuilders Sportcar AG, and a P-type by Hami also of Zürich. Swiss Keller made a WA look like a Mercedes parade car, Salmons like a Bentley.

In the 1940s the Y-type was the only chassis on offer and it was seized upon by a number of continental coachbuilders hoping for business. Pininfarina proved with its ground-breaking 1948 Cisitalia that it was possible to set a trend for a generation, even if the make of car it was set with vanished into oblivion. Zagato was ambitious and showed a YA at the Lugano Salon in 1949. It was also a mould-breaker but scarcely a trend-setter. Its cockpit was composed of curved-glass panels in the style of a second world war aircraft canopy. It must have given an airy ambience inside, unlike the rather gloomily trimmed YA saloon. The idea did not catch on and only one was ever made. Castagnata, another Italian carrozzeria from Milan, made a more elegant attempt with a theme taken up later by Bertone for the more successful Arnolt-MG.

BODY coupe, 2 doors, 4 seats; weight approx 20cwt (1016kg).
ENGINE 4 cylinders, in-line; front; 66.5mm x 90mm, 1250cc; compr 7.25:1; 46bhp (34.3kW) @ 4800rpm; 36.8bhp/L (27.4kW/L); 59lbft (79Nm) @ 2400rpm.
ENGINE STRUCTURE duplex roller chain-driven camshaft; pushrod ohv; cast iron block and top half of crankcase; aluminium ribbed sump; cast iron head; coil ignition; SU 1¨in carb; 3-bearing crankshaft; cooling by pump, fan, and thermostat.
TRANSMISSION rear wheel drive; 7¨in Borg & Beck single dry plate clutch; 4-speed manual gearbox; synchromesh on second, third, and top; Hardy Spicer needle roller bearing prop shaft;spiral bevel final drive 5.142:1.
CHASSIS DETAILS steel welded box-section side rails and tubular cross members, underslung at rear; independent front suspension by coil spring and wishbone, live rear axle with shackled semi-elliptic leaf springs and Panhard rod; Luvax-

Girling lever arm hydraulic dampers; Lockheed hydraulic brakes with 9in drums; rack and pinion; 13.5 Imp gal (16.2 US gal, 61.3L) fuel tank; 5.25 x 16 tyres; bolt-on steel disc wheels, Jackall hydraulic jacking system.
DIMENSIONS wheelbase 99in (251.5cm); track front 47.4in (120.4cm), rear 50in (127cm).
PERFORMANCE maximum speed 71mph (114kph); 0-60mph (96kph) @ 28.2sec; 22.1kg/bhp (29.6kg/kW); fuel consumption 27mpg (10.5L/100km).

Right: Zagato-bodied YA.

1949-1953 TD Midget

The YT tourer was a serious disappointment for Abingdon. There had been Riley-MG and uprated TC proposals, but they were adandoned in the quest for a new sports 2-seater. When they saw it, MG traditionalists were dismayed. The TD was introduced with disc, not centre-lock wire wheels, effete independent front suspension, and undignified front and rear bumpers. It even abandoned the traditional MG underslung rear chassis frame. Accommodating the American market was all very well but this seemed too much. The conclusion was a little hasty. Had it not been for the US market the whole MG culture might have died out. As it was, the TD was not only more comfortable; it was also more robust and cornered better. Independent suspension, a stiffer chassis, and lowered gearing more than made up for the increase in weight. The development programme for the TD consisted of little more than shortening a Y-type chassis by 5in (13cm) between the wheels, and reconfiguring a TC body. Formal drawings were produced, with a prototype in 1948, and a year later production commenced. One of the first modifications was to put holes in the disc wheels, ostensibly to help brake cooling. It may indeed have done so but the effect was to transform the car's appearance. Eight out of every ten TDs made went to the United States.

BODY roadster, 2 doors, 2 seats; weight 1930lb (875.5kg).
ENGINE 4 cylinders, in-line; front; 66.5mm x 90mm, 1250cc; compr 7.25:1; 54.4bhp (40.6kW) @ 5200rpm; 43.5bhp/L (32.5kW/L); 63.5 lbft (85Nm) @ 2600rpm.
ENGINE STRUCTURE duplex roller chain-driven camshaft; pushrod overhead valve; cast iron block and top half of crankcase; aluminium ribbed sump; cast iron head; coil ignition; two semi-downdraught SU carburettors; 3-bearing crankshaft; cooling by pump, fan, and thermostat.
TRANSMISSION rear wheel drive; single dry plate clutch; 4-speed manual gearbox, synchromesh on 2nd, 3rd, top; auto; hypoid final drive 5.125:1.
CHASSIS DETAILS steel welded box-section side rails and tubular cross members; independent front suspension by coil spring and wishbone, live rear axle with semi-elliptic leaf springs; Luvax-Girling lever arm hydraulic dampers; Lockheed hydraulic brakes with 9in drums, 2-leading shoe at front; rack and pinion steering; 12.5 Imp gal (15 US gal, 56.8L) fuel tank; 5.50 x 15 tyres; bolt-on steel disc wheels.
DIMENSIONS wheelbase 94in (239cm); track front 47.4in (120cm), rear 50in (127cm); turning circle 31.3ft (9.5m); ground clearance 6in (15cm); length 145in (368cm); width 58.3in (148cm); height 56in (142cm);
PERFORMANCE contemporary test maximum speed 77.2mph (124kph); 14.4mph (23kph) @ 1000rpm; 0-60mph (96kph) 21.3sec; 16.1kg/bhp (21.6kg/kW); fuel consumption 25mpg (11.3L/100km).
PRICE £751.19s.2d (£751.96).
PRODUCTION 29,664.

1949 George Phillips Le Mans TC

George Phillips, Fleet Street newspaper photographer and founder with Gregor Grant and John Bolster of *Autosport,* nursed a passion for motorsport, MGs and the Le Mans 24 Hours Race. He sought help from the factory on how to make his TC faster for the 1947 Brighton Speed Trials. Motor racing was beginning to understand the importance of reducing frontal area and elementary aerodynamics, so Phillips commissioned new bodywork first from Harry Lester, later of Lester MG, then Ted Goodwin. A TC might have been fine for amateur club racing, but at Le Mans Phillips and his co-driver R M "Curly" Dryden were up against four Talbot-Lagos, seven Delahayes, four Delages, six Aston Martins, an HRG, hordes of Simcas and two of the new Ferrari 166MMs. One of the Ferraris won and Culpan and Aldington were third in their Frazer-Nash, but Dryden suffered an electrical fault out on the circuit. A mechanic was despatched to instruct the driver on effecting a cure. Dryden, accustomed to the leisurely application of rules in British club racing, gave him a lift back to the pits and was immediately disqualified. Phillips was most disgruntled but he and Eric Winterbottom had more luck in 1950, finishing an astonishing 2nd in the 1½-litre class to a special Jowett Jupiter, averaging 73mph (117kph) over 24 hours.

BODY sports, 2 seats.
ENGINE 4 cylinders, in-line; front; 66.5mm x 90mm, 1250cc.
ENGINE STRUCTURE duplex roller chain-driven camshaft; pushrod overhead valve; cast iron block and top half of crankcase; aluminium ribbed sump; cast iron head; coil ignition; two semi-downdraught SU carburettors; 3-bearing crankshaft; cooling by pump, fan, and thermostat.
TRANSMISSION rear wheel drive; Borg & Beck sdp clutch; 4-speed manual gearbox; synchromesh on second, third, and top; spiral bevel final drive 5.125:1.
CHASSIS DETAILS parallel steel channel-section frame, underslung at rear, with four tubular cross-bracing and boxed-in round engine and gearbox; semi-elliptic springs front and rear with shackles; Luvax lever arm hydraulic dampers; Lockheed hydraulic brakes with 9in drums; Bishop cam gear steering; 16 Imp gal (19.2 US gal, 72.7L) fuel tank; 4.50 x 19.0 tyres; centre-lock wire wheels.

DIMENSIONS wheelbase 94in (239cm); track 45in (114cm); turning circle 37ft (11.3m); ground clearance 6in (15cm); length 139.5in (354.3cm); width 56in (142cm); height 53in (135cm).
PERFORMANCE fuel consumption 22mpg (12.8L/100km); 15.9mph (25.6kph) @ 1000rpm.
PRODUCTION 1.

From 1950 to 1953 the factory offered a tuned version of the TD to the chassis numbers of which TDC (for Competition) prefixes (later TD3) were added. These were not to be confused with TD2s identified by engine numbers XPAG TD2, which merely incorporated running changes including a bigger clutch. Centrepiece of the TDC conversion was the TC Stage I cylinder head modified to different stages of tune between 57bhp (42.5kW) and 61bhp (45.5kW). The suspension was stiffened at the front by means of extra, and rather old-fashioned looking, Andrex adjustable friction-type shock absorbers. The modified cylinder head increased the compression ratio and it had bigger valves. Identifying features on Mark IIs included a small bulge on the right side of the bonnet to accommodate the bigger inlet manifold, different badges and chrome radiator slats on some examples. It was possible to increase power still more for racing and the XPAG could be made to give half as much power again with a supercharger. The TD/C began as a motor racing project for Dick Jacobs, who took on and beat the benchmarking HRGs in the spring of 1950. Three works cars, FRX 941, 942 and 943 were prepared for Jacobs, Ted Lund and George Phillips to race at Silverstone, and in a drenching wet TT race at Dundrod they won a worthy team prize.

BODY roadster, 2 doors, 2 seats; weight 1930lb (875.5kg).

ENGINE 4 cylinders, in-line; front; 66.5mm x 90mm, 1250cc; compr 8.6:1, 8.1:1 optional; between 57bhp (42.5kW) and 61bhp (45.5kW), 45.6bhp/L (34kW/L) and 48.8bhp/L (36.4kW/L).

ENGINE STRUCTURE duplex roller chain-driven camshaft; pushrod overhead valve; cast iron block and top half of crankcase; aluminium ribbed sump; cast iron head; coil ignition, manual advance-retard; two semi-downdraught 1⅜in H4 SU carburettors, two SU fuel pumps; Lucas Sports Coil; 3-bearing crankshaft; cooling by pump, fan, and thermostat.

TRANSMISSION rear wheel drive; single dry plate clutch; 4-speed manual gearbox, synchromesh on 2nd, 3rd, top; auto; hypoid final drive 4.875, 4.55, or 5.125:1.

CHASSIS DETAILS steel welded box-section side rails and tubular cross members; independent front suspension by coil spring and wishbone, live rear axle with semi-elliptic leaf springs; Luvax-Girling lever arm hydraulic dampers, Andrex friction dampers at front; Lockheed hydraulic brakes with 9in drums, 2-leading shoe at front; rack and pinion steering; 12.5 Imp gal (15 US gal, 56.8L) fuel tank; 5.50 x 15 tyres; bolt-on steel disc wheels.

DIMENSIONS wheelbase 94in (239cm); track front 47.4in (120cm) rear 50in (127cm); turning circle 31.3ft (9.5m); ground clearance 6in (15cm); length 145in (368cm); width 58.3in (148cm); height 56in (142cm).

PERFORMANCE maximum speed 83mph (134kph); 0-60mph (96kph) 16.5sec; between 15.4kg/bhp (20.6kg/kW) and 14.4kg/bhp (19.2kg/kW); fuel consumption 25mpg (11.3L/100km)

PRICE £751.19s.2d (£751.96).

PRODUCTION 1,710.

135

1951 EX 172 George Phillips Le Mans TD

Having competed successfully in 1949 and 1950, Phillips had an automatic entry for the 1951 Le Mans, and with John Thornley hatched a new MG based on the TD to replace his TC. EX 172 was allocated to a design for a streamlined body on chassis TD/C5336. Syd Enever designed it and UMG 400 was the true inspiration of the MGA. The full-width sweeping wings, low rounded nose, and tapered tail were probably more shapely than strictly aerodynamic. There was a lot of talk at the time of ram air effect and a small scoop on the bonnet hopefully accelerated air into the carburettors. Phillips did not like the car much. He was unaccustomed to independent front suspension and was unhappy with the high driving position dictated by the TD chassis. Le Mans was not a success. Trouble was attributed to the quality of the fuel and despite lowering the compression ratio the car dropped a valve and put a hole in a piston. Phillips and his co-driver Allen Rippon carried on with three cylinders but eventually the car ran its bearings. Recriminations followed. Phillips felt he had not had much help from the factory and was disappointed at the preparation of the car. Thornley disapproved of his approach to driving. The car was broken up regarded, wrongly as it happened, as a disappointment all round.

BODY roadster, 2 doors, 2 seats.
ENGINE 4 cylinders, in-line; front; 66.5mm x 90mm, 1250cc; compr 8.1:1.
ENGINE STRUCTURE duplex roller chain-driven camshaft; pushrod overhead valve; cast iron block and top half of crankcase; aluminium ribbed sump; cast iron head; coil ignition; two semi-downdraught 1°in H4 SU carburettors, two SU fuel pumps; Lucas Sports Coil; 3-bearing crankshaft; cooling by pump, fan, and thermostat.
TRANSMISSION rear wheel drive; single dry plate clutch; 4-speed manual gearbox, synchromesh on 2nd, 3rd, top; auto; hypoid final drive 4.875, 4.55, or 5.125:1.
CHASSIS DETAILS steel welded box-section side rails and tubular cross members; independent front suspension by coil spring and wishbone, live rear axle with semi-elliptic leaf springs; Luvax-Girling lever arm hydraulic dampers, Andrex friction dampers at front; Lockheed hydraulic brakes with 9in drums, 2-leading shoe at front; rack and pinion steering; 12.5 Imp gal (15 US gal, 56.8L) fuel tank; 5.50 x 15 tyres; bolt-on steel disc wheels.
DIMENSIONS wheelbase 94in (239cm); track front 47.4in (120cm) rear 50in (127cm); turning circle 31.3ft (9.5m) ground clearance 6in (15cm); length 145in (368cm); width 58.3in (148cm); approx height 48in (122cm).
PERFORMANCE maximum speed 116mph (187kph).
PRODUCTION 1.

Right: Alec Hounslow at wheel, Syd Enever third from left.

1951-1953 YB saloon

After four years, improvements to the Y-type at the 1951 Motor Show at Earls Court corresponded to its shared features with the TD, including a barely noticeable increase in power. The hypoid final drive now used throughout the Nuffield range was quieter, and the front brakes were changed to two-leading shoe with two cylinders for each drum to even out wear and increase efficiency. Wheel sizes were reduced to 15in (38cm) instead of 16in (41cm) and the tyre section increased to 5.50. At the front an anti-roll bar was introduced and at the back heavier-duty Luvax-Girling lever arm dampers brought in as the Panhard rod was deleted. The result of these changes was a reduction in body roll. It was a pity the YB was so slow and low-geared, as its good handling could easily have accommodated more speed. Bodywork alterations to accommodate the smaller wheels included fuller rear wings, and larger-section tyres meant an amendment to the neat spare wheel stowage under the luggage boot.

Its modest rally successes continued. A team of works YBs driven by Len Shaw, Reg Holt, and Geoff Holt won the team prize in the 1953 RAC Rally, Shaw finishing a keenly contested sixth overall, and Dick Jacobs won his class in the production Touring car race at Silverstone three years in a row.

BODY saloon, 4 doors, 4 seats; weight 21cwt (1067kg).
ENGINE 4 cylinders, in-line; front; 66.5mm x 90mm, 1250cc; compr 7.25:1; 44bhp (34.3kW) @ 4800rpm; 35.2bhp/L (27.4kW/L); 59lbft (79Nm) @ 2400rpm.
ENGINE STRUCTURE duplex roller chain-driven camshaft; pushrod overhead valve; cast iron block and top half of crankcase; aluminium ribbed sump; cast iron head; coil ignition; SU 1¨in carburettor; 3-bearing crankshaft; cooling by pump, fan, and thermostat.
TRANSMISSION rear wheel drive; 7¨in Borg & Beck single dry plate clutch; 4-speed manual gearbox; synchromesh on second, third, and top; Hardy Spicer needle roller bearing prop shaft; hypoid bevel final drive 5.142:1.
CHASSIS DETAILS steel welded box-section side rails and tubular cross members, underslung at rear; independent front suspension by coil spring and wishbone, anti-roll bar; live rear axle with shackled semi-elliptic leaf springs; Luvax-Girling lever arm hydraulic dampers; Lockheed 2 leading-shoe (front) hydraulic brakes with 9in drums; rack and pinion steering; 13.5 Imp gal (16.2 US gal, 61.4L) fuel tank; 5.50 x 15 tyres; bolt-on steel disc wheels, Jackall hydraulic jacking system.
DIMENSIONS wheelbase 99in (251.5cm); track front 47.4in (120cm), rear 50in (127cm); length 161in (409cm).
PERFORMANCE maximum speed 71mph (114kph); 0-60mph (96kph) 28.2sec; 24.3kg/bhp (31.1kg/kW); fuel consumption 27mpg (10.5L/100km).
PRICE £671.11s 8d (£671 58) inc purchase tax.
PRODUCTION 1301.

Far right: Team car. The works YBs on the 1953 RAC Rally wore Lance Corporal, Corporal and Sergeant stripes. This corporal car was driven by Len Shaw.

1952 EX 175 prototype MGA

Morale at Abingdon was low as a result of BMC's reluctance to invest in new model development. Sales of the TD were in decline and competitors such as the Triumph TR2 looked threatening, so Syd Enever designed a new chassis frame to deal with the problem shown up by UMG 400's tall driving position He placed the side members wide apart, so that the driver and passengers could be lowered on each side of the transmission tunnel, and to compensate for loss of stiffness added a strong scuttle framework. Two such chassis were made, with a body along the lines of UMG 400, inspired by sports racing cars of the 1940s and 1950s, notably the 1939-1940 Mille Miglia BMW 328s. The shapely HMO 6 had hood, sidescreens, bumpers, and although the tall T-series engine demanded a bulge in the bonnet top, it was the shape adopted almost without alteration for the MGA. The commercially motivated L P Lord, who had just confirmed at the Earls Court Motor Show that he had bought the Austin-Healey 100, turned down EX175 in October 1952 and the design was put on ice. Enever streamlined the second EX 175 chassis in 1953 with wheel spats and a bubble cockpit, to see if it could be used as a record-breaker, but it proved unsuitable in wind-tunnel tests and was abandoned until incorporated in EX179.

BODY roadster, 2 doors, 2 seats; weight approx 1930lb (875.5kg).
ENGINE 4 cylinders, in-line; front; 66.5mm x 90mm, 1250cc; cr 7.25:1; 54.4bhp (40.6kW) @ 5200rpm; 43.5bhp/L (32.5kW/L); 63.5lbft (85Nm) @ 2600rpm.
ENGINE STRUCTURE duplex roller chain-driven camshaft; pushrod overhead valve; cast iron block and top half of crankcase; aluminium ribbed sump; cast iron head; coil ignition; two semi-downdraught 1"in H4 SU carburettors, two SU fuel pumps; Lucas Sports Coil; 3-bearing crankshaft; cooling by pump, fan, and thermostat.
TRANSMISSION rear wheel drive; single dry plate clutch; 4-speed manual gearbox, synchromesh on 2nd, 3rd, top; auto; hypoid final drive 4.875, 4.55, or 5.125:1.
CHASSIS DETAILS steel welded box-section perimeter side rails and tubular cross members; independent front suspension by coil spring and wishbone, live rear axle with semi-elliptic leaf springs; Luvax-Girling lever arm hydraulic dampers; Lockheed hydraulic brakes with 9in drums, 2-leading shoe at front; rack and pinion steering; 12.5 Imp gal (15 US gal, 56.8L) fuel tank; 5.50 x 15 tyres; bolt-on steel disc wheels.
DIMENSIONS wheelbase 94in (239cm); track front 47.4in (120cm), rear 50in (127cm); turning circle 31.3ft (9.5m); ground clearance 6in (15cm); length 145in (368cm); width 58.3in (148cm); height 56in (142cm).
PERFORMANCE 16.1kg/bhp (21.6kg/kW).
PRODUCTION 2 chassis frames, 1 body.

The raked grille, lowered bonnet, faired-in headlamps, and new interior of the TF were not at first highly regarded at Abingdon. It was looked on as something of a stop-gap and not a very happy one. The radiator was imitation, with a dummy filler cap and a header tank under the bonnet and, mindful of criticism of the disc wheels on the TD, new hubs were made so that wire wheels could be offered as an option. The engine was TD Mark II, otherwise not much had changed.

The TF was not even well received on its introduction at the 1953 motor show. The press and enthusiasts were mesmerised by streamlined TR2s and Austin-Healeys that did 100mph (160.9kph) for about the price of a TF. Jaguar was making cars that did 130mph (209kph) so the little MG seemed well outclassed.

It was years before the TF's elegant proportions and traditional structure were regarded as classic. New model development was still being done at Abingdon much as it had been thirty years before; there were no drawings for the new shape; Freddie Wake and Bert Wirdnam hammered out the flowing wings in a fortnight. Working with them was a panel beater Billy Wilkins, who had worked at Raworth, the firm that had built some of Kimber's first cars.

BODY roadster, 2 doors, 2 seats; weight 1930lb (875.5kg).
ENGINE 4 cylinders, in-line; front; 66.5mm x 90mm, 1250cc; compr 8.0:1; 57bhp (42.5kW) @ 5500rpm; 45.6bhp/L (34kW/L); 65lbft (87Nm) @ 3000rpm.
ENGINE STRUCTURE duplex roller chain-driven cam; pushrod ohv; cast iron block and top half of crankcase; aluminium ribbed sump; cast iron head with bathtub combustion chambers; coil ignition; two semi-downdraught SU carbs; 3-bearing crank; cooling by pump, fan, and thermostat.
TRANSMISSION rear wheel drive; 8in sdp clutch; 4-speed manual gearbox, synchromesh on 2nd, 3rd, top; auto; hypoid final drive 4.875:1.
CHASSIS DETAILS steel welded box-section side rails, tubular cross members, and scuttle reinforcement; ifs by coil spring and wishbone, live rear axle with semi-elliptic leaf springs; Luvax-Girling lever arm hydraulic dampers; Lockheed hydraulic brakes with 9in drums, 2-leading shoe at front; rack and pinion steering; 12.5 Imp gal (15 US gal, 56.8L); 5.5 x 15 tyres; bolt-on steel disc wheels, wire wheels optional.
DIMENSIONS wheelbase 94in (239cm); track 47.4in (120cm) front, 50in (127cm) rear, 48.4in (123cm)/ 50.8in (129cm) with wire wheels; turning circle 31.3ft (9.5m); ground clearance 6in (15cm); length 147in (373cm); width 58.3in (148cm); height 54.5in (138cm).
PERFORMANCE maximum speed 73.5mph (118kph); 15.3mph (24.5kph) @ 1000rpm; 0-60mph (96kph) 18.9sec; 15.4kg/bhp (20.6kg/kW); 25mpg (11.3L/100km).
PRICE £780.5s.10d (£780.29).
PRODUCTION 6,200.

CLIMBING

CORNERING

FLAT OUT

1953 Arnolt, Ghia-Aigle, and Shipsides

The shorter TD made a better basis for a coachbuilder than the YA. Nuccio Bertone's struggling Carrozzeria showed two with open and closed bodywork at the 1952 Turin Motor Show through Nuffield distributors Fattori and Mantani of Rome. They were in the fashionable full-width Italian style with an MG radiator shell upright at the front. It was a pretty car with good proportions and caught the attention of Chicago MG importer Harold 'Wacky' Arnolt, who also imported Aston Martins, Bentleys, and Bristols. He felt sure he could sell more TDs if they looked this good and did not have the quirkiness or frailty associated with Italian cars. He ordered 100 of each sort from Bertone and was immediately appointed a vice-president. They did not sell quickly. New York importer Inskip tried something the same with TDs stretched by 10in (25.4cm) to provide four seats and bigger doors. At $2925 only 12 were made.

Ghia-Aigle made six specially-bodied TDs for Swiss importer J H Keller. They too featured upright MG radiator shells and full-width bodywork. The open cars had tail-fins rather like the later Facellia, and MG took a keen interest in the result. Nottingham dealer Shipsides commissioned a rather bulbous coupe as an experiment but only one was ever built.

Arnolt 1¼-litre:
BODY coupe, convertible; 2 doors, 2+2 seats; weight 2103lb (954kg) coupe, 2083lb (945kg) convertible.
ENGINE 4 cylinders, in-line; front; 66.5mm x 90mm, 1250cc; compr 7.25:1; 54.4bhp (40.6kW) @ 5200rpm; 43.5bhp/L (32.5kW/L); 63.5lbft (85Nm) @ 2600rpm.
ENGINE STRUCTURE duplex roller chain-driven camshaft; pushrod overhead valve; cast iron block and top half of crankcase; aluminium ribbed sump; cast iron head; coil ignition; two semi-downdraught SU carburettors; 3-bearing crankshaft; cooling by pump, fan, and thermostat.
TRANSMISSION rear wheel drive; Borg and Beck sdp clutch; 4-speed manual gearbox, synchromesh on 2nd, 3rd, top; auto; hypoid final drive 5.125:1.
CHASSIS DETAILS steel welded box-section side rails and tubular cross members; independent front suspension by coil spring and wishbone, live rear axle with semi-elliptic leaf springs; Luvax-Girling lever arm hydraulic dampers; Lockheed hydraulic brakes with 9in drums, 2-leading shoe at front; rack and pinion steering; 12.5 Imp gal (15 US gal, 56.8L) fuel tank; 5.50 x 15 tyres; bolt-on steel disc wheels, Borrani wire wheels to Bertone Arnolt TD.
DIMENSIONS wheelbase 94in (239cm); track front 47.4in (120cm), rear 50in (127cm); turning circle 31.3ft (9.5m); ground clearance 6in (15cm); length 160in (406cm); width 60in (152cm); height 55in (140cm).
PERFORMANCE 17.5kg/bhp (23.5kg/kW); 14.4mph (23.2kph) @ 1000rpm; fuel consumption 25mpg (11.3l/100km).
PRICE US POE $2995 rising to $3585.
PRODUCTION 100 Arnolt MGs.

Left and right:
Arnolt MGs. Only
65 coupes and 35
roadsters were made
and it was several
years before the
last was sold.

1953-1956 Magnette ZA

The furore over the MG TF in October 1953 was nothing compared with the cynicism surrounding the launch at the same motor show of the Magnette. There was indignation about the adoption of an old MG name for what seemed a clone of the Wolseley 4/44, introduced the previous year. The rationale was the more obscure since the Wolseley had effectively an MG engine, the 1250cc XPAG, and the Magnette a BMC B-series engine descended from an Austin. It looked like BMC opportunism, yet both cars were conceived at the same time, the Magnette delayed to allow time for the engine, a fruit of the Nuffield-BMC merger, to be engineered into it. As so often with MGs the excellent qualities of the Magnette, designed by Gerald Palmer, only became apparent later. It was salutary that MG had for so long been seen as a marque in its own right that the association with volume manufacture was being disparaged. Certainly not much subtlety was shown about the distinguishing features, unlike the Y-type and its Morris duplicate the Series E. The Magnette's monocoque body was 2in lower than the Wolseley's and the differences extended to floor pan and many of the body pressings. The Magnette had a sporting central gear lever, the Wolseley a steering column change, and although both handled well the Magnette was certainly the superior.

BODY saloon, 4 doors, 4 seats; weight 2507lb (1137kg).
ENGINE 4 cylinders, in-line; front; 73mm x 89mm, 1489cc; compr 7.15:1; 60bhp (44.7kW) @ 4600rpm; 40.3bhp/L (30kW/L); 76.1lbft (102Nm) @ 3000rpm.
ENGINE STRUCTURE pushrod overhead valve; chain-driven camshaft; cast iron cylinder head and block; 2 SU inclined carburettors, 12-volt coil ignition; SU electric fuel pump; 3-bearing crankshaft; engine rubber-mounted.
TRANSMISSION rear wheel drive; 8in single dry plate clutch; 4-speed manual gearbox, synchromesh; Hardy Spicer prop shaft; hypoid bevel final drive 4.875:1.
CHASSIS steel monocoque structure; ifs by coil spring and wishbone; live back axle, semi-elliptic springs; telescopic dampers; hydraulic 10in drum brakes, 2LS at front; rack and pinion steering; 9.5 Imp gal (11.4 US gal, 43.2L) fuel tank; 5.50-15 tyres, steel disc wheels.
DIMENSIONS wheelbase 102in (259cm); track 51in (129.5cm); turning circle 37ft (11.3m); ground clearance 7in (18cm); length 169in (429cm); width 63in (160cm); height 58in (147cm).
PERFORMANCE maximum speed 79.5mph (128kph); 15.3mph (24.5kph) @ 1000rpm; 0-60mph (96kph) 22.6sec; 19kg/bhp (25.4kg/kW); fuel consumption 25.3mpg (11.2L/100km).
PRICE £914 17s 6d (£914.87).
PRODUCTION 12,754.

1954-1955 TF 1500

The last traditional MG was made with wooden formers in the bodywork, a proper Auster windscreen that folded flat, scuttle cowls, and doors hinged at the rear. Getting in and out easily was still thought more important than the risk of leg injuries. Private owners had already been boring out XPAG 1250cc engines to extract more power, but it was a chancy business given the thin cylinder walls. The factory re-cored some engines to allow 72mm to be bored out safely but these were not put into production.

In August 1954 EX179 ran with such an engine at Utah so the opportunity was taken to put it into production for a 1°-litre TF. Sufficient metal for the larger bores was achieved by doing away with the water spaces between cylinders 1 and 2, and 3 and 4. The increased bore brought a proportional increase in compression ratio. The only sign of the larger engine was a discreet "TF" 1500 badge on the bonnet. There was no explanation for the quotation marks. Performance was much improved, even though at high speed it ran up against an impenetrable aerodynamic wall of 16 sq ft of frontal area. The TF 1500 was never going to be as fast as its Triumph or Austin-Healey contemporaries but with production starting in July 1954 it bought time before the introduction of the MGA.

BODY roadster, 2 doors, 2 seats; weight 1930lb (875.5kg).
ENGINE 4 cylinders, in-line; front; 66.5mm x 90mm, 1466cc; compr 8.3:1; 63bhp (47kW) @ 5000rpm; 43bhp/L (32kW/L); 65lbft (87Nm) @ 3000rpm.
ENGINE STRUCTURE duplex roller chain-driven camshaft; pushrod overhead valve; cast iron block and top half of crankcase; aluminium ribbed sump; cast iron head; coil ignition; two semi-downdraught SU carburettors; 3-bearing crankshaft; cooling by pump, fan, and thermostat.
TRANSMISSION rear wheel drive; 8in single dry plate clutch; 4-speed manual gearbox, synchromesh on 2nd, 3rd, top; hypoid final drive 4.875:1.
CHASSIS DETAILS steel welded box-section side rails tubular cross members and scuttle reinforcement; independent front suspension by coil spring and wishbone, live rear axle with semi-elliptic leaf springs; Luvax-Girling lever arm hydraulic dampers; Lockheed hydraulic brakes with 9in drums, 2-leading shoe at front; rack and pinion steering; 12.5 Imp gal (15 US gal, 56.8L) fuel tank; 5.50 x 15 tyres; bolt-on steel disc wheels, wire wheels optional.
DIMENSIONS wheelbase 94in (239cm); track front 47.4in (120cm) rear 50in (127cm), or 48.4in (123cm) and 50.8in (129cm) with wire wheels; turning circle 31.3ft (9.5m); ground clearance 6in (15.2cm); length 147in (373cm); width 58.3in (148cm); height 54.5in (138cm).
PERFORMANCE maximum speed 88mph (142kph); 15.2mph (24.5kph) @ 1000rpm; 0-60mph (96kph) 16.3sec; 13.9kg/bhp (18.6kg/kW); fuel consumption 25mpg (11.3L/100km).
PRICE £780 5s 10d (£780.29).
PRODUCTION 3400.

THE NEW MG T.F. 1500
WITH THE RECORD
BREAKING 1½ LITRE ENGINE

Left: TF 1500 brochure
artist's drawings of cars
(with riding mechanics)
somehow omitted the "1500"
label on the bonnet sides.

George Eyston not only saw the publicity value of record-breaking, but as a director of Castrol he was in a position to do something about it. With EX 135, Goldie Gardner's car, effectively out of action, Castrol accordingly sponsored a new record-breaker. This was based on the redundant chassis of the MGA prototype EX175, and the approaching TF 1500's larger-bore (72mm not 66.5mm) XPAG (now XPEG) engine of 1466cc. Power was increased to 84bhp (62.6kW) at 6000rpm with a compression ratio of 9.3:1 and it ran on ordinary pump fuel. Wilson McComb described it picturesquely as "an extraordinarily inoffensive unit to use in a record-breaker." Not unlike the Gardner car in appearance, Eyston and American Ken Miles took eight Class F records at 153.69mph (246.72kph) and averaged over 120mph (192.6kph) for 12 hours at Bonneville.

In 1956 the car was taken back to the salt flats with an unsupercharged 1489cc Twin Cam engine and, driven by Ken Miles and former racing motorcyclist Johnny Lockett, took 16 records at up to 170.15mph (273.14kph). With a 948cc A-series engine from the yet to be announced Austin-Healey Sprite (and later MG Midget), giving 57bhp (42.5kW) it broke three international and 25 American standing-start records driven by Tommy Wisdom and David Ash, author of Automobile Almanac. An Austin-Healey development Sprite was found aerodynamically unsuitable so EX179 was redesignated as EX219 and became officially an Austin-Healey for the occasion. With Phil Hill at the wheel and the engine supercharged, this versatile car then did the flying mile at 143.47mph (230.31kph). BMC was thus enabled to advertise its new cars proudly, and perfectly truthfully, with a "record-breaking" engine.

BODY single-seat record breaker weight 2198lb (997kg) inc driver and 30 gals fuel.
ENGINE various 4 cylinders, in-line; front, see text.
TRANSMISSION rear wheel drive; sdp clutch; 4-speed manual gearbox, synchromesh on 2nd, 3rd, top; auto; hypoid final drive 4.875, 4.55, 5.125:1 or special gearing for records.
CHASSIS DETAILS steel welded square-section perforated tubing side rails and tubular cross members; ifs by coil spring and wishbone, live rear axle with semi-elliptic leaf springs; Luvax-Girling lever arm hydraulic dampers; Lockheed hydraulic brakes rear wheels only, with 9in drums, 2-leading and trailing shoe; rack and pinion steering; 12.5 Imp gal (15 US gal, 56.8L) tank; 5.50 x 15 tyres; bolt-on steel disc wheels.
DIMENSIONS wheelbase 95in (241cm); track front 47.4in (120cm), rear 50in (127cm); turning circle 31.3ft (9.5m); length 188.9in (480cm); width 63.5in (161.3cm); height to cockpit top 40.4in (102.6cm).
PERFORMANCE see text.
PRODUCTION 1.

1954 EX179 (2)

EX 179 was a vindication of Enever's low-built chassis although the car was mainly the work of Terry Mitchell, who became MG's chief chassis designer. It was one of the first tasks he undertook after moving from Cowley to Abingdon's re-established design office. Enever instructed Mitchell to keep up the appearance of the Gardner MG, and the bubble canopy was moved from left to right hand drive to suit the regulations. The aluminium body was made by Midland Sheet Metal.

Further vindication of the body design came with a series of wind-tunnel tests carried out by Michael Scarlett of *Autocar* in 1982. Drag coefficients of some notable cars were measured in the MIRA wind tunnel including the D-type Jaguar (Cd 0.49), Lotus Elite (Cd 0.35), and were compared with those obtained elsewhere. It is difficult to get a Cd of much under the Elite's 0.35 for a road car. A Porsche 924 of 0.37 was representative, a Citroen GSA's 0.34 was exceptional. The 0.26 of EX179 was higher than expected due to there being no undertray between the back of the nose and the toeboard. In other words the streamlining on top was amazingly good, but owing to the state of knowledge at the time the underside was neglected. It also showed more lift than expected for a 170mph (273kph) car. The figure that mattered, the Cd X frontal area of 3.0, was by far the lowest (the Jaguar was 6.32, the Lotus 5.26) and in a test to determine how the airflow behaved over the body, the only turbulence proved to be immediately behind the cockpit. The way the airflow clung to the entire length of the car Scarlett described as "a marvel".

1955 EX 182 Le Mans team cars

The Le Mans MGs of 1955 displayed, in their in their perimeter frame and maturity, the hallmarks of a production-ready car. They were prototypes in the spirit of regulations aimed at allowing manufacturers to try out new models in the full glare of publicity. The project known as EX182 resulted in four production look-alikes with aluminium bodies and Weslake-developed cylinder heads, true harbingers of things to come nevertheless. The bodies had the requisite seats and doors, the passenger side covered with a fairing. The 1955 race was a disaster. A Mercedes-Benz 300SLR crashed into the crowd, killing its driver Pierre Levegh and over 80 spectators. Almost at the same time one of the MGs crashed, badly injuring Dick Jacobs, a staunch MG supporter whose connections with the cars went back to 1937. The race went on as abandonment would only have created further mayhem, and the MGs acquitted themselves well finishing 5th and 6th in the class behind three Porsches. They averaged 86.17mph (138.67kph) and 81.97mph (131.9kph), finishing 12th and 17th overall. In September the Ulster TT was also marred by fatal accidents.

Two works MGs had twin overhead camshaft engines, one designed by Austin, the other by Morris engines. The Morris version became the prototype for the MGA Twin Cam.

BODY sports, 2 seats; weight 1596lb (724kg).
ENGINE 4 cylinders, in-line; front; 73.025mm x 88.9mm, 1489cc; compr 9.4:1; 82.5bhp (61.5kW) @ 6000rpm; 55.3bhp/L (41.3kW/L); 85lbft (114Nm) @ 4500rpm.
ENGINE STRUCTURE pushrod ohv; chain-driven camshaft; cast iron cylinder head and block, no gasket; two 1⌡in SU inclined carburettors, 12-volt coil ignition; two SU electric fuel pumps; 3-bearing crank with lead-bronze shell bearings.
TRANSMISSION rear wheel drive; Borg & Beck sdp 8in clutch; 4-speed manual close-ratio gearbox, synchromesh 2nd, 3rd, top; hypoid final drive with bevel-type differential 3.7:1.
CHASSIS DETAILS steel perimeter frame with scuttle reinforcement; ifs by coil spring and unequal length wishbone; live rear axle with semi-elliptic springs; Armstrong lever arm dampers front and rear; Lockheed hydraulic brakes10in drums, 2LS at front; rack and pinion steering; 20

Imp gal (24 US gal, 90.9L) fuel tank; front 5.60–15tyres, rear 6.00-15; centre-lock wire wheels.
DIMENSIONS wheelbase 94in (239cm); track front 47.5in (127cm), rear 48.8in (124cm); turning circle 28ft (8.5m); ground clearance 6in (15cm); length 150in (381cm); width 58in (147cm); height 41in (104cm).
PERFORMANCE maximum speed 103mph (165.8kph) (with windscreen and 4.3 axle), 119.5mph (192.3kph) at Le Mans with metal cover on passenger seat and racing screen; 21mph (33.8kph) @ 1000rpm; 0-60mph (96kph) 13.8sec; 8.8kg/bhp (11.8kg/kW); fuel consumption 23.8mpg (11.9L/100km).
PRODUCTION 4.

Right: one of the Le Mans cars racing at the 1955 TT with Ted Lund at the wheel.

1955-1959 MGA

If Abingdon's plans had worked, the Le Mans cars would have been even closer to production MGAs. Pressed Steel wanted to stamp out the bodies for the new car with so-called soft dies. These would be cheap and for relatively small production runs should have been perfectly adequate. In the event they were nothing of the sort. The plastic dies broke after only a few stampings and the whole MGA production schedule was put back several months.

The A appellation was applied because with the ZA and ZB the end of the alphabet had been reached. It was also supposed to represent a fresh start for MG, so the first car was known as the MGA. Its spring 1955 announcement was put off until the autumn. By that time the clever perimeter frame into which Enever had built such strength, the B-series BMC engine, and the well-balanced style were no longer a mystery. All that remained was to confirm that the ride and handling were up to scratch and although not as fast as the TR2 or Austin-Healey 100, the MG pedigree and its superior handling would carry the day. More than 13,000 were produced during the first full year of production, far exceeding the total production of the TC in the four post-war years it was made. In sports car terms the MGA was off to a flying start.

BODY sports, 2 doors, 2 seats; weight 1988lb (902kg).
ENGINE 4 cylinders, in-line; front; 73.025mm x 88.9mm, 1489cc; compr 8.3:1; 68bhp (50.7kW) @ 5500rpm; 45.7bhp/L (34kW/L); 77.4lbft (104Nm) @ 3500rpm.
ENGINE STRUCTURE pushrod overhead valve; chain-driven camshaft; cast iron cylinder head and block; 2 SU inclined carburettors, 12-volt coil ignition; SU electric fuel pump; 3-bearing crankshaft; engine rubber-mounted
TRANSMISSION rear wheel drive; Borg & Beck sdp 8in clutch; 4-speed manual gearbox, synchromesh 2nd, 3rd, top; hypoid bevel final drive 4.3:1; 4.55 optional.
CHASSIS DETAILS steel perimeter frame with scuttle reinforcement; ifs by coil spring and unequal length wishbone; live rear axle with semi-elliptic springs; Armstrong lever arm dampers front and rear; Lockheed hydraulic brakes 10in drums, 2LS at front; rack and pinion steering; 10 Imp gal (12 US gal, 45.5L) fuel tank;

5.60–15; centre-lock wire wheels optional.
DIMENSIONS wheelbase 94in (239cm); track front 47.5in (121cm), rear 48.8in (124cm); turning circle 28ft (8.5m); ground clearance 6in (15cm); length 156in (396cm); width 58in (147cm); height 50in (127cm).
PERFORMANCE maximum speed 98mph (157.7kph); 17mph (27.4kph) @ 1000rpm; 0-60mph (96kph) 15.6sec; 13.3kg/bhp (17.8kg/kW); fuel con 27mpg (10.5L/100km).
PRICE £844 0s 10d (£844.04).
PRODUCTION 58,750.

Top right: stripped for action with aero screens, shorn of bumpers and with a Lucas Flamethrower in the grille like the Le Mans car, an MGA at Goodwood.

Far right: Classic MGA. MG historian Wilson McComb feels at home during his spell of duty in the Abingdon press office.

1956-1959 MGA Coupe

Soon after launch the MGA's engine power was increased slightly, and late in 1956 came the closed coupe. Its 117lb (53kg) of extra weight was more than compensated for by better aerodynamics. Historically there were plenty of precedents in the MG tradition of salonettes, contemporaneously Jaguar had enjoyed huge success with the stylish two-seat XK 120, and the MG with deeply curved front and rear windows was an immediate success. Many aspiring sports two-seater drivers disliked the draughtiness of soft-tops and sidescreens in the British climate, and among the proprietary detachable hard-tops was an aluminium one from coachbuilders Vanden Plas, used on the Alpine Rally in July. The huge class area of the Coupe banished most feelings of claustrophobia and the enhanced stiffness of the body improved the handling. Detailing was exemplary, from the neat upward-pull door handles to the well carpeted and upholstered interior; however it was noisy inside and there were difficulties in making the wind-up windows truly draught proof. Reputedly the coupe was designed round the back window of the A55 Austin Cambridge, which fitted precisely in place of the detachable windscreen of the MGA sports. With the BMC parts bin able to supply the glass, no outside supplier was needed for the relatively few involved.

BODY sports coupe, 2 doors, 2 seats; weight 2105lb (955kg).
ENGINE 4 cylinders, in-line; front; 73.025mm x 88.9mm, 1489cc; compr 8.3:1; 72bhp (53.7kW) @ 5500rpm; 48.4bhp/L (36.1kW/L); 77.4lbft (104Nm) @ 3500rpm.
ENGINE STRUCTURE pushrod ohv; chain-driven cam; cast iron cyl head and block; 2 SU inclined carbs, 12-volt coil ignition; SU electric fuel pump; 3-bearing crankshaft; engine rubber-mounted.
TRANSMISSION rear wheel drive; Borg & Beck sdp 8in clutch; 4-speed manual gearbox, synchromesh 2nd, 3rd, top; hypoid bevel final drive 4.3:1;

4.55 optional.
CHASSIS DETAILS steel perimeter frame with scuttle reinforcement; ifs by coil spring and unequal length wishbone; live rear axle with semi-elliptic springs; Armstrong lever arm dampers front and rear; Lockheed hydraulic brakes 10in drums, 2LS at front; rack and pinion steering; 10 Imp gal (12 US gal, 45.5L) fuel tank; 5.60–15; centre-lock wire wheels optional.
DIMENSIONS wheelbase 94in (239cm); track 47.5in (121cm), rear 48.8in (124cm); turning circle 28ft (8.5m); ground clearance 6in (15cm); length 156in (396cm); width 58in (147cm); height 50in (127cm).
PERFORMANCE maximum speed 100.5mph (161.7kph); 17mph (27.4kph) @ 1000rpm; 0-60mph (96kph) 15sec; 13.3kg/bhp (17.8kg/kW); 27mpg (10.5L/100km).
PRICE £1087. 7s (£1087.35).
PRODUCTION 58,750 (all MGA 1500).

Sleek lines of author's
MGA (below) in 1960
and (right) pausing on
a club rally. Navigator
Gilbert Harper urges haste.

1956-1958 Magnette ZB

The second Magnette had a more powerful engine and the axle ratio was raised for quieter cruising. Some aspects of production were still somewhat archaic. The big wrap-round back window had to be hand-cut on finished bodies on the Pressed Steel line at Cowley. Two-colour paintwork was known as Varitone although quite a lot of ZB Magnettes were soberly finished in one colour. It was distinguished in its top speed of nearly 90mph, rack and pinion steering, cornering poise, and a calm air of well-being and good taste. "The air of quality which follows from the use of first-class hide upholstery and pleasingly grained wood for the facia panel and door cappings is immediately apparent. It is matched by small details … well-positioned pedals … generous parcel tray… and high quality carpets firmly fixed to the floor," said *The Motor*.

The re-established competitions department at Abingdon under Marcus Chambers tentatively entered Magnettes in rallies and they won their class in the 1958 BRSCC saloon car championship, but they were heavy and their competition career was brief.

Manumatic transmission, in which the clutch was operated by an electrical switch in the gear lever knob, was no more of a success in the Magnette than anywhere else.

BODY saloon, 4 doors, 4 seats; weight 2507lb (1137kg).
ENGINE 4 cylinders, in line; front; 73mm x 89mm, 1489cc; compr 8.3:1; 68bhp (50.7kW) @ 5200rpm; 45.7bhp/L (34kW/L); 83llbft (111Nm) @ 3000rpm.
ENGINE STRUCTURE pushrod overhead valve; chain-driven camshaft; cast iron cylinder head and block; 2 SU inclined carburettors, 12-volt coil ignition, vacuum timing control; SU electric fuel pump; 3-bearing crankshaft; engine rubber-mounted.
TRANSMISSION rear wheel drive; 8in single dry plate clutch; 4-speed manual gearbox, synchromesh; Hardy Spicer prop shaft; hypoid bevel final drive 4.55:1.
CHASSIS DETAILS steel monocoque structure; ifs by coil spring and wishbone; live back axle, semi-elliptic springs; telescopic dampers; hydraulic 10in drum brakes, 2LS at front; rack and pinion steering; 9.5 Imp gal (11.4 US gal, 43.2L) fuel tank; 5.50-15 tyres, steel disc wheels.

DIMENSIONS wheelbase 102in (259cm); track 51in (129.5cm); turning circle 37ft (11.3m); ground clearance 7in (17.8cm); length 169in (429.3cm); width 63in (160cm); height 58in (147.3cm).
PERFORMANCE maximum speed 85.8mph (138kph); 16.4mph (26.4kph) @ 1000rpm; 0-60mph (96kph) 20.8sec; 16.7kg/bhp (22.4kg/kW); fuel consumption 25.5mpg (11.1L/100km).
PRICE £1072 7s (£1072.35).
PRODUCTION 23,846.

The appeal of the Magnette in a world of Standard Ensigns, Ford Consuls, Hillman Minxes, and Morris Oxfords was easily understood.

Syd Enever decided that the last of the Abingdon record-breakers should be a classic teardrop, like an aircraft drop-tank with slots for the wheels. It was reputed to give 30 percent less drag than EX179, and with Abingdon's tradition for irreverent nicknames was soon known as the Roaring Raindrop. Following the successful centre-seat Cooper-Bristol, prejudice against engines behind the driver (a legacy of the supposedly "difficult" Auto Unions) was diminishing, and EX181's was duly located aft. The chassis was a tubular affair, the engine a supercharged 1489cc Twin Cam, and the car appeared with and without the tail-fin that Eyston advocated.

The goal in 1957 was 250mph but the team would have been content with 240mph, or four miles a minute. Stirling Moss, five days after winning a famous victory at Pescara for Vanwall, achieved 245.64mph (394.33kph) on damp salt. It was 50mph faster than he had ever driven in his life and he described the experience many years later as quite unnerving, particularly when he found he could not use the gearbox to slow up. Phil Hill, who began his career in a TC MG, set EX181's 1959 records using a 1506cc version of the engine for Class E. It was now delivering 300bhp (223.7kW), or some three times its standard output. It was the last occasion the car was driven competitively.

BODY single-seater record breaker; weight 1655lb (751kg) dry.
ENGINE 4 cylinders, in-line; front; 75.4mm x 89mm, 1588cc, later 1506cc; 290bhp (216.3kW) @ 7300rpm; 182.6bhp/L (136.2kW/L).
ENGINE STRUCTURE two chain-driven overhead camshafts; cast iron block, aluminium cylinder head; finned aluminium sump; twin 3/16" SU carbs; 3-bearing crank; Shorrock s/charger running at 32psi (2.206bar) @ 7000rpm.
TRANSMISSION rear wheel drive; 7⌡ 3-plate clutch; 4-speed manual gearbox; final drive 1.94:1 and 1.825:1.
CHASSIS DETAILS tubular steel structure; ifs by coil spring and unequal length wishbone; De Dion rear with quarter elliptic springs; single hydraulic disc brake on half shaft; rack and pinion steering; 7.9 Imp gal (9.5 US gal, 36L) fuel tank; Dunlop ultra-high speed tyres on 15" steel disc wheels.

DIMENSIONS wheelbase 96in (244cm); length 181.5in (461cm); width 64.3in (163cm); height 38.3in (97cm).
PERFORMANCE maximum speed 254.91mph (409.2kph); 2.6kg/bhp (3.5kg/kW).
PRODUCTION 1.

Below: Moss eases himself into the cramped cockpit of a car that he described as one of the most uncomfortable he had ever driven.

1957-1959 EX 186 proposed Le Mans car

A more radical car was planned for a continuing assault on Le Mans after 1955. Preparations were in hand even before the 1955 event, and a model made and drawings done before the racing programme was abandoned in 1955. Work on the car was well under way in 1957 and continued until 1959. The basis was a Twin Cam engine in a much-modified MGA chassis with De Dion rear suspension, a favourite of chassis designer Terry Mitchell. The body was the work of Denis Williams, based on typical long-distance endurance cars of the time with a low full width windscreen and head fairing, and made by Midland Sheet Metal.

It is unclear how many cars were proposed, perhaps as many as ten might have been laid down if MG had continued in racing but only one was ever built. Ted Lund tried to get it released and run as a private entry at Le Mans in 1959 but was unsuccessful.

BODY racing, 2 seats.
ENGINE 4 cylinders, in-line; front; 75.4mm x 89mm, 1588cc; compr 9.9:1 (later reduced to 8.3); 108bhp (80.5kW) @ 6700rpm; 68bhp/L (50.7kW/L); 104lbft (140Nm) @ 4500rpm.
ENGINE STRUCTURE 2 chain-driven overhead camshafts; cast iron block, aluminium cylinder head; finned aluminium sump 2 SU H6 carburettors, 12-volt coil ignition; SU electric fuel pump; 3-bearing crankshaft; engine rubber-mounted.

TRANSMISSION rear wheel drive; Borg & Beck sdp 8in clutch; 4-speed manual gearbox, synchromesh 2nd, 3rd, top; Hardy Spicer prop shaft; hypoid bevel final drive 4.3:1.
CHASSIS DETAILS tubular steel frame; ifs by coil spring and unequal length wishbone; De Dion rear axle; Armstrong lever arm dampers front and rear; Dunlop disc brakes; Cam Gears rack and pinion steering; 10 Imp gal (12 US gal, 45.5L) fuel tank; 5.50x15 (front), 6.00x15 (rear) tyres; centre-lock ventilated disc wheels.
PRODUCTION 1.

MG historian David Knowles has uncovered evidence that John Thornley and Syd Enever had the car built sub rosa, and around Christmas 1960 the order came for it to be disposed of. It was shipped off to Californian MG distributor Kjell Qvale who sold it on many years later to a Californian enthusiast.

The inspiration of Nuffield designer Gerald Palmer was a double overhead camshaft conversion of the B-series engine. A classic racing layout dating back to 1911, it was rarely used for production engines on account of cost, noise, and complication. Jaguar was one that managed it in an era before toothed belt drives, and the chain-driven arrangement off a jackshaft located where the B-series camshaft was on the ordinary engine, was a bold one. The valves were inclined at 80deg, the crankshaft stiffened, and different con-rods were used. The polished alloy valve covers made a brave sight but accessibility could be problematical.

By the time it was put into production Palmer had left for Vauxhall, never understanding why its piston problems were not put right by the engineers at Morris Engines. Development was left to Twin Cam owners who learned how to maintain reliable oil-tight engines. Dearth of 100 octane fuel was a problem, and the Twin Cam was withdrawn owing to heavy warranty claims. The engine was noisy and oil consumption of a pint every 120miles (193km) was not unusual. Four cars were available for the press launch at Chobham, but there was trouble with overheating and running-on, and one of the cars was crashed.

BODY sports, 2 doors, 2 seats; weight 2184 lb (991kg).
ENGINE 4 cylinders, in-line; front; 75.4mm x 89mm, 1588cc; compr 9.9:1 (later reduced to 8.3); 108bhp (80.5kW) @ 6700rpm; 68bhp/L (50.7kW/L); 104lbft (140Nm) @ 4500rpm.
ENGINE STRUCTURE two chain-driven overhead camshafts; cast iron block, aluminium cylinder head; finned aluminium sump 2 SU H6 carburettors, 12-volt coil ignition; SU electric fuel pump; 3-bearing crankshaft; engine rubber-mounted.
TRANSMISSION rear wheel drive; Borg & Beck sdp 8in clutch; 4-speed manual gearbox, synchromesh 2nd, 3rd, top; Hardy Spicer prop shaft; hypoid bevel final drive 4.3:1.
CHASSIS steel perimeter frame with scuttle reinforcement; ifs by coil spring and unequal length wishbone; live rear axle with semi-elliptic springs; Armstrong lever arm dampers front and rear; Dunlop disc brakes; Cam Gears rack and pinion; 10 Imp gal (12 US gal, 45.5L) fuel tank; 5.60–15; centre-lock ventilated disc wheels.
DIMENSIONS wheelbase 94in (239cm); track 47.5in (121cm) front, 48.8in (124cm) rear; turning circle 28ft (8.5m); ground clearance 6in (15cm); length 156in (396cm); width 58in (147cm); height 50in (127cm).
PERFORMANCE maximum speed 115mph (185kph); 17mph (27.4kph) @ 1000rpm; 0-60mph (96kph) 9.1sec; 9.2kg/bhp (12.3kg/kW); fuel consumption 22.2mpg (12.7L/100km).
PRICE £1195 7s 6d (£1195.37.5p); coupe £1281 15s 10d (£1281.79p).
PRODUCTION 2111.

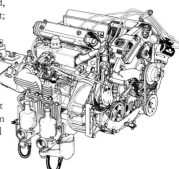

Dunlop disc brakes and
centre-lock perforated steel
wheels completed the Twin
Cam's specification,
justifying its steep
increase in price.

Left: record-breaker
supercharged Twin Cam
engine.

Right: Famous Twin Cam
(here) 1MTW and sister car
2MTW, ex Dick Jacobs
team cars, raced for the
best part of forty years.

Little eagerness was shown on the introduction of the Farina-styled range of 1°-litre BMC saloons. *Motor Sport* was unequivocal: "The Mark III Magnette does not fill the individualistic niche which caused enthusiasts to regard the ZB Magnette with such warm affection. It remains (to be seen) whether one might as well just order a 15/60 Wolseley or an Austin A55." It could have added a Morris Oxford, or a Riley 4/68; they were all the same. The best *Motor Sport* could find to say about the new Magnette concerned the torsion bar boot lid support and the dimming of direction flasher warning lights at night. *The Motor* was critical of it having 17 points requiring lubrication by grease-gun every 1,000 miles: "an anachronism on a modern design." Testers were not impressed either with oil consumption of a pint every 200 miles. Taking driving excitement out of a car in which it was such a vital ingredient was ill-conceived; the regression to cam and lever from rack and pinion steering was particularly insensitive. "The steering is better at high speed than low ones, when apparent friction at some point in the linkage makes it too heavy for parking and causes slight weaving at town speeds." The Magnette's price of £200 over the Morris and Austin equivalents gave a livelier turn of speed and superior furnishings, but not much else.

BODY saloon, 4 doors; 4 seats; weight 2407.9lb (1092.2kg).

ENGINE 4 cylinders, in line; front; 73.025mm x 88.9mm, 1489cc; compr 8.3:1; 66.5bhp (49.6kW) @ 5200rpm; 44.7bhp/L (33.3kW/L); 85lbft (114Nm) @ 3300rpm.

ENGINE STRUCTURE pushrod overhead valve, chain-driven camshaft; cast iron cylinder block and head; 2 SU HD 4 carburettors; SU PD electric fuel pump; centrifugal and vacuum ignition; 3-bearing crankshaft.

TRANSMISSION rear wheel drive; Borg & Beck 8in sdp clutch; 4-speed manual gearbox, synchromesh; Hardy Spicer open prop shaft; hypoid bevel final drive 4.3:1.

CHASSIS DETAILS steel monocoque structure; ifs by coil springs and wishbones; live axle and semi-elliptic springs; Armstrong lever arm hydraulic dampers; Girling hydraulic 9in drum brakes (2LS front); Cam and lever steering;10.5 Imp gal (12.6 US gal, 47.7L) fuel tank; 5.90–14 tubeless tyres; steel disc wheels.

DIMENSIONS wheelbase 99.25in (252cm); track 50in (127cm) front, 48.5in (123cm) rear; turning circle 34.5ft (10.5m); ground clearance 7in (17.8cm); length 178in (452cm); width 63.25in (160.7cm); height 59.25in (150.5cm).

PERFORMANCE maximum speed 87.7mph (140.8kph); 16.6m (26.7kph) @ 1000rpm; 0-60mph (96kph) 19.7sec; 16.4kg/bhp (22kg/kW); fuel consumption 26.8mpg (10.5L/100km).

PRICE £1012 12s 6d (£1012. 62.5p).

PRODUCTION 15,676.

1959-1961 MGA 1600 Tourer and Coupe

After earning $60 million from exports to the United States, increasing the MGA's B-series engine's capacity to match the Twin Cam's 1588cc simplified cylinder block machining brought an extra 6bhp (4.5kW) or some 10%. Crucially it was accompanied by a 17% increase in torque. Acceleration was swifter and even the open car, production of which began in May, could now reach a genuine 100mph. Lockheed disc brakes were fitted to the front wheels but without a servo they were on the heavy side. It was all a bit late to recapture the Triumph and Austin-Healey market but MG still had the edge in handling and pedigree. The engine was no quieter than before and fuel consumption suffered slightly. Among the improvements for dealing with approaching competition from open cars with better weather protection were sliding sidescreens of clear plastic laminate instead of instead of soft transparent material that became scratched and opaque. Plastic detachable hardtops proliferated; the works one was well proportioned and fitted snugly. Luggage space remained at a premium and on 1600 Coupes the spare wheel in the boot was moved rearwards to provide suitcase room in the carpeted area behind the seats. Coupes were made complete with the top welded on at Morris Bodies in Cowley and had a fabric-covered facia.

BODY sports, 2 doors, 2 seats; weight 1988lb (902kg), Coupe 2105lb (955kg).

ENGINE 4 cylinders, in-line; front; 75.39mm x 88.9mm, 1588cc; compr 8.3:1; 79.5bhp (59.3kW) @ 5600rpm; 50.1bhp/L (37.3kW/L); 87.4lbft (117Nm) @ 3800rpm.

ENGINE STRUCTURE pushrod overhead valve; chain-driven camshaft; cast iron cylinder head and block; 2 SU inclined carburettors, 12-volt coil ignition; SU electric fuel pump; 3-bearing crankshaft; engine rubber-mounttted

TRANSMISSION rear wheel drive; Borg & Beck sdp 8in clutch; 4-speed manual gearbox, synchromesh 2nd, 3rd, top; hypoid bevel final drive 4.3:1; 4.55 optional.

CHASSIS DETAILS steel perimeter frame with scuttle reinforcement; ifs by coil spring and unequal length wishbone; live rear axle with semi-elliptic springs; Armstrong lever arm dampers front and rear; Lockheed hydraulic brakes 11in discs at front, 10in drums at back, 2LS at front; rack and pinion steering; 10 Imp gal (12 US gal, 45.5L) fuel tank; 5.60–15; centre-lock wire wheels optional.

DIMENSIONS wheelbase 94in (238.8cm); track 47.5in (120.7cm) front, 48.8in (123.8cm) rear; turning circle 28ft (8.5m); ground clearance 6in (15.2cm); length156in (396.2cm); width 58in (147.3cm); height 50in (127cm).

PERFORMANCE maximum speed 100.5mph (161.7kph); 17mph (27.4kph) @ 1000rpm; 0-60mph (96kph) 15.0sec; 11.3kg/bhp (15.2kg/kW) tourer, 12kg/bhp (16.1kg/kW) coupe; fuel con 27mpg (10.5L/100km).

PRICE £940 7s 6d (£940 37.5p), Coupe £1026 15s 10d (£1026.79).

PRODUCTION 31,501.

1960 Ted Lund Colin Escott Le Mans coupe

Thoroughly alarmed by the heavy accident rate that seemed to follow the works MGAs, the BMC directors withdrew official backing for racing. In future the factory would take part only in rallies. As something of a subterfuge to get back to Le Mans, the factory built a car with a twin-cam engine as tried out in the 1955 TT, registered it SRX 210 and passed it on to Ted Lund. A member of the Le Mans driver team, Lund raced the car at Le Mans in 1959, 1960, and 1961.

The body may have incorporated some of the aluminium shell built for the 1955 Le Mans cars but it was always described as a private venture and was entered for the race by the North West Centre of the MG Car Club. Co-driver Colin Escott hit a dog at night, putting paid to the car's cooling system (and the dog) in 1959. For 1960 Lund bought the car from the factory, it was equipped with Coupe doors and fastback bodywork, won the 2.0 litre class, and finished 12th at 91.195mph (146.395kph); a creditable performance.

This versatile vehicle came back in 1961, highly tuned, but lapping at 101.6mph (163.1kph) proved too much for it and the engine failed early in the race. The car then went on to a long career in club racing, a distinctive survivor of the MG competitions department.

BODY sports, 2 seats; weight of 1959 open car approx 1600lb (726kg).

ENGINE 4 cylinders, in-line; front; 75.4mm x 89mm, 1588cc, for 1960 79.4mm x 89mm, 1763cc, for 1961 128bhp (95.5kW); 80.6bhp/L (60.1kW) 1.6, 54.2bhp/L (54.2kW/L) 1.7.

ENGINE STRUCTURE two chain-driven overhead camshafts; cast iron block, aluminium cylinder head; finned aluminium sump; two twin-choke Weber carburettors; 12-volt coil ignition; two SU electric fuel pumps; 3-bearing crankshaft.

TRANSMISSION rear wheel drive; Borg & Beck sdp 8in clutch; 4-speed manual close-ratio gearbox, synchromesh 2nd, 3rd, top; hypoid final drive with bevel-type diff 4.1:1.

CHASSIS DETAILS steel perimeter frame with scuttle reinforcement; ifs by coil spring and unequal length wishbone; live rear axle with semi-elliptic springs; Armstrong lever arm dampers front and rear; Lockheed hydraulic brakes 10in drums, 2LS at front; rack and pinion steering; 20 Imp gal (24 US gal, 90.9L) fuel tank; front 5.60–15tyres, rear 6.00-15; centre-lock steel wheels.

DIMENSIONS wheelbase 94in (238.8cm); track 47.5in (120.7cm) front, 48.75in (123.8cm) rear; turning circle 28ft (8.5m); ground clearance 6in (15.24cm); length 150in (381cm); width 58in (147.3cm); height 41in (104.1cm).

PERFORMANCE 1959, approximately 125mph (201kph) with metal cover on passenger seat and racing screen; 1960, 130mph (209kph); 1961, 140mph (225kph).
PRODUCTION 1.

The advent of the Mini changed perceptions of sporting handling and road holding. Aspiring racing and rally enthusiasts turned to Minis and Mini-Coopers because they could often outperform contemporary sports cars of greater power. Front wheel drive could out-corner and outmanoeuvre old-style rear-drive in rally driving test competitions, yet a sports car with front wheel drive proved in the end too radical. It was seriously considered, and several experimental schemes were drawn up and modelled. Syd Enever laid plans for it before the Mini was even launched. EX220 was subsequently awarded an Austin Drawing Office (ADO) code for development. EX220 was among the best known because prototypes were built, one of which survived.

A sports car using the Mini's transverse engine would have suited MG's tradition of corresponding to volume-produced cars. The prototype bore a strong family resemblance to the up-coming MGB, but Alec Issigonis believed a sports car should have rear wheel drive and opposed production. Technical difficulties with scuttle shake owing to the absence of a roof could have been overcome. The running prototype was based on Minivan underpinnings with a deep central backbone tunnel.

BODY roadster, 2 doors, 2 seats.
ENGINE 4 cylinders, in-line; front, transverse; 64.58mm x 83.72mm, 1098cc; compr 8.9:1, 8.0 optional; 56bhp (41.7kW) @ 5500rpm; 51bhp/L (38kW/L); 62lbft (83Nm) @ 3250rpm.
ENGINE STRUCTURE pushrod overhead valve, chain-driven camshaft; cast iron cylinder head, block; 2 SU HS2 1˝ in carburettors, SU electric fuel pump; 3-bearing crankshaft.
TRANSMISSION front wheel drive; sdp clutch; 4-speed manual gearbox, synchromesh; helical gear final drive 4.22:1.
CHASSIS DETAILS independent suspension by Hydrolastic cone rubber springs; telescopic dampers; hydraulic disc and drum brakes; rack and pinion steering.
PRODUCTION 2.

Pininfarina designed a stylish body but the sporty Mini was destined to be the Mini-Cooper and not an open two-seater.

1961-1962 MGA 1600 Mk II Tourer and Coupe

The next change in MGA engine size was also carried out to achieve economies in engine production. In April the 1600 was discontinued, replaced by a 1600 Mk II, identifiable by vertical, not sloping grille bars.

The increase from 1588cc to 1622cc meant new cylinder block and head castings and, although the 88.9mm stroke never altered, the new 76.2mm bore meant two pairs of cylinders were conjoined, and porting and airflow improved. The combustion chambers were reshaped with bigger inlet valves, and the concave pistons became flat-topped. Comfortingly for old-style engineers the cylinder dimensions were now memorably 3in x 3°in.

Time was however catching up with the MGA. Softly sprung cars like the Sunbeam Alpine were appearing, and while their handling and roadholding were not in the same class as the MG, their ride and roadworthiness had to be matched. "By modern standards," said *The Autocar* in October 1959, "the suspension must be considered firm; on smooth roads this is no disadvantage … this does not apply on rougher surfaces however, and a feeling that the wheels were hopping and jumping, accompanied by intermittent tyre squeal indicated that the tyres were not maintaining full contact with the road."

BODY sports, 2 doors, 2 seats; weight 1985lb (900kg); coupe 2045lb (928kg).

ENGINE 4 cylinders, in-line; front; 76.2mm x 88.9mm, 1622cc; compr 8.9:1; 90bhp (67.1kW) @ 5500rpm; 55.5bhp/L (41.4kW/L); 97.4lbft (131Nm) @ 4000rpm.

ENGINE STRUCTURE pushrod overhead valve; chain-driven camshaft; cast iron cylinder head and block; 2 SU inclined carburettors, 12-volt coil ignition; SU electric fuel pump; 3-bearing crankshaft; engine rubber-mounted

TRANSMISSION rear wheel drive; Borg & Beck sdp 8in clutch; 4-speed manual gearbox, synchromesh 2nd, 3rd, top; hypoid bevel final drive 4.1:1.

CHASSIS DETAILS steel perimeter frame with scuttle reinforcement; ifs by coil spring and unequal length wishbone; live rear axle with semi-elliptic springs; Armstrong lever arm dampers front and rear; Lockheed hydraulic brakes 11in discs at front 10in drums rear; rack and pinion

steering; 10 Imp gal (12 US gal, 45.5L) fuel tank; 5.60–15; centre-lock wire wheels optional.

DIMENSIONS wheelbase 94in (239cm); track 47.5in (121cm) front, 48.75in (124cm) rear; turning circle 28ft (8.5m); ground clearance 6in (15cm); length 156in (396cm); width 58in (147cm); height 50in (127cm).

PERFORMANCE maximum speed 101.4mph (162.8kph); 17.9mph (28.7kph) @ 1000rpm; 0-60mph (96kph) 13.7sec; 10kg/bhp (13.4kg/kW), coupe 10.3kg/bhp (13.8kg/kW); fuel consumption 22.3mpg (12.7L/100km).

PRICE £940 7 6 (£940 37.5p).

PRODUCTION 8,719.

The new MGA had an encouraging debut in competition, when a Coupe driven by Don and Erle Morley won its class and finished 28th in the 1962 Monte Carlo Rally.

1961-1962 MGA 1600 De Luxe; 1962 1600 De Luxe Mark II

Not for the first time when a new model failed to meet expectations, MG created something new to use up component stocks ordered for 2,500 cars. Once the Twin Cam was discontinued, the 1600 De Luxe and Mark II De Luxe were introduced to use up redundant body shells, incorporating as many Twin Cam features as possible except for the troublesome engine.

Two distinct Marks were made, 82,1600 De Luxe models (70 Tourers and 12 Coupes) with 1588cc engines, and 313,1600 De Luxe Mark IIs with 1622cc engines (290 Tourers and 23 Coupes). They were all equipped with disc brakes, centre-lock ventilated pressed steel Dunlop wheels, and leather facias but there were wide differences in trim and specification. They did not figure in official price-lists or catalogues, suggesting an emergency that seems to have continued well into 1962 and the imminent introduction of the MGA's successor. There was some uncertainty among production cars over specifications, some having optional equipment such as oil coolers, close ratio gearboxes, and special seats as standard. They seem not to have been sold through the usual channels, suggesting MG dealers and the sporting establishment were amongst the eager clientele for one of the most prized classics of MG history.

1600 De Luxe Mark II:
BODY sports, 2 doors; 2 seats; weight 2184 lb (991kg).
ENGINE 4 cylinders, in-line; front; 76.2mm x 88.9mm, 1622cc; cr 8.9:1; 90bhp (67.1kW) @ 5500rpm; 55.5bhp/L (41.4kW/L); 97.4lbft (131Nm) @ 4000rpm.
ENGINE STRUCTURE pushrod ohv; chain-driven camshaft; cast iron cylinder head and block; 2 SU inclined carburettors, 12-volt coil ignition; SU electric fuel pump; 3-bearing crankshaft; engine rubber-mounted
TRANSMISSION rear wheel drive; Borg & Beck sdp 8in clutch; 4-speed manual gearbox, synchromesh 2nd, 3rd, top; Hardy Spicer prop shaft; hypoid bevel final drive 4.3:1.
CHASSIS DETAILS steel perimeter frame with scuttle reinforcement; ifs by coil spring and unequal length wishbone; live rear axle with semi-elliptic springs; Armstrong lever arm dampers front and rear; Dunlop disc brakes; Cam Gears rack and pinion steering; 10 Imp gal (12 US gal, 45.5L) fuel tank; 5.60–15; centre-lock ventilated disc wheels.
DIMENSIONS wheelbase 94in (239cm); track 47.5in (121cm) front, 48.75in (124cm) rear; turning circle 28ft (8.5m); ground clearance 6in (15cm); length156in (396cm); width 58in (147cm); height 50in (127cm).
PERFORMANCE maximum speed 102mph (163.7kph); 17mph (27.4kph) @ 1000rpm; 0-60mph (96kph) 15.5sec; 11kg/bhp (14.8kg/kW); fuel consumption 22.2mpg (12.7L/100km).
PRICE see text.
PRODUCTION 395.

Twin Cam components were seized upon by the Competitions Department as catalogued items for Sebring racers and the last MGA rally car.

1961-1968 Magnette MkIV

Approval of the Farina Magnette was a long time coming. It had failed to produce the affection and respect felt for its predecessor, yet in Mark IV form with a number of useful detail improvements, it was quite a worthy car.

The engine was increased in size and power by rounding off the bore to 3in (76.2mm). The stroke was 3.5in (88.9mm) and the result was a steeper torque curve, and an all-round improvement in performance with little effect on fuel consumption, although the fuel tank was too small to provide a useful range. About 250 miles was its limit. Doubling the valve springs diminished but did not altogether cure valve bounce at high engine speeds.

The Mark IV Magnette was the first MG offered with fully automatic transmission, and the ride and handling were improved by the addition of anti-roll bars at front and back, as well as an increase in wheelbase and track. *The Autocar* was pleased at having itself offered these solutions to the car's "…somewhat bucking ride." After testing the Mark III: "Today's Magnette is well up to standard for a conventional design with a rigid back axle, offering its rear-seat occupants almost as easy travelling as those in the front." What it called "lost movement" in the steering was however still a shortcoming.

BODY saloon; 4 doors; 4 seats; weight 2534lb (1150kg).
ENGINE 4-cylinders; in-line; front; 76.2mm x 88.9mm, 1622cc; compr 8.3:1; 68bhp (50.7kW)@ 5000rpm; 41.9bhp/L (31.3kW/L); 89lb ft (119Nm) @ 2500rpm.
ENGINE STRUCTURE pushrod overhead valve, chain-driven camshaft; cast iron cylinder block and head; 2 SU H4 carburettors; SU electric fuel pump; centrifugal and vacuum ignition; 3-bearing crankshaft.
TRANSMISSION rear wheel drive; Borg & Beck 8in sdp clutch; 4-speed manual gearbox, synchromesh; optional Borg Warner automatic; Hardy Spicer open prop shaft; hypoid bevel final drive 4.3:1.
CHASSIS DETAILS steel monocoque structure; ifs by coil springs and wishbones; live axle and semi-elliptic springs; anti-roll bars front and rear; Armstrong lever arm hydraulic dampers; Girling hydraulic 9in drum brakes (2LS front); Cam and lever steering; 10.5 Imp gal (12.6US gal, 47.7L) fuel tank; 5.90-14tubeless tyres; steel disc wheels.
DIMENSIONS wheelbase 100.2in (254.5cm); track 50.2in (127.5cm) front, 51.4in (130.5cm) rear; turning circle 36ft (11m); ground clearance 7in (17.8cm); length 178in (452cm); width 63.25in (160.7cm); height 59.25in (150.5cm).
PERFORMANCE maximum speed 86mph (138kph); 16.6mph (26.7kph) @ 1000rpm; 0-60mph (96kph) 19sec; 16.9kg/bhp (22.7kg/kW); fuel consumption 25.2mpg (11.2L/100km).
PRICE £997. 17s 9d (£997 88.75p).
PRODUCTION 13,738.

1961-1962 Midget GAN1

Any lingering feelings over L P Lord's adoption of the Austin-Healey in what looked like Abingdon's hour of need were assuaged when the Abingdon factory undertook the assembly of, among other cars, Austin-Healeys. There was little opportunity for rancour when the Austin-Healey Sprite was adopted for production at Abingdon as a new MG Midget. Purloining a name from Riley, the Sprite was in the idiom of the old Midget, borrowing components from a small production saloon, the Austin A35, and splicing them into a plain, simple, and easily manufactured open 2-seater. Donald Healey was in the Kimber mould of practicality and achievement. The result was probably the car MG ought to have been building all along, and soon it was making the cheerful frog-eyed two-seater, with its precise steering and nimble handling.

In 1961 as Sprite sales began to falter BMC decided the shortage of luggage room and pert visage had no place in the modern world and ordered a re-skin, seizing the opportunity to co-produce it as an MG. In the Byzantine world of BMC the Healeys produced a new front and Syd Enever a new tail. It was a wonder it ever got made at all, far less matched up, to produce the Mark II Sprite and the reborn Mark I Midget of modern times coded GAN 1.

BODY sports, 2 doors, 2 seats; weight 1566lb (710kg).
ENGINE 4 cylinders, in-line; front; 62.94mm x 76.2mm, 948cc; cr 9.0:1; 46bhp (34.3kW) @ 5500rpm; 48.5bhp/L (36.2kW/L); 52.8lbft (71Nm) @ 3000rpm.
ENGINE STRUCTURE pushrod overhead valve, chain-driven camshaft; cast iron cyl head, block; 2 SU HS2 1ˇ in carbs, mechanical fuel pump; 3-bearing crankshaft.
TRANSMISSION rear wheel drive; 6ˇ in sdp clutch; 4-speed manual gearbox, synchromesh; hypoid final drive 4.22:1.
CHASSIS DETAILS steel platform chassis; ifs by coil springs and wishbones; live rear axle quarter-elliptic 15-leaf springs, radius arms, lever arm hydraulic dampers; Lockheed hydraulic brakes 7in drums; rack and pinion; 6 Imp gal (7.2 US gal, 27.3L) tank; 5.20–13 Dunlop tubeless tyres; ventilated steel; disc wheels, wire wheels optional.
DIMENSIONS wheelbase 80in (203.2cm); track 45.25in (114.9cm) front, 44.75in (113.7cm) rear; turning circle 30.1ft (9.2m); ground clearance 5in (12.7cm); length135.25in (346.1cm); width 53in (134.5cm); height 49.75in (126.4cm).
PERFORMANCE maximum speed 84.7mph (136kph); 15.4mph (24.7kph) @ 1000rpm; 0-60mph (96kph) 20.2sec; 15.4kg/bhp (20.7kg/kW); fuel consumption 33.4mpg (8.5L/100km).
PRICE £669 15s 10d (£669 79.16p).
PRODUCTION 16,084.

Right: original BMC publicity picture has (top left) the Midget's ancestor, a Mark 1 Austin-Healey Sprite complete with winter hardtop.

Even though Purchase Tax was increased in 1961, the Midget introduced in June remained at under £700 about the price of an Austin A40, Ford Anglia or Morris Minor four-door. The only real competition came from the Austin-Healey Sprite at £660 or the Triumph Herald Coupe £729, and Convertible £776. The Turner A35 Sports was £839; there was nothing remotely like the open two-seater Midget/Sprite. Differences between them were purely cosmetic. The MG had fancy wheel trim, a prettier grille, chrome strips, and the cachet of the MG name, although even that was open to dispute. Austin-Healey enthusiasts could be fiercely loyal and looked upon the Midget as essentially their car titivated as an MG and not engineered at Abingdon at all. The first major revision came at the Earls Court London Motor Show in October 1962 with a sort of Mark 1½ when the capacity of the BMC A-series engine was raised, putting the performance up to the level of the Riley 1.5 or Alfa Romeo Giulietta ti. It was still not a fast car in absolute terms but the new engine, disc brakes, and gearbox with baulk-ring synchromesh gave it a lift at a time when the traditional sports car was being challenged by small front wheel drive saloons like the Mini-Cooper. A padded roll was added to the facia coaming as a token safety feature.

BODY sports, 2 doors, 2 seats; weight 1566lb (710kg).
ENGINE 4 cylinders, in-line; front; 64.58mm x 83.72mm, 1098cc; compr 8.9:1, 8.0 optional; 56bhp (41.7kW) @ 5500rpm; 51bhp/L (38kW/L); 62lb ft (83Nm) @ 3250rpm.
ENGINE STRUCTURE pushrod ohv, chain-driven camshaft; cast iron cylinder head, block; 2 SU HS2 1˝ in carburettors, SU electric fuel pump; 3-bearing crankshaft.
TRANSMISSION rear wheel drive; 7˝ in sdp clutch; 4-speed manual gearbox, synchromesh; hypoid final drive 4.22:1.
CHASSIS DETAILS steel platform chassis; ifs by coil springs and wishbones; live rear axle quarter-elliptic 15-leaf springs, radius arms, lever arm hydraulic dampers; Lockheed hydraulic brakes 8¼ in discs front, 7in drums rear; rack and pinion steering; 6 Imp gal (7.2 US gal, 27.3L) fuel tank; 5.20–13 Dunlop tubeless tyres; ventilated steel; disc wheels; wire wheels optional.
DIMENSIONS wheelbase 80in (203.2cm); track 45.25in (114.9cm) front, 44.75in (113.7cm) rear; turning circle 30.1ft (9.2m); ground clearance 5in (12.7cm); length135.25in (346.1cm); width 53in (134.5cm); height 49.75in (126.4cm).
PERFORMANCE maximum speed 88.6mph (142.2kph); 15.4mph (24.7kph) @ 1000rpm; 0-60mph (96kph) 16.9sec; 12.7kg/bhp (17kg/kW); fuel consumption 29.9mpg (9.4L/100km).
PRICE 1962 £598 13s 9d (£598 69p).
PRODUCTION 9601.

Left: Ubiquitous
A-series with lifting lugs
and heat shield behind
the carburettors used
almost throughout the
life-span of the Midget.

The 1100 was not the first MG to have Issigonis ingredients. The long-lasting MG front suspension also came from his drawing board, although a good deal earlier than the front wheel drive transverse-engined Hydrolastic-suspended saloon ranges that became the mainstay of BMC. The cars may not in the end have been commercial successes, but the formula produced three million of them, and for many years they were among the top-selling cars in Britain.

The principle of MGs being twin-carburettored, leather upholstered versions of others in the same series was well established. It was a logical progression from the 1930s Nuffield Group when the big MG saloons borrowed components from Wolseley and Morris. It was less subtly done in the 1960s. Chrome stripes and dummy radiator grilles did not fool customers, who knew the cars were coming off production lines a long way from Abingdon. William Morris's old principle of assembling cars from components "made by experts" elsewhere held good so long as the host plant applied the finishing touches. Rolls-Royces were no less Rolls-Royces through the bodies being made by Pressed Steel at Cowley. They would not have been Rolls-Royces had they been made wholly at Cowley and much the same went for MGs.

BODY saloon, 2/4 doors, 4 seats; weight 1820lb (825.5kg).
ENGINE 4 cylinders, in-line; front, transverse; 64.58mm x 83.72mm, 1098cc; compr 8.9:1, optional 8.1:1; 55bhp (41kW) @ 5500rpm; 50.1bhp/L (37.3kW/L); 61lbft (82Nm) @ 2750rpm.
ENGINE STRUCTURE pushrod overhead valve, chain-driven camshaft; cast iron cylinder head, block; 2 SU HS2 1¨ in carburettors, SU electric fuel pump; centrifugal and vacuum ignition; 3-bearing crank.
TRANSMISSION front wheel drive; 7.125in sdp clutch; 4-speed manual gearbox, synchromesh; helical gear final drive 4.133:1.
CHASSIS steel monocoque structure; independent suspension by interconnected Hydrolastic units and rubber-cone springs; transverse wishbone at front, trailing arms at rear with anti-toll bar and two torsion bars for pitch stiffness; Lockheed brakes, 8in disc front 8in drum rear with pressure limiting valve; Cam Gears rack and pinion; 8 Imp gal (9.5 US gal, 38.4L) fuel tank; 5.50-12 tubeless tyres.
DIMENSIONS wheelbase 93.5in (237.5cm); track 51.5in (130.8cm) front, 50.75in (128.9cm) rear; turning circle 32.5ft (9.9m); ground clearance 5.25in (13.3cm); length 146.75in (372.7cm); width 60.25in (153cm); height 53.25in (135.3cm).
PERFORMANCE maximum speed 87.3mph (140kph); 14.9mph (23.9kph) @ 1000rpm; 0-60mph (96kph) 20.2sec; 15kg/bhp (20.1kg/kW); 30mpg (9.4L/100km).
PRICE £713 9s 7d (£713 48p).
PRODUCTION 116,827.

Two-colour paintwork was an option and there was a two-door version that went for export.

Far right: Hydrolastic suspension.

1962-1967 MGB

One of the best known and best loved sports cars of all time, the MGB was right from the word go. It had a mid-life crisis in the dog days of British Leyland, and went downhill to its demise in 1980 with the customary afflictions of the elderly, overweight and incontinent. Yet it stood the tests of time astonishingly well. It may not have quite kept up with the opposition in terms . of speed and acceleration, but it was well up to the mark in comfort and accommodation. As a pioneer of open two-seater monocoques it was ahead of the field. The MGB was probably over-engineered, but it solved the problems of a structure with wide door apertures that threatened its beam strength far better than many of its successors from rival manufacturers. It may have been heavy but it never suffered from the scuttle shake that bedevilled others in the succeeding half century. Although an inspired car, it did not have the crisp handling or nimbleness of its immediate predecessor the MGA, but it was strong, safe, and stylish, true to the prescription laid down by Cecil Kimber for MG half a century before.

True to tradition it also had a strong link to volume production components, so it had a well-tried engine and familiar, relatively cheap components. An entire industry was created dedicated to its restoration and preservation.

BODY roadster, 2 doors, 2 seats; weight 2030lb (921kg).
ENGINE 4 cylinders, in-line; front; 80.26mm x 88.9mm, 1798cc; compr 8.8:1; 95bhp (70.8kW) @ 5400rpm; 52.8bhp/L (39.4kW/L); 110lbft (147.5Nm) @ 3000rpm.
ENGINE STRUCTURE pushrod overhead valve; chain-driven camshaft; cast iron cylinder head and block; 2 SU inclined H4 carburettors, SU electrical fuel pump; centrifugal and vacuum ignition control; 3-bearing crankshaft; engine rubber-mounted; optional oil cooler.
TRANSMISSION rear wheel drive; Borg & Beck 8in diaphragm spring clutch; 4-speed manual gearbox, synchromesh; single-piece open prop shaft; hypoid bevel final drive 3.91:1.
CHASSIS steel monocoque structure; ifs by coil springs and unequal wishbones; live axle with semi-elliptic springs; Armstrong lever arm dampers; Lockheed hydraulic brakes, front 10.75in discs, rear 10in drums; rack and helical pinion steering; 10 Imp gal (12 US gal, 45.5L)

fuel tank; Dunlop Road Speed 5.90-14 tyres; 4J rims; wire wheels optional.
DIMENSIONS wheelbase 91in (231.1cm); track 49in (124.5cm); turning circle 30.5ft (9.3m); ground clearance 4.25in (10.8cm); length 153.75in (390.5cm); width 60in (152.4cm); height 49.25in (125cm).
PERFORMANCE maximum speed 108.1mph (173.5kph);16.4mph (26.3kph) @ 1000rpm; 0-60mph (96kph) 12.1sec; 9.7kg/bhp (13kg/kW); fuel consumption 23.0mpg (12.3L/100km).
PRICE £870 2s 3d (£870 30p).
PRODUCTION 513,276 all MGB.

Changes to the third Midget, known as the Mark II, were more fundamental than with the Mark 1° GAN2 of 1962. Sports cars of the 1960s still handled much as in the 1950s with sharp steering, firm ride resulting from small spring amplitudes, and little body roll. Essentially rear wheel drive over-steerers, they were being caught out by small front wheel drive cars, which although not all smooth-riding, captured much of the clubman sporting market. The Spridget had to change from quarter-elliptic rear springs, which had used the bump stops as an integral feature of the suspension, to semi-elliptics. There was a small advantage in reducing unsprung weight through abandonment of the torque arm and mounting bracket. The ride improved, which was just as well in view of competition from the independently sprung but somewhat wayward Triumph Spitfire. The wider main crankshaft bearings gave better reliability and refinement but led to demand for improved furnishings like the black crackle-finish facia with its angled dials. Seats constantly changed and a new windscreen and winding windows were another response to opposition from the Spitfire. The unfortunate corollary was loss of elbow room; the cockpit environment was a far cry from the cowled scuttle and cutaway door of the TC, though a good deal drier and less draughty.

BODY sports, 2 doors, 2 seats; weight 1540lb (698.5kg).
ENGINE 4 cylinders, in-line; front; 64.58mm x 83.72mm, 1098cc; compr 8.9:1, 8.0 optional; 59bhp (44kW) @ 5750rpm; 53.7bhp/L (40.1kW/L); 62lbft (83Nm) @ 3250rpm.
ENGINE STRUCTURE pushrod overhead valve, chain-driven camshaft; cast iron cylinder head, block; 2 SU HS2 1˜ in carburettors, SU electric fuel pump; 3-bearing crankshaft.
TRANSMISSION rear wheel drive; 7˜ in sdp clutch; 4-speed manual gearbox, synchromesh; hypoid final drive 4.22:1.
CHASSIS DETAILS steel platform chassis; ifs by coil springs and wishbones; live rear axle semi-elliptic leaf springs, Armstrong lever arm hydraulic dampers; Lockheed hydraulic brakes 8˜in disc front, 7in drums rear; rack and pinion steering; 6 Imp gal (7.2 US gal, 27.3L) fuel tank; 5.20–13 Dunlop tubeless tyres; steel disc wheels; wire wheels optional.

DIMENSIONS wheelbase 80in (203.2cm); track 45.25in (114.9cm) front, 44.75in (113.7cm) rear; turning circle 30.1ft (9.2m); ground clearance 5in (12.7cm); length 135.25in (346.1cm); width 53in (134.5cm); height 49.75in (126.4cm).
PERFORMANCE maximum speed 91.8mph (147.4kph);15.4mph (24.7kph) @ 1000rpm; 0-60mph (96kph) 14.9sec; 11.8kg/bhp (15.8kg/kW); fuel consumption 29.2mpg (9.7L/100km).
PRICE £622 17s 1d (£822 85.4p).
PRODUCTION 26,601.

The first Sprite's abrasive ride was abhorrent to Abingdon, and its quarter-elliptic rear springs were soon changed to half-elliptics. Experiments in improving the Sprite/Midget's ride quality with BMC's Hydrolastic coupled fluid suspension began late in 1962 and carried on for some 18 months under EX 229 and 231. Cost considerations led to the abandonment of a coil sprung back axle for the MGB, but when proposals for the car's replacement were drawn up in 1964 Hydrolastic was once again given consideration. EX234 could, with different engines, have been capable of replacing both the Midget and MGB.

Pininfarina built a stylish body that was designed by MG with hints of MGB, and a prototype was made and test-driven at Silverstone with encouraging results. The 2+2 interior was beautifully furnished with a central console. Roy Brocklehurst, who succeeded Syd Enever as chief engineer in 1971, worked in strictest secrecy on the car's underpinnings in the Abingdon boiler house. The prototype was equipped with an A-series engine driving the rear wheels through an Austin Gipsy final drive.

Hydrolastic suspension was used throughout the BMC front wheel drive range, and extensive experiments needed to be carried out to adapt it for rear wheel drive.

BODY roadster, 2 doors, 2 seats.
ENGINE 4 cylinders, in-line; front, transverse; 70.6mm x 81.3mm, 1275cc; compr 9.75:1; 70bhp (52.2kW) @ 6000rpm; 54.9bhp/L (40.9kW/L); 77lbft (103Nm) @ 3000rpm. Option for fitting 1798cc B-series.
ENGINE STRUCTURE pushrod overhead valve, chain-driven camshaft; cast iron cylinder head, block; 2 SU HS2 1˜ in carburettors, SU electric fuel pump; centrifugal and vacuum ignition; 3-bearing crankshaft.
TRANSMISSION front wheel drive; 7.125in sdp clutch; 4-speed manual gearbox, synchromesh; helical gear final drive 4.133:1.
CHASSIS DETAILS steel monocoque structure; independent suspension by interconnected Hydrolastic units and rubber-cone springs; transverse wishbone at front, trailing arms at rear with anti-toll bar; sub-frame mounted; Lockheed brakes, 8in disc front 8in drum rear with pressure limiting valve; Cam Gears rack and pinion steering; 8.5 Imp gal (10.2 US gal, 38.6L) fuel tank; 13in wheels.
DIMENSIONS wheelbase 80in (203.2cm).
PRODUCTION 1.

Development work on EX234 was gradually diminished as demands for engineering effort increased to cope with safety and emissions research.

1964 O-series MGB

For an engine whose origins went back to the dark days of the war, the pushrod B-series had an astonishing lifespan. It was subject to continuous development and a number of attempts at replacement, such as the E-series built at a new plant at Cofton Hackett. This was quite a small power unit developed for front wheel drive transverse engined cars; the rationale was that it could have two cylinders added for bigger cars. It would not have fitted into an MGB however, and among the alternatives explored was a narrow-angle V4 and even a V6. A 2-litre version of the 5-bearing B-series was designed as something of a stop-gap. This was the O-series, with an overhead camshaft aluminium cylinder head, which unfortunately took a long time to develop as US emission control measures grew more demanding. It was fitted in the Rover SD1 2000 in 1982 and tried experimentally in MGBs in the late 1970s. With the model approaching the end of its useful life however, it remained a tantalising might-have-been.

The O-series evolved into the M16 twin overhead camshaft fuel injected Rover 820 engine, mooted as a possibility for the revived MGB of the 1990s. The V8 was chosen instead leaving private owners such as MG expert Roger Parker to build one-offs.

BODY roadster and GT, 2 doors, 2 seats; weight approx 2442lb (1108kg) (GT).

ENGINE 4 cylinders, in-line; front; 84.4mm x 89mm, 1994cc; compr 9.0:1; 101bhp (75.3kW) @ 5250rpm; 50.7bhp/L (37.8kW/L); 120lbft (161Nm) @ 3250rpm.

ENGINE STRUCTURE single toothed belt driven overhead camshaft; cast iron block, aluminium cylinder head; two SU HIF 44 carburettors; contact-breaker ignition; 5-bearing crankshaft.

TRANSMISSION rear wheel drive; sdp clutch; 5-speed manual synchromesh gearbox; hypoid bevel final drive.

CHASSIS DETAILS steel monocoque structure; ifs by coil springs and unequal wishbones; live axle with semi-elliptic springs, anti-roll bars front and rear; Armstrong lever arm dampers; Lockheed hydraulic brakes with vacuum servo, front 10.75in discs, rear 10in drums; rack and pinion steering; 11 Imp gal (13.2 US gal, 50L) fuel tank; 165SR -14 tyres; 5J rims.

DIMENSIONS wheelbase 91in (231.1cm); track 49in (124.5cm); turning circle 30.5ft (9.3m); ground clearance 5in (12.7cm); length 158.25in (402cm); width 60in (152.4cm); height 49.25in (125.1cm).

PERFORMANCE 11kg/bhp (14.7kg/kW).

PRODUCTION nil, development cars only.

Author's pet project, an M-16 engined MGB Twin-Cam. Heritage bodyshell, Sherpa bellhousing, and SDI 5-speed gearbox gave a 120mph top speed and lively acceleration.

1964 Dick Jacobs Midget Coupe

Following a long association with MG as a driver and, as the proprietor of the Mill Garage at South Woodford a dealer, Dick Jacobs was the means by which MG returned to the track in the 1960s. His racing Magnettes and MGA Twin Cams 1 and 2 MTW had been outstandingly successful, so when three Midgets were specially prepared for racing, two were assigned to him. The third went to Scottish enthusiast and MG works rally driver John Milne. Using a Midget platform as a basis they had hand-made aluminium bodies secured with a mixture of rivets and epoxy-resin adhesive. They conformed to the shape of the standard car with the addition of a sloping fastback roof and a rounded nose. Disc brakes, soon to be incorporated in the standard car, were added and the suspension was modified with high-rate springs and Armstrong competition shock absorbers, those at the back of variable rate. Engines were enlarged as development continued with BMC Formula Junior experience. Alan Foster and Andrew Hedges gained a fine reputation for speed and reliability, not only in British club racing in which they scored a class win and third place in the 1963 Autosport Championship, but also in the 1964 100-kilometre race at Nürburgring where they were first and second in class. Andrew Hedges and Roger Mac won their class in one at Sebring.

BODY coupe, 2 doors, 2 seats; weight 1242lb (563.4kg).
ENGINE 4 cylinders, in-line; front; 63.73mm x 76.2mm, 972cc; compr 9.0:1; 75bhp (55.9kW) @ 5750rpm; 77.2bhp/L (57.5kW/L). Various engines: 995cc, 1139cc, and 1293cc to comply with racing capacity classes.
ENGINE STRUCTURE pushrod ohv, chain-driven camshaft; cast iron cylinder head, block; twin-choke Weber carb, mechanical fuel pump; 3-bearing crank, four-branch exhaust; machined polished combustion chambers and ports. Among the engine variations was a 1293cc dry-sump unit for the Nürburgring.
TRANSMISSION rwd; sdp clutch; 4-spd close-ratio gearbox, synchro; hypoid final drive 4.875:1.
CHASSIS DETAILS steel platform chassis; ifs by coil springs and wishbones, anti-roll bar; live rear axle quarter-elliptic leaf springs, radius arms, lever arm hydraulic dampers; Lockheed hydraulic brakes disc front, 7in drums rear; rack and pinion steering; 6 Imp gal (7.2 US gal, 27.3L) fuel tank; racing tyres; wire wheels.
DIMENSIONS wheelbase 80in (203.2cm); track 45.25in (114.9cm) front, 44.75in (113.7cm) rear; turning circle 30.1ft (9.2m); ground clearance 4in (10.2cm); length 135.25in (346.1cm); width 53in (134.5cm); height 48in (121.9cm).
PERFORMANCE maximum speed 120mph (192.6kph).
PRODUCTION 3.

1964 MGB Sebring racer

Among the 15 or so MGBs campaigned by the Abingdon Competitions Department under Stuart Turner, three were GTs, two of which were special lightweight cars. Open cars were raced and rallied with and without hardtops, and among the engine permutations were three or five-bearing blocks, and cross-flow or aluminium heads. Compression ratios could be as high as 11:1, and tuning experts such as Daniel Richmond at Downton and Morris Engines were consulted. For Le Mans the cars had smoothed-off nose-cones to improve the aerodynamics, not unlike the Dick Jacobs Midgets, and profiled plastic headlamp covers. In 1964 Paddy Hopkirk and Andrew Hedges averaged 99.9mph (160.4kph) at Le Mans in No. 37 BMO 54B, finishing 19th overall. At Sebring in 1965 an MGB came second in class and at Le Mans in 1965 Hopkirk and Hedges finished 11th, the best an MGB achieved there, and second in its class. It was the last MGB to tackle Le Mans, but glory was still to come in the Marathon de la Route 84-hour race at the Nürburgring. Julien Vernaeve and Andrew Hedges, driving MGB No. 47 GRX 307D, won after 5260 miles (8465km) of racing, a great testimony to the strength of the MGB and to team manager Peter Browning. Hopkirk and Hedges won their class at Sebring in a newly built MGB GT LBL 591E in 1967.

BODY Roadster, coupe, 2 doors, 2 seats; weight 2030lb (908kg).
ENGINE 4 cylinders, in-line; front; 81.32mm x 88.9mm, 1847cc; compr 8.8:1 or more; 130bhp (96.9kW) @ 6500rpm; 70.4bhp/L (52.5kW/L).
ENGINE STRUCTURE pushrod overhead valve; chain-driven camshaft; cast iron cylinder head and block; Weber twin choke 45DCOE carburettor; SU electric fuel pump; centrifugal and vacuum ignition control; 5-bearing crankshaft (3-bearing for some events); engine rubber-mounted; oil cooler; tubular exhaust manifold.
TRANSMISSION rear wheel drive; Borg & Beck sdp clutch; 4-speed close-ratio gearbox, overdrive fitted according to event; single-piece open prop shaft; Salisbury hypoid bevel final drive 3.91:1 (or to suit event); limited slip differential.
CHASSIS steel monocoque structure; ifs by coil springs and unequal wishbones; live axle with semi-elliptic springs, anti-roll bar; Armstrong competition adjustable dampers; disc brakes; rack and pinion steering; 23 Imp gal (27.6 US gal, 104.6L) fuel tank (or additional tank to standard); racing tyres; wide rimmed aluminium or wire wheels depending on event.
DIMENSIONS wheelbase 91in (231.1cm); track 49in (124.5cm); turning circle 30.5ft (9.3m); length 153.75in (390.5cm).
PERFORMANCE maximum speed 140mph (224.7kph) in Le Mans trim; 7kg/bhp (9.4kg/kW).
PRODUCTION approx 15.

The A-series engine dated from 1943 when Austin was instructed to look for an alternative power unit for the Jeep. Two cylinders were lopped off a 6-cylinder truck engine that was adapted for Austin's first post-war Sixteen saloon. Reduced to 1.0-litre, it went into the Austin A35 and Morris Minor. Overcrowding on the pushrod side meant siamesing the inlet and exhaust ports, common tracts leading to two valves, an arrangement of which engine consultant Harry Weslake disapproved. The engine was turned sideways for the Mini, developed to 1071 cc for the Mini-Cooper, then in 1964 with staggered cylinders for the 1275 Mini-Cooper S, had an increase on its original 803cc by some 60 per cent. This developed 72bhp (53.7kW) but was detuned for the Midget enabling cheaper materials to be used in manufacture. It had smaller valves and a compression ratio of 8.8 against the Mini's 9.7:1 by virtue of dished piston crowns. Only the Cooper had the nitrided E40 steel crankshaft, changed later to tuftrided.

The Midget III of October 1966 had a more sophisticated hood and a bigger cockpit aperture, yet the interior still seemed cramped as seats grew bigger and the bulkhead hampered their rearward adjustment. Praiseworthy brakes and gearbox kept Midgets abreast of the market.

BODY sports, 2 doors, 2 seats; weight 1575lb (714kg).

ENGINE 4 cylinders, in-line; front; 70.61mm x 81.28mm, 1275cc; compr 8.8:1 8.0 optional; 65bhp (48.5kW) @ 6000rpm; 51bhp/L (38kW/L); 72lbft (97Nm) @ 3000rpm.

ENGINE STRUCTURE pushrod ohv, chain-driven cam; cast iron cylinder head, block; 2 SU HS2 1¨ in carbs, SU electric fuel pump; 3-bearing crankshaft.

TRANSMISSION rear wheel drive; 6¨ in diaphragm spring sdp clutch; 4-speed manual gearbox, synchro; hypoid final drive 4.22 later 3.9:1.

CHASSIS DETAILS steel platform chassis; ifs by coil springs and wishbones; live rear axle semi-elliptic 5-leaf springs, Armstrong lever arm hydraulic dampers; optional anti-roll bar; Lockheed hydraulic brakes 8¨in disc front, 7in drums rear; rack and pinion steering; 6 Imp gal (7.2 US gal, 27.3L) fuel tank; 5.20–13 Dunlop tubeless tyres; steel disc wheels, wire wheels optional.

DIMENSIONS wheelbase 80in (203.2cm); track 45.25in (114.9cm) front, 44.75in (113.7cm) rear; turning circle 30.1ft (9.2m); ground clearance 5in (12.7cm); length 135.25in (346.1cm); width 53in (134.5cm); height 49.75in (126.4cm).

PERFORMANCE maximum speed 94mph (151kph); 15.4mph (24.7kph) later 16.5mph (26.5kph) @ 1000rpm; 0-60mph (96kph) 14.1sec; 11kg/bhp (14.7kg/kW); 29.6mpg (9.5L/100km) fuel consumption.

PRICE £683 18s 2d (£683 90p).

PRODUCTION 13,722.

Among claimants to have pioneered the hatchback, the opening rear window giving access to luggage space, was Aston Martin with the DB2/4 of 1953. It created a new kind of sports coupe, better suited to autobahn speeds than were open cars before really wind-tight hoods. A closed-top MGB was planned in advance of the car's announcement but Abingdon was so busy satisfying demand for the open car there was scarcely time to divert the necessary resources. Besides, there was no consensus on its shape. Coachbuilders and hardtop-makers including Coune of Belgium (see right) tried to meet John Thornley's demand for a poor man's Aston Martin. He might well have added the E-type Jaguar.

Syd Enever took a quarter-scale model to Morris Bodies branch at Coventry to discuss manufacturing practicalities and it was pointed out to him that BMC had a long-standing arrangement with Pininfarina to design things like that. Pininfarina's first effort at drawing one up was no better than Abingdon's but when it had been sent a full-sized MGB the result was instantly successful. The key difference was the height of the windscreen. There was some argument about whether this was an inspiration of Abingdon or Turin; either way the result was one of the best-proportioned cars of the day.

BODY coupe, 2 doors, 2+2 seats; weight 2379lb (1079kg).
ENGINE 4 cylinders, in-line; front; 80.26mm x 88.9mm, 1798cc; compr 8.8:1; 95bhp (70.8kW) @ 5400rpm; 52.8bhp/L (39.4kW/L); 110lbft (148Nm) @ 3000rpm.
ENGINE STRUCTURE pushrod ohv; chain-driven camshaft; cast iron cylinder head and block; 2 SU inclined H4 carburettors, SU electrical fuel pump; centrifugal and vacuum ignition control; 5-bearing crankshaft; engine rubber-mounted; oil cooler.
TRANSMISSION rear wheel drive; Borg & Beck 8in diaphragm spring clutch; 4-speed manual gearbox, synchromesh; o/d opt 0.8:1; single-piece open prop shaft; Salisbury

hypoid bevel final drive 3.91:1.
CHASSIS steel monocoque structure; ifs by coil springs and unequal wishbones, anti-roll bar; live axle with semi-elliptic springs; Armstrong lever arm dampers; Lockheed hydraulic brakes, front 10.75in discs, rear 10in drums; rack and helical pinion steering; 12 Imp gal (14.4US gal, 54.6L) fuel tank; Dunlop C41 5.60-14 or SP41 165-14 tyres; 4°J rim wire wheels opt, 4J steel wheel rims.
DIMENSIONS wheelbase 91.75in (233cm); track 50in (127cm); turning circle 30.5ft (9.3m); ground clearance 5.25in (13.3cm); length 153.75in (390.5cm); width 60in (152.4cm); height 49.5in (125.7cm).
PERFORMANCE maximum speed 107mph (171.8kph); 22.4mph (36kph) o/d top, 11.2mph (18kph) top @ 1000rpm; 0-60mph (96kph) 13.2sec; 11.4kg/bhp (15.2kg/kW); 20.9mpg (13.5L/100km).
PRICE £998 8s 9d (£998 43.75p).
PRODUCTION 125,621 all MGB GTs.

1967-1969 MGB

The MGB, like many cars with long lifespans, was subject to continuous change especially during the Leyland years of cosmetic makeovers. One of the most significant changes took place as a result of BMC engine policy. The old B-series was insufficiently smooth-running for the new Austin 1800 so it was altered to five main bearings instead of three from 1965 model year. The change was accomplished without affecting the engine externally but the extra bearings made it less freely revving than before. The result was more refinement and greater reliability but less speed. A 12-gallon tank came in at the same time. An all-synchromesh gearbox was introduced, entailing a structural change to the transmission tunnel. An alternator replaced the dynamo in 1968 as more emisson control measures came into use and American-specification cars brought increasing changes. Energy-absorbing dashboards and rocker switches were necessary to comply with new regulations, and MG production suffered as resources were diverted to deal with them.

The GT with its stiffer springing and anti-roll bar prospered, with the attraction of luggage accommodation 38in (96.5cm) wide by 30in (76.2cm) deep with the seat backrest up, and 38in (96.5cm) square with it down.

BODY roadster, 2 doors, 2 seats; weight 2030lb (920.8kg).
ENGINE 4 cylinders, in-line; front; 80.26mm x 88.9mm, 1798cc; compr 8.8:1; 95bhp (70.8kW) @ 5400rpm; 52.8bhp/L (39.4kW/L); 110lbft (147.5Nm) @ 3000rpm.
ENGINE STRUCTURE pushrod overhead valve; chain-driven camshaft; cast iron cylinder head and block; 2 SU inclined H4 carburettors, SU electrical fuel pump; centrifugal and vacuum ignition control; 5-bearing crankshaft; engine rubber-mounted; oil cooler.
TRANSMISSION rear wheel drive; Borg & Beck 8in diaphragm spring clutch; 4-speed manual gearbox, all-synchromesh; single-piece open prop shaft; Salisbury hypoid bevel final drive 3.91:1.
CHASSIS DETAILS steel monocoque structure; ifs by coil springs and unequal wishbones; live axle with semi-elliptic springs, optional anti-roll bar; Armstrong lever arm dampers; Lockheed hydraulic brakes, front 10.75in discs, rear 10in drums; rack and helical pinion steering; 12 Imp gal (14.4 US gal, 54.6L) fuel tank; Dunlop Road Speed 5.90-14 tyres; 4J rims; wire wheels optional.
DIMENSIONS wheelbase 91in (231.1cm); track 49in (124.5cm); turning circle 30.5ft (9.3m); ground clearance 4.25in (10.8cm); length 153.75in (390.5cm); width 60in (152.4cm); height 49.25in (125cm).
PERFORMANCE maximum speed 108.1mph (173.5kph); 16.4mph (26.3kph); 0-60mph (96kph) 12.1sec; 9.8kg/bhp (13kg/kW); fuel consumption 23mpg (12.3L/100km). PRICE £870 2s 3d (870 11.25p). PRODUCTION 513,276 all MGB.

Raised transmission tunnel (top right) was among the modifications necessary for the MGC introduction. The space required for the all-synchromesh gearbox allowed the option of an automatic gearbox that continued until 1973.

205

1967-1969 MGC

The politics of BMC/British Leyland that had brought the Healeys in during LP Lord's time now banished them in Donald Stokes's. Yet Austin-Healey production was important to Abingdon, and a replacement was sought for the 3000 model due to be phased out at the end of 1967. A number of prototype schemes were launched including some that continued to use the Healey name, but time was short and there was a good deal of pressure from American dealers to secure the succession. The result was a hurried compromise that, had it only been given time to mature, would have resulted in a highly satisfactory car. The basis, the substantial MGB monohull in both open and GT form, was there and there should have been sufficient wit to produce a satisfactory six-cylinder engine once it was decided not to use the existing BMC C-series. The Healeys fostered a move up-market with a big 4.0-litre Princess R Rolls-Royce engine. Morris engines, faced with adapting a six-cylinder for a forthcoming saloon as well as a sports car, drew one up that turned out unsatisfactory for both and not much different from the abandoned C-series. Its weight estimates were badly awry. A new floor pan was needed, with torsion bar front suspension because the cross member that picked-up the coil springs would not fit under the six-cylinder's sump.

BODY roadster, 2 doors, 2 seats; weight 2460lb (1116kg).

ENGINE 6 cylinders, in-line; front; 83.36mm x 88.9mm, 2912cc; compr 9.0:1; 145bhp (108.1kW) @ 5250rpm; 49.8bhp/L (37.1kW/L); 170lbft (228Nm) @ 3400rpm.

ENGINE STRUCTURE pushrod ohv; chain-driven camshaft; cast iron cylinder head and block; 2 SU HS6 1⅛in carburettors, SU electrical fuel pump; centrifugal and vacuum ignition control; 7-bearing crankshaft; engine rubber-mounted; oil cooler

TRANSMISSION rear wheel drive; Borg & Beck 9in diaphragm spring clutch; 4-speed manual gearbox, all-synchromesh; single-piece open prop shaft; hypoid bevel final drive 3.307:1, optional Laycock LH overdrive 0.82:1, Salisbury final drive 3.7:1; optional auto Borg Warner Type 35.

CHASSIS DETAILS steel monocoque structure; ifs by unequal length parallel wishbones and torsion bars, with anti-roll bar; live axle on semi-elliptic springs; Armstrong telescopic dampers front, lever arm rear; Girling brakes, front 11.25in discs, rear 9in drums; Cam gears rack and pinion steering; 12 Imp gal (14.4 US gal, 54.6L) fuel tank; Dunlop SP 41 165–15 tyres; 5J rims; wire wheels optional.

DIMENSIONS wheelbase 91in (231.1cm); track 50in (127cm) front, 49.5in (125.7cm) rear; turning circle 36ft (11m); ground clearance 4.5in (11.4cm); length 153.2in (389.1cm); width 60in (152.4cm); height 49.25in (125.1cm).

PERFORMANCE maximum speed 118mph (189kph); 27mph (43.3kph) o/d top; 22.1mph (35.5kph) direct top @ 1000rpm; 0-60mph (96kph) 10.0sec; 7.7kg/bhp (10.3kg/kW); 19.3mpg (14.6L/100km).

PRICE £1101 16s 6d (£1101 82.5p).

PRODUCTION 4542.

1967-1969 MGC GT

Bonnet bulge and fatter tyres apart, there was little to distinguish the MGC GT from the B, yet it was quite different to drive. With 55.7 per cent of its weight on the front wheels against the B's 52.5 per cent, the B's nimble handling was gone, and the MGC's splendid long-legged qualities were not immediately apparent. It was withdrawn within two years. University Motors, a long-standing MG dealers, sure the car was not at all bad bought the last 141, 118GTs and 23 roadsters. The MGC may have been best suited for cruising along motorways, but it looked the part, and rode serenely. Remembering how demand continued for the MGA Twin Cam after it was withdrawn, instead of selling off the remaining MGCs cheaply, University Motors sold them at a premium. With Downton Stage II engine conversions they were £1620 instead of £1386. The modified MGC was a revelation. It had the old Healey's strident appeal, the engine was smooth and lively; acceleration was 20 per cent faster, and top speed 130mph (208.7kph). There were some cosmetic additions; a different grille and a small leather steering wheel instead of the standard over-large one. It exaggerated the heaviness of the steering at parking speeds but it looked good. If the MGC had been made like this at first there might have been no need to abandon it.

BODY coupe, 2 doors, 2+2 seats; weight 2615lb (1186kg) (automatic). ENGINE 6 cylinders, in-line; front; 83.36mm x 88.9mm, 2912cc; compr 9.0:1; 145bhp (108kW) @ 5250rpm; 49.8bhp/L (37.1kW/L); 170lbft (228Nm) @ 3400rpm.
ENGINE STRUCTURE pushrod ohv; chain-driven camshaft; cast iron cyl head and block; 2 SU HS6 1⅛in carbs, SU electrical fuel pump; centrifugal and vacuum ign control; 7-bearing crank; engine rubber-mounted; oil cooler.
TRANSMISSION rear wheel drive; Borg & Beck 9in diaphragm spring clutch; 4-speed manual gearbox, all-synchromesh; single-piece open prop shaft; hypoid bevel final drive 3.307:1, optional Laycock LH overdrive 0.82:1, Salisbury final drive 3.7:1; opt auto Borg Warner Type 35 final drive 3.35:1.
CHASSIS steel monocoque; ifs by unequal length parallel wishbones and torsion bars, with anti-roll bar; live axle on semi-elliptic springs; Armstrong telescopic dampers front,

lever arm rear; Girling brakes, front 11.25in discs, rear 9in drums; cam gears rack and pinion steering; 12 Imp gal (14.4 US gal, 54.6L); Dunlop SP 41 165-15 tyres; 5J rims; wire wheels optional; 72-spoke optional.
DIMENSIONS wheelbase 91in (231cm); track 50in (127cm) front, 49.5in (125.7cm) rear; turning circle 36ft (11m); ground clearance 4.5in (11.4cm); length 153.2in (389cm); width 60in (152.4cm); height 50in (127cm).
PERFORMANCE max 120mph (193kph); 27mph (43.3kph) o/d top, 22.1mph (35.5kph) direct top and auto @ 1000rpm; 0-60mph (96kph) 10sec; 8.2kg/bhp (11kg/kW); 19.3mpg (14.6L/100km).
PRICE £1249.
PRODUCTION 4457.

Top: University Motors MGC tested by Eric Dymock in 1969.

1968 MGC GTS Sebring racer

The last cars from BMC Competitions were ready before the 1967 production MGC they were based on. They were raced as prototypes, which meant they had to bear more than a superficial resemblance to the production version.

The first car with a 2004cc MGB engine and 150bhp (111.9kW) @ 6000rpm came ninth in the 1967 Targa Florio. In 1968 at Sebring 'Mabel' (MBL 546E) No44 driven by Paddy Hopkirk and Andrew Hedges won class, was third prototype and 10th overall with a 3.0 litre engine. It also raced in the 84-hour Marathon de la Route on the Nürburgring and came sixth after a heroic performance by Tony Fall who drove two laps without brakes.

Another car was built with an aluminium engine, and they raced again at Sebring in 1969, the final appearance of works cars under the flag of British Leyland, not BMC. Number 35 (RMO 699F), driven by Hopkirk and Hedges, finished ninth prototype and 15th overall. Number 36 (MBL 546E) driven by Craig Hill and Bill Brack, finished 15th prototype and 34th overall behind a private MGB driven by John Colgate and Don Parks.

BODY coupe, 2 doors, 2 seats; weight 2240lb (1016kg).
ENGINE 6 cylinders, in-line; front; 84.1mm x 88.9mm, 2956cc; compr 9.0:1; 210bhp (156.6kW) @ 6000rpm; 71bhp/L (53kW/L).
ENGINE STRUCTURE pushrod overhead valve; chain-driven camshaft; aluminium cylinder head and cast iron block (one engine made with aluminium block); 3 twin choke Weber carburettors; centrifugal and vacuum ignition control; 7-bearing crankshaft; engine rubber-mounted; oil cooler.
TRANSMISSION rear wheel drive; Borg & Beck 9in diaphragm spring clutch; 4-speed manual gearbox, all-synchromesh; single-piece open prop shaft; hypoid bevel final drive 3.307:1, optional Laycock LH overdrive 0.82:1, Salisbury final drive 3.7:1; optional auto Borg Warner Type 35.
CHASSIS steel monocoque structure; ifs by unequal length parallel wishbones and torsion bars adjustable from within car; anti-roll bar; live rear axle on semi-elliptic springs with locating arms and anti-roll bar; Armstrong adjustable telescopic dampers; Girling disc brakes; Cam gears rack and pinion steering; 24 Imp gal (28.8 US gal, 109.1L) fuel tank; racing tyres, centre-lock alloy wheels.
DIMENSIONS wheelbase 91in (231.1cm); track 50in (127cm) front, 49.5in (125.7cm) rear; turning circle 36ft (11m); length 153.2in (389.1cm); width 65in (165.1cm).
PERFORMANCE maximum speed 150mpg (241.4kph) approx.
PRODUCTION 2.

As with the Dick Jacobs Midgets, the basis was the steel platform with an aluminium body conforming to the GT shape, with flares for racing tyres and wheels.

1968 MG 1300

Obediently joining in when the 1100 became the 1300, the MG variant had ten per cent more power, raising its top speed to nearly 100mph. Radial-ply tyres were standardised, it dispensed with the 1100's strip speedometer and had closer ratio gears although there were still only four of them. The engine was still firmly A-series, with three main bearings and noisy transfer gears. Harmony in the specifications of Wolseley, Riley, and MG 1300s means that they became almost indistinguishable from one another except that the MG was available only with two doors. It still had praiseworthy ride and handling, despite reservations about how the front tended to dive to the inside if the throttle was closed suddenly in mid-corner. The radial-ply tyres magnified road noise, and among the qualitative problems that varied from car to car were obstructive gearshifts and sticky rack and pinion steering. Economy was a little below average, top speed up, and acceleration about par. In a triumph of miniaturisation in 1965 an automatic transmission developed by Automotive Products (AP) was developed that fitted into the sumps of Minis and 1100/1300s. It was a good deal less smooth than full-sized automatics, invariably noisy, and seldom as reliable. It also made the MG a good deal less lively and increased the consumption of fuel quite markedly.

BODY saloon, 2 doors, 4 seats; weight 1847lb (838kg), 1936lb (879kg) automatic.
ENGINE 4 cylinders, in-line; front, transverse; 70.6mm x 81.3mm, 1275cc; cr 9.75:1; 70bhp (52.2kW) @ 6000rpm; 54.9bhp/L (40.9kW/L); 77lbft (103Nm) @ 3000rpm.
ENGINE STRUCTURE pushrod ohv, chain-driven camshaft; cast iron cyl head, block; 2 SU HS2 1ⁱin carbs, SU electric fuel pump; centrifugal and vacuum ignition; 3-bearing crank.
TRANSMISSION front wheel drive; 7.125in sdp diaphragm spring clutch; 4-speed manual gearbox, all-synchromesh; helical gear final drive 3.65:1; opt AP 4-speed auto with torque converter, final drive 3.76:1.
CHASSIS DETAILS steel monocoque; independent suspension by interconnected Hydrolastic units and rubber-cone springs; transverse wishbone at front, trailing arms at rear with anti-toll bar and two torsion bars for pitch stiffness; Lockheed brakes, 8in disc front 8in drum rear, pressure limiting valve; Cam Gears

rack and pinion; 8.5 Imp gal (10.2 US gal, 38.6L) fuel tank; 145-12in radial ply Dunlop SP68 tyres 4.0in rim.
DIMENSIONS wheelbase 93.5in (237.5cm); track 51.5in (130.8cm) front, 50.75in (128.9cm) rear; turning circle 32.5ft (9.9m); ground clearance 5.25in (13.3cm); length 146.75in (372.7cm); width 60.25in (153cm); height 53.25in (135.3cm).
PERFORMANCE maximum speed 97mph (155.7kph), 93mph (149kph) auto; 16.8mph (27kph) @ 1000rpm, 16.3mph (26.2kph) auto @ 1000rpm; 0-60mph (96kph) 14.1sec, 14.3sec auto; 12kg/bhp (16.1kg/kW), 12.6kg/bhp (16.8kg/kW) auto; fuel consumption 30mpg (9.4L/100km), 27mpg (10.5L/100km) auto.
PRICE £925 11s 8d (£925 58p), £1021 8s 4d (£1021 42p)
PRODUCTION Mk I & II 26,240.

213

1969-1974 Midget Mk 3/4 GAN 4/5

Upheavals during the birth-pangs of British Leyland blurred the transition of the Mark III (announced October 1966) into the Mark IV Midget (announced October 1969). Design and development was nominally moved to Abingdon, although more as a way of writing the Healey family out of the script than giving decision-making to MG.

The Sprite was withdrawn from export markets and the Healey name was dropped. All vestiges of the MG grille were swept away in a rash of corporate harmonisation, with Leyland symbols predominating. Trendy cast alloy wheels, matt black sills and seat trim with narrow central panels and horizontal ribbing came in. The cast wheels were replaced with cheaper Rostyle wheels and the up-to-the-minute matt black windscreen surround was dropped within a year. The rear wheel arches were rounded instead of being squared-off, but this turned out to weaken the press-work which then crumpled in rear-end impacts so was also changed back.

One of the more useful changes was an increase in the size of the fuel tank. Fuel consumption had deteriorated as a result of exhaust emission controls and increased weight, reducing the car's effective range to well under 200miles (322km).

BODY sports, 2 doors, 2 seats; weight 1548lb (702kg).
ENGINE 4 cylinders, in-line; front; 70.61mm x 81.28mm, 1275cc; compr 8.8:1 8.0 optional; 65bhp (48.5kW) @ 6000rpm; 60bhp/L (38kW/L); 72lbft (97Nm) @ 3000rpm.
ENGINE STRUCTURE pushrod overhead valve, chain-driven camshaft; cast iron cylinder head, block; 2 SU HS2 1˝in carburettors, SU electric fuel pump; 3-bearing crankshaft.
TRANSMISSION rear wheel drive; 6˝ in diaphragm spring sdp clutch; 4-speed manual gearbox, synchromesh; hypoid final drive 3.9:1.
CHASSIS DETAILS steel platform chassis; ifs by coil springs and wishbones; live rear axle semi-elliptic 5-leaf springs, Armstrong lever arm hydraulic dampers; optional anti-roll bar; Lockheed hydraulic brakes 8˝in disc front, 7in drums rear; rack and pinion steering; 7 Imp gal (8.4 US gal, 31.8L) fuel tank; 145-13 Michelin radial-ply tyres; cast alloy wheels, later Rostyle steel, wire wheels optional.

DIMENSIONS wheelbase 80in (203.2cm); front track 46.5in (118.1cm) with Rostyles or 45.25in (114.9cm), rear 45in (114.3cm) with Rostyles, or 44.75in (113.7cm); turning circle 30.1ft (9.2m); ground clearance 5in (12.7cm); length 135.25in (346.1cm); width 53in (134.5cm); height 49.75in (126.4cm).
PERFORMANCE maximum speed 94mph (151kph); 16.5mph (26.5kph) @ 1000rpm; 0-60mph (96kph) 14.1sec; 10.8kg/kW (14.5kg/kW); fuel consumption 29.6mpg (9.5L/100km).
PRICE £915 14s 9d (£915 74p). PRODUCTION GAN 4 13,722, GAN 5 86,650, total 100,372.

Radial ply tyres were standardised in 1972, the suspension was raised half an inch to meet American headlamp and bumper regulations, and an alternator replaced the dynamo.

1972 SSV1 Experimental safety vehicle

Compliance with world safety and emission control regulations was a contentious issue throughout the 1970s. Increasing demands on engineering resources, research and development changed the nature of the motor industry. Planned obsolescence and the round of annual facelifts had to go by the board as serious studies were undertaken in order to keep pace with legislation.

Determined to show it could keep abreast of developments, British Leyland Motor Corporation (BLMC) asked MG to create an Experimental Safety Vehicle (SSV1) incorporating a number of as-yet untried safety features. These included a Lockheed anti-roll system that seems to have led to a deterioration in handling, run-flat tyres, low-level soft bumpers designed to reduce pedestrian injuries, air-bags, and passive seat belts. There was a big rear-view mirror in the roof, and body box-sections were filled with polyurethane foam to increase their strength in an accident.

The Triumph engineers at BLMC were assigned anti-lock brakes, self-levelling headlamps, and the development of an idea that Lucas had tried in 1962, a radar (Lucas used infra-red technology) cruise control that closed the throttle and applied the brakes when it approached the car ahead.

BODY coupe, 2 doors, 2 +2 seats.
ENGINE 4 cylinders, in-line; front; 80.26mm x 88.9mm, 1798cc; compr 8.8:1; 95bhp (70.8kW) @ 5400rpm; 52.8bhp/L (39.4kW/L); 110lbft (148Nm) @ 3000rpm.
ENGINE STRUCTURE pushrod overhead valve; chain-driven camshaft; cast iron cylinder head and block; 2 SU inclined H4 carburettors, SU electrical fuel pump; centrifugal and vacuum ignition control; 5-bearing crankshaft; engine rubber-mounted; oil cooler.
TRANSMISSION rear wheel drive; Borg & Beck 8in diaphragm spring clutch; 4-speed manual gearbox, all-synchromesh; single-piece open prop shaft; Salisbury hypoid bevel final drive 3.91:1.
CHASSIS DETAILS steel monocoque structure; ifs by coil springs and unequal wishbones; live axle with semi-elliptic springs, optional anti-roll bar; Armstrong lever arm dampers; Lockheed hydraulic brakes, front 10.75in discs, rear 10in drums; rack and helical pinion steering; 12 Imp gal (14.4 US gal, 54.6L) fuel tank; Dunlop Road Speed 5.90 - 14 tyres; 4J rims.
DIMENSIONS wheelbase 91in (231.1cm); track 49in (124.5cm); turning circle 30.5ft (9.3m); ground clearance 4.25in (10.8cm); width 60in (152.4cm).
PERFORMANCE 16.4mph (26.3kph) @ 1000rpm.
PRODUCTION 1.

A novelty of the SSV1 was the British Leyland Alcohol Simulation Test (BLAST) that set the driver a simple coloured lights test to determine sobriety.

1973-1976 MGB GT V8

In 1969 former Mini racer Ken Costello of Farnborough fitted an aluminium Oldsmobile V8 into an MGB. Rover had bought the V8 from GM for the Rover 3.5 and Range Rover, and Costello's second conversion was of an MGB GT with a British-made engine. Beyond an MGC 9°in clutch and a 3.07:1 back axle the modifications required were fairly elementary and Costello Motor engineering began making them in steady numbers. The car was 90lb (40.8kg) lighter than the standard MGB, and did nearly 130mph (208.7kph). Costello's request to British Leyland for a supply of engines was his undoing. If there was a market for an MGB V8, BL wanted it for itself. A prototype was commissioned and production commenced even though the output of engines was scarcely sufficient for Rover's use, and supplies to Costello were severely constrained. It scarcely mattered, Costello obtained Oldsmobile or Buick cylinder blocks of which there were plenty, and carried on as before. Made only as GTs and not exported because the engine was not de-toxed, the car's announcement, within two months of the Arab-Israel war that brought the first world oil crisis, was unfortunate. From a peak of 176 in October 1973, within a year production had shrunk to 18. It recovered to 93 in April 1975 then stopped the following year.

BODY coupe, 2 doors, 2+2 seats; weight 2387lb (1082.7kg).
ENGINE 8 cylinders, 90deg V; front; 88.96mm x 71.1mm, 3528cc; compr 8.25:1; 137bhp (102.2kW) @ 5000rpm; 38.8bhp/L (29kW/L); 193ftlb (259Nm) @ 2900rpm.
ENGINE STRUCTURE pushrod overhead valve; hydraulic tappets; aluminium cylinder block and heads; two 1∫in SU HIF6 carburettors; SU electric fuel pump; 5-bearing crankshaft.
TRANSMISSION rear wheel drive; Borg & Beck diaphragm spring sdp clutch; 4-speed manual synchromesh gearbox, Laycock LH overdrive 0.82:1 standard; hypoid bevel final drive 3.07:1.

CHASSIS DETAILS steel monocoque structure; ifs by wishbones, coil springs, anti-roll bar and lever-type dampers; Live rear axle with semi-elliptic springs and lever-type dampers; 10.7in disc front 10in drum rear hydraulic servo brakes; rack and pinion steering; 12 Imp gal (14.4 US gal, 54.6L) fuel tank; alloy and steel composite wheels, 175HR x 14 tyres 5J rims.
DIMENSIONS wheelbase 91in (231.1cm); track 49in (124.5cm); turning circle 34ft (10.4m); ground clearance 4.5in (11.4cm); length 154.7in (392.9cm), 158.25in (402cm) from autumn 1974; width 60in (152.4cm); height 50in (127cm), 51in (129.5cm) from autumn 1974.
PERFORMANCE maximum speed 125.3mph (201.7kph); 28.5mph (45.8kph) o/d top, 23.4mph (37.6kph) top @ 1000rpm; 0-60mph (96kph) 7.7sec; 7.9kg/bhp (10.6kg/kW); 19.8mpg (14.3L/100km).
PRICE £2293.96 on announcement, £3317 in autumn 1976.
PRODUCTION 2591.

Leyland was run mostly by former Triumph executives, and with the A-series at the end of its useful life, it was scarcely surprising that the Spitfire engine found its way into the Midget. For the first time since the introduction of baulk-ring synchromesh in 1962 there was also a major revision to the gearbox. The new all-synchromesh unit evolved round the single-rail design of the Morris Marina, with wider ratios, but making the car under-geared. There was not much more power, and the improved torque of the engine was necessary in view of the extra weight of the new bumpers deemed indispensable to meet approaching US safety legislation. The "rubber" bumpers, moulded in urethane foam over a steel base, made a major contribution to the weight of 1850lb (839kg), up from the safe, simple Mark 1 Sprite's 1400lb (635kg), and the small air intake in them caused overheating until changes were made.

The ride height was raised by another inch through changes to the front cross-member mounting and decambering the rear springs. This had a profound effect on the ride and handling, an undeserving fate for a popular little car.

In 1977 the specification included head restraints, inertia-reel safety belts, and later a radio console and two-speed wipers.

BODY sports, 2 doors, 2 seats; weight 1774lb (805kg).

ENGINE 4 cylinders, in-line; front; 73.7mm x 87.5mm, 1493cc; compr 9.0:1; 66bhp (49.2kW) @ 5500rpm; 44.2bhp/L (33kW/L); 77lbft (103Nm) @ 3000rpm.

ENGINE STRUCTURE pushrod overhead valve, chain-driven camshaft; cast iron cylinder head, block; 2 SU HS4 1° in carburettors, SU mechanical fuel pump; 3-bearing crankshaft.

TRANSMISSION rear wheel drive; 7˝ in diaphragm spring sdp clutch; 4-speed manual gearbox, all-synchromesh; hypoid final drive 3.9:1.

CHASSIS DETAILS steel platform chassis; ifs by coil springs and wishbones; live rear axle semi-elliptic 6-leaf springs, Armstrong lever arm hydraulic dampers; optional anti-roll bar; Lockheed hydraulic brakes 8˝in disc front, 7in drums rear; rack and pinion steering; 7 Imp gal (8.4 US gal, 31.8L) fuel tank; 145-13 Michelin radial-ply tyres; Rostyle steel wheels, wire wheels optional.

DIMENSIONS wheelbase 80in (203.2cm); track 46.3in (118cm) with Rostyles or 45.25in (114.9cm) front, 45in (114.3cm) with Rostyles or 44.75in (113.7cm) rear; turning circle 30.1ft (9.2m); ground clearance 3.25in (8.25cm); length 141in (358.1cm); width 60.25in (153cm); height 48.25in (122.6cm).

PERFORMANCE maximum speed 101mph (163kph); 16.5mph (26.5kph) @ 1000rpm; 0-60mph (96kph) 12.3sec; 12.2kg/bhp (16.4kg/kW); fuel consumption 27.9mpg (10.1L/ 100km).
PRICE £1,418.04.
PRODUCTION 72,185.

Cecil Kimber, with his distrust of hydraulics, would have welcomed the addition of a brake failure warning light.

1975-1980 MGB (rubber bumper)

In a despairing effort to meet increasingly severe American safety regulations, the MGB was equipped with energy absorbing bumpers. Heavy reinforcement lay behind them, the car's weight went up by 70lb (31.8kg), length by 5in (12.7cm) and power was diminished. Another increase in the camber of the rear springs added a further 1.5in (3.8cm) to the ride height, and there was more packing in the front suspension to bring the bumpers up to an American minimum height. The result was a disaster for the car's handling. The additional weight induced more body roll, so it became necessary to fit an anti-roll bar at the rear as well thickening the one at the front. The car felt lugubrious and its appearance suffered, yet the Leyland management failed to address the underlying problem; investment in one of the smallest factories in the group. The US-market modifications were so far-reaching and fundamental that there was no longer any practical way that production could be separated. The massive bumpers and nearly all the US-market ancillaries save the automatic seat belts and asthmatic Stromberg carburettor with its associated emission control plumbing, were incorporated for the home market as well. MGB sales dropped by 10,000 a year, and although down to 24,576 in 1975 astonishingly recovered to 29,558 in 1976.

BODY coupe, 2 doors, 2+2 seats; weight 2781lb (1095kg). Roadster, 2 seats, 2304lb (1045kg).
ENGINE 4 cylinders, in-line; front; 80.26mm x 88.9mm, 1798cc; compr 9.0:1; 84bhp (62.6kW) @ 5500rpm; 46.7bhp/L (34.8kW/L); 105lbft (142Nm) @ 2500rpm.
ENGINE STRUCTURE pushrod overhead valve; chain-driven camshaft; cast iron cylinder head and block; 2 SU inclined HIF4 carburettors, SU electrical fuel pump; centrifugal and vacuum ignition control; 5-bearing crankshaft; engine rubber-mounted; oil cooler.
TRANSMISSION rwd; Borg & Beck 8in diaphragm spring clutch; 4-speed manual gearbox, all-synchromesh; single-piece open prop shaft; hypoid bevel final drive 3.91:1.
CHASSIS DETAILS steel monocoque structure; ifs by coil springs and unequal wishbones; live axle with semi-elliptic springs, anti-roll bars front (increased in size 1977) and rear; Armstrong lever arm dampers; Lockheed hydraulic brakes with

vacuum servo, front 10.75in discs, rear 10in drums; rack and pinion steering; 11 Imp gal (13.2 US gal, 50L) fuel tank; Pirelli Cinturato 165SR -14 tyres; 5J rims, wire wheels optional.
DIMENSIONS wheelbase 91in (231.1cm); track 49.5in (125.7cm); turning circle 32ft (9.75m); ground clearance 4.19in (11cm); length 158.25In (402cm); width 60in (152.4cm); height 49.25In (125.1cm).
PERFORMANCE maximum speed 99mph (158.9kph); 17.9mph (28.7kph), 21.8mph (35kph) o/d top @ 1000rpm; 0-60mph (96kph) 14.0sec; 13kg/bhp (17.5kg/kW) coupe, 12.4kg/bhp (16.7kg/kW) roadster; fuel consumption 27.0mpg (10.5L/100km).
PRICE £2,539.
PRODUCTION 513,276 all MGB.

Manufactured by Marley Foam, from Bayflex 90 polyurethane, the bumpers were required to withstand a 5mph impact without deforming.

1975 MGB GT Anniversary

With an enthusiasm that overcame the niceties of history, 750 specially prepared MGB GTs celebrated what British Leyland's spin doctors decided was 50 years' production of MGs. The company's history was so equivocal that it depended on the definition of MG and of production.

The limited edition anniversary cars incorporated a number of the more useful developments that came with maturity such as the replacement of the two six-volt batteries behind the seats with one 12-volt battery. The steering ratio was changed from 3° turns lock to lock to 3 turns and the dashboard altered to include, rather belatedly since MGB drivers had been complaining about it since 1962, a new glove-locker lock. The switch for the new LH overdrive was moved to the gear lever. MGB GT body shells were now engineered for the discontinued V8, so they had a cross-flow radiator and thermostatically controlled electric cooling fan, which made up for a few of the horse power lost on emission control equipment. Wheels were the V8 cast alloy and steel pattern with 175 section tyres. Halogen headlights, tinted windows, and head restraints were all standard, and the cars were all painted British Racing Green with a gold side-stripe and commemorative badge.

BODY coupe; 2-doors; 2+2-seats; weight 2781lb (1095kg).
ENGINE 4 cylinders, in-line; front; 80.26mm x 88.9mm, 1798cc; compr 9.0:1; 84bhp (62.6kW) @ 5500rpm; 46.7bhp/L (34.8kW/L); 105lbft (142Nm) @ 2500rpm.
ENGINE STRUCTURE pushrod ohv; chain-driven camshaft; cast iron cylinder head and block; 2 SU inclined HIF4 carburettors, SU electrical fuel pump; centrifugal and vacuum ignition control; 5-bearing crankshaft; engine rubber-mounted; oil cooler.
TRANSMISSION rear wheel drive; Borg & Beck 8in diaphragm spring clutch; 4-speed manual gearbox, all-synchromesh; single-piece open prop shaft; hypoid bevel final drive 3.91:1.
CHASSIS steel monocoque structure; ifs by coil springs and unequal wishbones; live axle with semi-elliptic springs, anti-roll bars front and rear; Armstrong lever arm dampers; Lockheed hydraulic brakes, front 10.75in discs, rear 10in drums;

rack and pinion steering; 11 Imp gal (13.2 US gal, 50L) fuel tank; Pirelli Cinturato 175SR -14 tyres; 5J rims, wire wheels optional.
DIMENSIONS wheelbase 91in (231.1cm); track 49.5in (125.7cm); turning circle 32ft (9.75m); ground clearance 4.19in (11cm); length 158.25In (402cm); width ·60in (152.4cm); height 49.25In (125.1cm).
PERFORMANCE max speed 99mph (158.9kph); 17.9mph (28.7kph) @ 1000rpm, 21.8mph (35kph) o/d top; 0-60mph (96kph)14.0sec; 13kg/bhp (17.5kg/kW); fuel consumption 27.0mpg (10.5L/100km).
PRICE £2,669.
PRODUCTION 750.

A certificate and dashboard plaque detailing the production number from the commemorative run completed the ensemble.

1980 MGB Limited Edition

Even after closing Speke, BL still suffered from over-capacity and Abingdon was deemed surplus to requirements. The announcement on 10 September 1979 followed celebrations of 50 years' of MG production in rural Berkshire. It also followed closure of AEC at Park Royal and the end of car manufacturing at Canley. John Thornley urged American dealers to get BL to reconsider but to no avail, as a loss of £900 was claimed on every MGB. MG clubs mounted a protest rally but Sir Michael Edwardes pointed out that 100,000 jobs in BL as a whole were his main preoccupation rather than 1,100 at strike-free Abingdon. Still, mindful of opportunities for profit, BL made a special edition of the last 1000 MGBs.

The production run had a chin spoiler, with roadsters finished in metallic bronze and gold LE stripes, GTs in pewter metallic with silver stripes. Orange and brown striped cloth upholstery completed the ensemble on roadsters; GTs had a silver grey interior. MGB power output for the UK increased to as much as 97bhp (72.3kW) but a Limited Edition roadster, finished in black, was also sold in America, and although not as asthmatic as the 65bhp (48.5kW) Zenith-Stromberg cars of the mid-1970s, had smaller valves, one carburettor, and emission control equipment.

BODY coupe, 2 doors, 2+2 seats, weight 2781lb (1095kg). Roadster, 2 seats, 2304lb (1045kg).
ENGINE 4 cylinders, in-line; front; 80.26mm x 88.9mm, 1798cc; compr:1; 90bhp (67.1kW) @ 5500rpm; 50.1bhp/L (37.3kW/L); 105lbft (142Nm) @ 2500rpm.
ENGINE STRUCTURE pushrod ohv; chain-driven camshaft; cast iron cylinder head and block; 2 SU inclined HIF4 carbs, SU electrical fuel pump; centrifugal and vacuum ignition control; 5-bearing crank; engine rubber-mounted; oil cooler.
TRANSMISSION rear wheel drive; Borg & Beck 8in diaphragm spring clutch; 4-speed manual gearbox, all-synchromesh; single-piece open prop shaft; hypoid bevel final drive 3.91:1.
CHASSIS DETAILS steel monocoque structure; ifs by coil springs and unequal wishbones; live axle with semi-elliptic springs, anti-roll bars front and rear; Armstrong lever arm dampers; Lockheed hydraulic brakes, front 10.75in discs, rear 10in drums;

rack and pinion steering; 11 Imp gal (13.2 US gal, 50L)) fuel tank; Pirelli Cinturato 175SR -14 tyres, 185-70 optional; 5J rims, wire wheels optional.
DIMENSIONS wheelbase 91in (231.1cm); track 49.5in (125.7cm); turning circle 32ft (9.75m); ground clearance 4.19in (11cm); length 158.25In (402cm); width 60in (152.4cm); height 49.25In (125.1cm).
PERFORMANCE maximum speed 105mph (168.6kph); 17.9mph (28.7kph), 21.8mph (35kph) o/d top; 0-60mph (96kph) 14.0sec; 12.2kg/bhp (16.3kg/kW) coupe, 11.6kg/bhp (15.6kg/kW) roadster; fuel consumption 27mpg (10.5L/100km). PRICE £6,108 roadster, £6,376 GT. PRODUCTION 420 roadsters, 580 GTs.

Stag-pattern alloy wheels, an option since 1977, were standard but roadster buyers could specify wire wheels and 208 of them did so.

1980 MG Aston Martin proposal

As a demonstration of the takeover consortium's viability, a prototype Aston Martin MG was built at Newport Pagnell by Aston Martin. Managing Director Alan Curtis's instructions to designer William Towns was to use as much of the existing MGB as possible but enhance its appeal to buyers in America, Continental Europe, and Japan, emerging as a market where MGs were becoming firm favourites. The aim was to keep production up to the current 600 cars a week, use the O-series engine (with an unspecified V6 as a later option) and Rover 3500 gearbox and back axle, under licence from BL.

Towns drew on the experience of BL's American subsidiary to gauge the market, and a standard MGB coupe was delivered to Aston Martin at Newport Pagnell as the basis for a facelift. The plan was to use the model as a platform for a new range that included a Midget and the B prototype, built inside a week, to convince the government and the backers to take the project seriously. Towns raised the windscreen, tidied up the BL safety bumpers, and improved the cosmetics inside. It scarcely mattered that there was no time to engineer a fuel filler flap; the project was stillborn, and Towns' renderings of a family of MGs were consigned to the realm of romantic might-have-beens.

BODY roadster; 2 doors, 2 seats.
ENGINE 4 cylinders, in-line; front; 80.26mm x 88.9mm, 1798cc; compr 8.8:1; 95bhp (70.8kW) @ 5400rpm; 52.8bhp/L (39.4kW/L); 110lbft (149Nm) @ 3000rpm.
ENGINE STRUCTURE pushrod ohv; chain-driven camshaft; cast iron cylinder head and block; 2 SU inclined H4 carburettors, SU electrical fuel pump; centrifugal and vacuum ignition control; 5-bearing crankshaft; engine rubber-mounted; oil cooler.
TRANSMISSION rear wheel drive; Borg & Beck 8in diaphragm spring clutch; 4-speed manual gearbox, all-synchromesh; single-piece open prop shaft; Salisbury hypoid bevel final drive 3.91:1.
CHASSIS steel monocoque structure; ifs by coil springs and unequal wishbones; live axle with semi-elliptic springs, optional anti-roll bar; Armstrong lever arm dampers; Lockheed hydraulic brakes, front 10.75in discs, rear 10in drums; rack and helical pinion steering; 12 Imp gal (14.4 US gal, 54.6L) fuel tank; Dunlop Road Speed 5.90 - 14 tyres; 4J rims; wire wheels optional.
DIMENSIONS wheelbase 91in (231.1cm); track 49in (124.5cm); turning circle 30.5ft (9.23m); ground clearance 4.25in (10.8cm); length 153.75in (390.5cm); width 60in (152.4cm); height 49.25in (125cm).
PERFORMANCE maximum speed 108.1mph (173.5kph); 16.4mph (26.3kph) @ 1000rpm; 0-60mph (96kph) 12.1sec; fuel consumption 23.0mpg (12.3L/100km).
PRODUCTION 1.

New unregistered MGBs were still on sale when MG reappeared on a production car. BL reorganised itself as Austin-Rover and applied MG to a sporting Metro in May 1982 by way of introduction to a turbocharged MG Metro due at the motor show. This was the first genuine 100mph Metro, and true to tradition the designers given the job of applying MG identity were liberal with appliqué octagons and red piping. More to the point they replaced steel wheels with ventilated alloy ones shod with low-profile tyres. A plastic surround to the rear window was claimed to produce a drag coefficient reduction of two decimal places. An additional 12bhp (8.9kW) was extracted from the venerable A-series engine, now known as A-Plus, by means of quite extensive modifications, including a new cam profile that gave more overlap and was even more extreme than the old Mini Cooper S. The compression ratio was raised from 9.4 to 10.5:1 by reducing combustion chamber volume and the size of the cavities in the short-skirt pistons. Traditionally MG engines had twin carburettors, but this Metro had one, with clever detailing in a water-heated inlet manifold to stabilise the temperature of the ingoing mixture. The MG Metro was not quite in the Mini-Cooper class, but it achieved its performance with a good deal less fuss and commotion.

BODY saloon, 2 doors, 4 seats; weight 1785lb (811kg).
ENGINE 4 cylinders, in-line; front, transverse; 70.61mm x 81.28mm, 1275cc; compr 10.5:1; 72bhp (53.7kW) @ 6000rpm; 56.5bhp/L (42.1kW/L); 73lbft (98Nm) @ 4000rpm.
ENGINE STRUCTURE pushrod ohv; chain-driven camshaft; cast iron cylinder block and head; SU HIF44 carburettor; contact-breaker ignition; electric fan; 3-bearing crankshaft.
TRANSMISSION front wheel drive; sdp 7.13in clutch; 4-speed manual synchromesh gearbox; helical spur final drive 3.4441:1.
CHASSIS steel monocoque structure; independent front suspension by wishbones and Hydragas springs, telescopic dampers; independent rear suspension by trailing arms and Hydragas units with integral damping; dual circuit brakes disc front 8.4in, rear 7in drums, vacuum servo; rack and pinion steering; 7 Imp gal (8.4 US gal, 32L) fuel tank; 155/70SR-12 radial-ply tyres, 5in rims.
DIMENSIONS wheelbase 88.6in (225cm); track 50.2in (127.4cm); turning circle 34.1ft (10.4m) L, 32.25ft (9.9m) R; ground clearance 6.5in (16.5cm); length 134.1in (340.4cm); width 60.9in (154.7cm); height 53.6in (135.9cm).
PERFORMANCE maximum speed 103mph (166kph); 17.2mph (27.6kph) @ 1000rpm; 0-60mph (96kph) 10.9sec; 11.3kg/bhp (15.1kg/kW); fuel consumption 38.3mpg (7.3 L/100km).
PRICE £4,799.
PRODUCTION 120,197.

1983-1990 MG Metro Turbo

Turbo Technics, a British private tuning firm, produced the first turbocharged A-series in1982, but Austin Rover with Lotus engineering as consultants was not far behind. A turbocharger was duly strapped on to produce the most powerful production A-series ever. Its 93bhp (69.4kW) at 6130rpm was well over three times the output of the original A30, and 21 per cent more than the 1275S Mini-Cooper. Although a Garrett AiResearch T3 turbocharger blowing at 7.5psi (0.52kg-cm) straight through an SU carburettor sounded fairly rough and ready, more modern technology was on hand. Ducellier contactless ignition was an important step forward in electronic engine management. Fifty years to the month after the supercharged 1100cc MG K3 Magnette was planned for racing, the MG Metro Turbo gave a good account of itself, only ceasing production when all Metros were rebadged as Rover 100s. It was perhaps not the most refined small hot hatch, with quite a lot of fore and aft movement of the transverse engine even on its new mountings. Power delivery was more progressive than many turbos of the day. The chief shortcoming was low gearing; there was no space for a fifth gear. It was only at high speeds that the extra power went to the edge of the Metro's handling and roadholding envelope.

BODY saloon, 2 doors, 4 seats; weight 1826lb (828kg).
ENGINE 4 cylinders, in-line; front, transverse; 70.61mm x 81.28mm, 1275cc; compr 9.4:1; 93bhp (69.4kW) @ 6130rpm; 72.9bhp/L (54.4kW/L); 85lbft (114Nm) @ 4000rpm.
ENGINE STRUCTURE pushrod ohv; chain-driven cam; cast iron cyl block & head; Garret AiResearch T3 turbocharger, 7.5psi (.517bar) boost, SU HIF44 carb; Ducellier breakerless ignition; electric fan; 3-bg crank.

TRANSMISSION front wheel drive; sdp 7.13in clutch; 4-speed manual synchromesh gearbox; helical spur final drive 3.21:1.
CHASSIS steel monocoque structure; ifs by wishbones and Hydragas springs, telescopic dampers; irs by trailing arms and Hydragas units with integral damping; dual circuit brakes disc front 8.4in, rear 7in drums, vacuum servo; rack and pinion steering; 7 Imp gal (8.4 US gal, 32L) fuel tank; 165/60SR-12 radial-ply tyres 5½in rims.
DIMENSIONS wheelbase 88.6in (225cm); track 50.2in (127.4cm); turning circle 34.1ft (10.4m) L, 32.25ft (9.9m) R; ground clearance 6.5in (16.5cm); length 134.1in (340.4cm); width 60.9in (154.7cm); height 53.6in (135.9cm).
PERFORMANCE maximum speed 112mph (180.2kph); 18.6mph (29.9kph) @ 1000rpm; 0-60mph (96kph) 9.4sec; 8.9kg/bhp (11.9kg/kW); 30.3mpg (9.3L/100km).
PRICE £5,650.
PRODUCTION 21,968.

1983-1984 MG Maestro 1600

The first MG Maestro had the Austin-Rover R-series engine with a chain-driven overhead camshaft, two Weber carburettors, and a short eight-port inlet manifold. It had breakerless electronic ignition to meet emission control endurance running and unleaded fuel. A versatile car with back seats that could be folded flat asymmetrically, it had good ride quality. Austin-Rover abandoned the interconnected Hydrolastic and Hydragas of the unlamented Allegro in favour of coil springs. Among its innovations was an electronic facia with solid state vacuum fluorescent displays, and a voice synthesiser, neither of which caught on. The Volkswagen-derived 5-speed gearbox had close ratios and a high final drive that made fifth an overdrive at 0.91:1. It was a heavy car with some serious shortcomings that included difficult hot starting, drive-line shunt, and poor fuel economy. Austin-Rover's quality problems were exacerbated by shortage of time and money to develop new cars, and the Maestro suffered accordingly. After only 17 months the R-series was replaced in the Austin Maestro by the S-series with a toothed belt drive to the camshaft. The cylinder head was turned through 180deg so that the inlet side faced the bulkhead. The S-series was also installed in the MG but not many were made before the opportunity was seized to set it quietly aside.

Data for R-series:
BODY saloon, 5 doors, 4 seats; weight 2190 lb (993kg).
ENGINE 4 cylinders, in-line; front, transverse; 76.2mm x 87.6mm, 1598cc; compr 9.7:1; 103bhp (76.8kW) @ 6000rpm; 64.5bhp/L (48.1kW/L); 100lbft (134Nm) @ 4000rpm.
ENGINE STRUCTURE chain-driven ohv; cast iron cylinder block and head; twin dual fixed-choke downdraught Weber 40DCNF carburettors; breakerless electronic ignition; electric fan; 5-bearing crank.
TRANSMISSION front wheel drive; sdp 7.9in clutch; 4-speed manual synchromesh gearbox, helical spur final drive 3.65:1.
CHASSIS steel monocoque structure; ifs by strut and lower arm, coil springs, telescopic dampers and anti-roll bar. Semi independent rear by trailing arms, torsion beam, coil springs telescopic dampers and anti-roll bar; hydraulic servo diagonally split circuit brakes 9.5in discs, 8.0in drums; rack and pinion steering; 11.7 Imp gal (14 US gal, 53L) fuel tank; P8 radial ply 175/65SR tyres 5°in rims, aluminium alloy wheels.
DIMENSIONS wheelbase 98.7in (250.7cm); track front 59in (149.9cm), rear 58in (147.3cm); turning circle 35ft (10.7m); ground clearance 5.8in (14.7cm); length 159.5in (405cm); width 66.4in (168.7cm); height 56.3in (142.9cm).
PERFORMANCE maximum speed 111mph (179kph); 19.9mph (31.9kph) @ 1000rpm; 0-60mph (96kph) 9.6sec; 9.6kg/bhp (12.9kg/kW); 26.8mpg (10.5L/100km).
PRICE £6245.
PRODUCTION 12,427 R-series, 2,762 S-series.

1984 MG Metro 6R4

Built under rules changed prematurely for safety's sake, club drivers could buy 6R4s with 250bhp (186.4kW). Works cars could have up to 380bhp (283.4kW). The 1984 prototype had been under development for three years by Frank Williams Grand Prix engineering, to a design by Patrick Head, and bore a superficial resemblance to a Metro. Its mid engine was a V6 cut down from a Rover V8, and it had four-wheel drive to compete with Audi Quattro, Peugeot 205, and Lancia Delta. The engine evolved as a highly original Austin-Rover design by David Wood. Cosworth cast new blocks and heads, and electronic engine management was by Lucas Micos, a research and development offshoot of Lucas. Ferguson technology was incorporated in the four wheel drive system, with a propeller shaft to the right of the engine, and strut suspension was adopted to distribute the chassis loads widely. Had Group B for which it was designed continued, the 6R4 would probably have been more successful, its light weight and low inertia having proved convincing to enthusiastic ARG motor sport chief John Davenport and its drivers. The engine found an unexpected lease of life when Tom Walkinshaw acquired rights to it for the Jaguar XJR-10. As the JRV-6 with two turbochargers it took part in 26 races in 1989-1991, winning six.

BODY saloon, 2 doors, 2 seats; weight 2266lb (1030kg).
ENGINE 6 cylinders, 90 deg V; mid, lengthwise; 92mm x 75mm, 2991cc; compr 12.0:1; 410bhp (305.7kW) @ 9000rpm; 137.1bhp/L (102.2kW/L); 270lbft (362Nm) @ 6500rpm.
ENGINE STRUCTURE two belt-driven overhead camshafts per bank; 4 valves per cylinder; Mahle slipper pistons, dry liners; aluminium cylinder heads and block; Lucas Micos mapped electronic ignition and 6-point fuel injection; 4-bearing crankshaft; rally version machined from solid En40b, Club version forged; dry sump lubrication.
TRANSMISSION four wheel drive; Borg & Beck twin plate diaphragm spring clutch; 5-speed manual dog-engaged gearbox, synchromesh on Club; spiral bevel final drive, interchangeable ratios; epicyclic torque-splitting differential, viscous coupling.
CHASSIS DETAILS space-frame tubular steel and aluminium structure; integral roll cage; body aluminium, carbon fibre-reinforced grp; ifs and irs by coil springs, struts, Bilstein telescopic dampers anti-roll bar, all fully adjustable; adjustable ratio split dual circuit 12in ventilated disc brakes; rack and pinion steering centre take-off; two 13.2 Imp gal (15.8 US gal, 60L) fuel tanks; various competition tyres, Dymag cast magnesium alloy wheels.
DIMENSIONS wheelbase 94.1in (239.1cm); track front 59.45in (151cm), rear 59.7in (151.5cm); length 131.9in (335cm); width 74in (188cm); height 59.1in (150cm) depending on suspension level.
PERFORMANCE maximum speed 155mph (248.8kph); 0-60mph (96kph) 4.3sec; 2.5kg/bhp (3.4kg/kW).
PRICE £40,000.
PRODUCTION 200 plus.

1984-1991 MG Montego 2.0EFi

The Montego was effectively a three-box version of the Maestro but rather more distinguished. The wheelbase was 2.3in (5.8cm) longer and common bodywork parts were the front bulkhead, floorpan, inner front wings, and parts of the doors. A roomy car with a big boot, from 1984 Austin versions had S-series engines, but the MG had the O-series 2.0-litre with a slightly rudimentary (by comparison with sophisticated successors) fuel injection system developed jointly by Austin-Rover and Lucas. This measured intake airflow by the electrical resistance of a heated wire for regulating the fuel to the cylinders. It worked in conjunction with electronic transistorised ignition along the lines of Bosch Motronic that mapped load, speed, and temperature. MG was into the new age of engine management. Austin and Vanden Plas Montegos laboured on with carburettors. The Vanden Plas was the best-equipped and had as standard the power-assisted steering that cost an extra £285 on the MG. ARG management meanwhile decreed that MGs, besides a sprinkling of octagons, would be distinguished by red stripes in the bumpers, red seat belts, red graphics on the instruments, and red trim on the upholstery. The Montego was lively, well-equipped, and rode comfortably, but still not quiet or refined enough to beat the opposition from BMW.

BODY saloon, 4 doors, 5 seats; weight 2300lb (1043kg).
ENGINE 4 cylinders, in-line; front, transverse; 84.5mm x 89.0mm, 1994cc; compr 9.0:1; 115bhp (85.8kW) @ 5500rpm; 57.7bhp/L (43kW/L); 134lbft (180Nm) @ 2800rpm.
ENGINE STRUCTURE belt-driven overhead camshaft; cast iron block, aluminium cylinder head, block; electronic breakerless ignition, Lucas L-type fuel injection; 5-bearing crank.
TRANSMISSION front wheel drive; sdp diaphragm spring clutch; 5-speed manual all synchromesh gearbox; helical spur final drive 3.875:1.
CHASSIS steel monocoque structure; ifs by struts and lower arms, coil

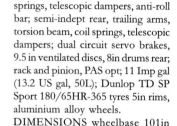

springs, telescopic dampers, anti-roll bar; semi-indept rear, trailing arms, torsion beam, coil springs, telescopic dampers; dual circuit servo brakes, 9.5 in ventilated discs, 8in drums rear; rack and pinion, PAS opt; 11 Imp gal (13.2 US gal, 50L); Dunlop TD SP Sport 180/65HR-365 tyres 5in rims, aluminium alloy wheels.
DIMENSIONS wheelbase 101in (256.5cm); track front 56.7in (144cm), rear 57.4in (145.8cm); turning circle 34.1ft (10.4m) L, 35.75ft (10.9m) R; ground clearance 6.2in (15.7cm); length 175.9in (446.8cm); width 67.3in (171cm); height 55.9in (142cm).
PERFORMANCE maximum speed 114mph (183kph); 20.6mph (33kph) @ 1000rpm; 0-60mph (96kph) 8.9sec; 9.1kg/bhp (12.2kg/kW); fuel consumption 29.3mpg (9.6L/100km). PRICE £8,165.20.
PRODUCTION 34,476.

Left: original Austin Montego belt-driven overhead camshaft engine with one carburettor.

1984-1991 MG Maestro 2.0 EFi

In October 1984 the 2.0-litre belt-driven overhead camshaft fuel injected O-series engine replaced the ill-starred 1600, and a Honda gearbox purloined from the joint Austin Rover Group (ARG)-Honda project XX replaced the Volkswagen one. The result, as at least one dealer put it, "…was how the car should have been in the first place."

Power and torque were enhanced, and the performance was now a match for opposition such as the Golf GTi and the Astra GTE. The digital dashboard was now an option; the Maestro's instruments were once again analogue, and there were some exterior enhancements such as a body-colour grille and bumpers. Although refinement was never a feature of the O-series on start-up, at least it did start up whether warm or cold, which was more than could be said for its predecessor.

The 2.0-litre also scored on fuel consumption with an improvement on the 1600 by 7mpg (40.4L/100km). The standard steering was too low-geared for a sporty car but a higher-geared power-assisted option was available. ARG was catching up with modern technology in the O-series engine management system, from the Montego, incorporating Lucas L-type multi-point fuel injection, and electronic ignition with knock sensing.

BODY saloon, 5 doors, 4 seats; weight 2150lb (975.2kg).
ENGINE 4 cylinders, in-line; front, transverse; 84.5mm x 89.0mm, 1994cc; compr 9.1:1; 115bhp (85.8kW) @ 5500rpm; 57.7bhp/L (43kW/L); 134lbft (180Nm) @ 2800rpm.
ENGINE STRUCTURE chain-driven overhead camshaft; cast iron cylinder block and aluminium head; Lucas L-type fuel injection; breakerless electronic ignition; electric fan; 5-bearing crankshaft.
TRANSMISSION front wheel drive; sdp diaphragm spring clutch; 5-speed manual synchromesh gearbox; helical spur final drive 3.93:1.
CHASSIS steel monocoque structure; ifs by strut and lower arm, coil springs, telescopic dampers and anti-toll bar. Semi independent rear by trailing arms, torsion beam, coil springs telescopic dampers and anti-roll bar; hydraulic vacuum servo diagonally split circuit brakes 9.5in ventilated discs, 8.0in drums; rack and pinion steering, optional PAS; 11 Imp gal (14 US gal, 50L) fuel tank; MXV radial ply 175/65SR tyres 5°in rims aluminium alloy wheels.
DIMENSIONS wheelbase 98.7in (250.7cm); track front 59in (149.9cm); rear 58in (147.3cm); turning circle 33ft 8in (10.3m); ground clearance 5.8in (14.7cm); length 159.5in (404.9cm); width 66.4in (168.7cm); height 56.3in (142.9cm).
PERFORMANCE maximum speed 115mph (185kph); 21.9mph (35.2kph) @ 1000rpm; 0-60mph (96kph) 8.5sec; 8.5kg/bhp (11.4kg/kW); fuel consumption 33.4mpg (8.5L/100km).
PRICE £7,249.
PRODUCTION 32,725.

Increasingly onerous emission control regulations, which demanded engines run for 50,000 miles and remain in tune without attention, was bringing out the best in engineering.

241

1985-1991 MG Montego Turbo

It may have seemed logical to believe that since the Montego EFi had been a modest success, so adding 33bhp (24.6kW) to make it even faster would compound the achievement. The first examples in 1985 however were unruly. Turbo lag was well known. It took a great deal of experience with turbos working at incandescent temperatures, and spinning at limits of materials' integrity, to reduce it to an acceptable level. Rather less was known about torque steer in conjunction with turbo lag. There never had been front wheel drive cars with enormous power surges occurring in arrears of a driver's plans. In the wet it demanded deft handling. The trouble was not only that the extra 35lbft of extra torque arrived at 3500rpm instead of 2800rpm, but also the turbo breathed in through a solitary SU and did not delivery power smoothly. It also lost its tune quicker than it would have with good, although complicated and expensive, fuel injection. In 1986 the front suspension was modified, the steering rack lowered, the gearing raised and the track control arms altered. The springs and dampers were already stiffener than the non-turbo. Owners complained about stability, and in an effort to improve it the front air dam was redesigned. In the end the Montego Turbo was civilised and good value at the lower end of the turbocharged price spectrum.

BODY saloon, 4 doors, 5 seats; weight 2380lb (1079.6kg).
ENGINE 4 cylinders, in-line; front, transverse; 84.5mm x 89.0mm, 1994cc; compr 8.5:1; 150bhp (111.9kW) @ 5500rpm; 75.2bhp/L (56.1kW/L); 169lbft (227Nm) @ 3500rpm.
ENGINE STRUCTURE belt-driven overhead camshaft; sodium-filled exhaust valves; cast iron block, aluminium cylinder head, block; electronic breakerless electronic ignition; Garrett AiResearch T3 turbocharger and intercooler, 10psi (0.7bar) boost; ARG (SU-type) single variable choke carburettor; 5-bearing crankshaft.
TRANSMISSION front wheel drive; sdp diaphragm spring clutch; 5-speed manual all synchromesh gearbox; helical spur final drive 3.647:1.
CHASSIS steel monocoque structure; ifs by struts and lower arms, coil springs, telescopic dampers, anti-roll bar (+2mm); semi-independent rear, trailing arms, torsion beam, coil springs, anti-roll bar, telescopic dampers; dual circuit servo brakes, 9.5 in ventilated discs, 8in drums rear; rack and pinion PAS; 11 Imp gal (14 US gal, 50L) fuel tank; radial ply 190/65HR-365 tyres 5.3in rims, aluminium alloy wheels.
DIMENSIONS wheelbase 101in (256.5cm); track front 56.7in (144cm), rear 57.4in (145.8cm); turning circle 35.1ft (10.7m) L, 35.75ft (10.9m) R; ground clearance 6.2in (15.7cm); length 175.9in (446.8cm); width 67.3in (171cm); height 55.9in (142cm).
PERFORMANCE maximum speed 125mph (200.7kph); 25mph (40.1kph) @ 1000rp; 0-60mph (96kph) 7.5sec; 7.2kg/bhp (9.6kg/kW); fuel consumption 23.0mpg (12.3L/100km).
PRICE £10,300.55.
PRODUCTION 7,276.

Right: "Old Number One" pulled out of retirement for publicity shot of Montego Turbo.

1985 MG EX-E

Five years after the demise of Abingdon and the MGB, the first glimmer of hope that MG as a make in its own right might not be dead but only resting, came at the 1985 Frankfurt Motor Show. Austin Rover morale had been low, but chairman and chief executive Harold Musgrove had installed Royden Axe, formerly of Rootes and Chrysler as director of design in 1982. Roy Axe's Canley studio had two directors; Gordon Sked responsible for exterior, and Richard Hamblin for interior design. Included in a number of projects was an open two-seater MG Midget based on the Metro drawn up by Gerry McGovern.

The EX-E had grp body panels by Specialised Mouldings, a Huntingdon firm associated with Lola cars, on an aluminium frame, to a modular design developed by Gaydon Technology. A Cd of 0.24 was claimed and it also incorporated a number of concept-car features of the mid-1980s such as a hands-free cellular phone and a satellite navigation system. There was talk of a production version of EX-E with a Rover M16 engine. It certainly had the makings of a road car but such was the pressure to sustain the volume end of the business that neither the government nor British Aerospace that bought Austin-Rover in 1988 were ever likely to put up the cash.

BODY coupe, 2 doors, 2 seats.
ENGINE 6 cylinders, 90 deg V; mid, lengthwise; 92mm x 75mm, 2991cc; compr 12.0:1; 250bhp (186.4kW) @ 7000rpm; 83.6bhp/L (62.3kW/L); 225lbft (302Nm) @ 6500rpm.
ENGINE STRUCTURE two belt-driven overhead camshafts per bank; 4 valves per cylinder; Mahle slipper pistons, dry liners; aluminium cylinder heads and block; Lucas Micos mapped electronic ignition and 6-point fuel injection; 4-bearing forged crank; dry sump lubrication.
TRANSMISSION four wheel drive; Borg & Beck twin plate diaphragm spring clutch; 5-speed synchromesh gearbox; spiral bevel final drive; epicyclic torque-splitting differential, viscous coupling.
CHASSIS DETAILS space-frame tubular steel and aluminium structure; ifs and irs by double wishbones coil springs, telescopic dampers anti-roll bar; experimental ride-height selection; dual circuit 12in ventilated disc brakes with ABS; rack and pinion steering centre take-off; 000 fuel tanks; 215/45VR17 tyres, cast aluminium alloy 17in wheels, 7Jrims.
PERFORMANCE maximum speed estimated 170mph (272.9kph); 0-60mph (96kph) estimated 5.0sec.
PRODUCTION 1.

EX-E was unveiled at the Frankfurt motor show to astonished applause from the assembled European press that had assumed the British industry no longer capable of such flights of fancy.

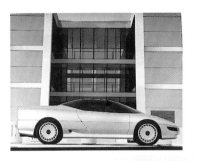
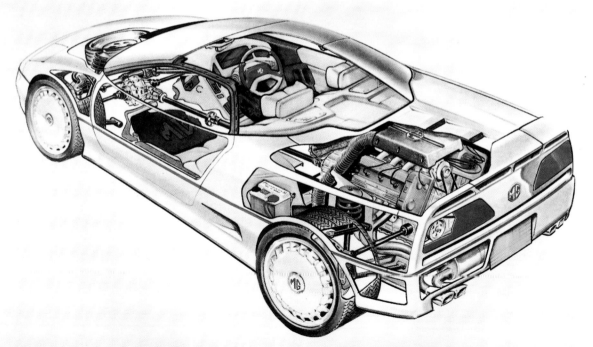

1989-1991 MG Maestro Turbo

The last Austin Rover Group (ARG) model put the turbocharged Montego engine in the Maestro. It was a short-lived tour de force, although the fastest production MG to date at just under 130mph (208.7kph). It was less refined than its direct competitor the Peugeot 309GTi but it was £1000 cheaper.

The changes in the car's appearance were commissioned from Tickford coachbuilders in a bizarre return to a firm which, as Salmons, had been making MG bodies on and off for well over 50 years. It was now emerging from Aston Martin ownership, making its own version of the MG Metro, and now completed the Maestros at its works in Bedworth near Coventry.

ARG's attempts to improve the handling of the Maestro/Montego pair had borne some fruit. Spring rates, anti-roll bars, and camber settings had all been revised and the latest gas-filled dampers contributed to handling that was tamed but still fell some way short of the competition. Low-speed ride suffered too. The problem remained wheelspin coming out of corners in the lower gears. A limited slip differential might have improved matters and electronic anti-wheelspin measures were not yet generally available.

BODY saloon, 4 doors, 4 seats; weight 2379lb (1080kg).
ENGINE 4 cylinders, in-line; front, transverse; 84.5mm x 89.0mm, 1994cc; cr 8.5:1; 152bhp (113.3kW) @ 5100rpm; 76.2bhp/L (56.8kW/L); 169lbft (227Nm) @ 3500rpm.
ENGINE STRUCTURE belt-driven overhead camshaft; sodium-filled exhaust valves; cast iron block, aluminium cylinder head, block; electronic breakerless electronic ignition; Garrett AiResearch T3 turbocharger and intercooler, 10psi (0.7bar) boost; ARG (SU-type) single variable choke carb; 5-bearing crank.
TRANSMISSION front wheel drive; sdp diaphragm spring clutch; 5-speed manual all synchro gearbox; helical spur final drive 3.647:1.
CHASSIS steel monocoque structure; ifs by strut and lower arm, coil springs and anti-toll bar. Semi independent rear by trailing arms, torsion beam, coil springs and anti-roll bar, Telescopic gas-filled dampers front ad rear; hydraulic servo diagonally split circuit brakes 9.5in ventilated discs, 8.0in drums; rack and pinion PAS; 11.7 Imp gal (14 US gal, 53L) fuel tank; MXV2 radial ply 185/55 VR15 tyres 6in rims, aluminium alloy wheels.
DIMENSIONS wheelbase 98.7in (250.7cm); track 58.3in (148cm) front, 57.3in (145.5cm) rear; turning circle 33.8ft (10.3m); ground clearance 7in (17.8cm); length 157.6in (400.3cm); width 76in (193cm) including mirrors; height 56.1in (14.2cm).
PERFORMANCE maximum speed 129mph (208kph); 25mph (40.1kph) @ 1000rpm; 0-60mph (96kph) 6.9sec; 7.1kg/bhp (9.5kg/kW); 20.1mpg (14.1L/100km).
PRICE £12,999.
PRODUCTION 501.

It looked for a time as though this would be the last car to carry the MG badge, as production was discontinued in anticipation of a new range of cars that would be Rovers only.

247

The rebirth of MG in the 1990s drew warm applause. By the summer of 1992 pictures were released of what was being called "the MG that never was," the RV8, and speculation on PR3, codename for the MGF, was rife. The RV8 took up where the MGB left off. It might have been more logical to start with an engine based on the stillborn O-series (there was a perfectly appropriate one, the M16 that used O-series bottom end and a splendid twin-cam head) but it was a time of cheap fuel and a revival of interest in classics like the Cobra.

Rover, it seems, was apprehensive about being down-sized. Using the remanufactured MGB bodyshell as a basis, it developed a car that had classic overtones, elegant furnishings and an exciting performance. Unlike the 1980 Limited Editions that were essentially valedictory and sold slowly, the 2000 RV8s sold out quickly and soon commanded premium prices.

The body was 25 per cent MGB, with floor pan, doors, and boot lid carried over. Almost everything else was new;

BODY roadster, 2 doors, 2 seats; weight 2822lb (1280kg).
ENGINE 8 cylinders, 90deg V; front; 94mm x 71mm, 3946cc; compr 9.35:1; 187bhp (139.4kW) @ 4750rpm; 47.4bhp/L (35.3kW/L); 231lbft (310Nm) @ 3200rpm.
ENGINE STRUCTURE pushrod ohv; hydraulic tappets; aluminium cylinder block and heads; breakerless electronic ignition, Lucas multi-point

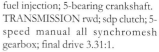

fuel injection; 5-bearing crankshaft.
TRANSMISSION rwd; sdp clutch; 5-speed manual all synchromesh gearbox; final drive 3.31:1.
CHASSIS steel monocoque structure; ifs by double wishbone and coil springs, telescopic dampers, anti-roll bar; live axle with control arms, tapered leaf semi-elliptic springs, telescopic dampers, anti-roll bar; hydraulic servo ventilated 270mm disc front brakes 280mm drums at rear; rack and pinion steering; 11 Imp gal (13.2 US gal, 51L); 205-65VR tyres, 15in cast alloy wheels, 6J rims.
DIMENSIONS wheelbase 92in (233cm); track front 49in (124.5cm), rear 52in (132cm); length 158in (401cm); width 67in (169.4cm); height 52in (132cm).
PERFORMANCE maximum speed 135mph (216.7kph); 29mph (46.6kph) @ 1000rpm; 0-60mph (96kph) 5.9sec; 6.8kg/bhp (9.2kg/kW); fuel consumption 20.2mpg (14L/100km).
PRICE £26,500.
PRODUCTION 2000.

body sills, wings, bonnet, and effectively all four corners. The opportunity to have a proper MG grille was passed up, a great shame especially when everything else was done with such style. The huge wheels were alloy split rims with large-section tyres which accounted for the heavy steering. The cockpit was beautifully trimmed. The black-framed windscreen was the same shape as the old MGB, but inside the luxurious trim would have done credit to a Bentley. The wood and leather was sumptuous.

If you were to paint a picture of the RV-8 client – 50-something, couldn't afford a decent MG when he was 25 – now was his chance. He was not interested in anything very racy but wanted to keep up with the traffic. He had become accustomed to wood and leather in his executive saloon and did not much want to give it up. There were walnut cappings on the doors and leather door casings, very upper-crust. The instruments looked a little mean but they were excellent units, as was the Philips radio and CD player. It had an air of quality throughout, with the feel of a carefully hand-made car.

As a thoroughbred car for touring in the grand manner as opposed to GT and driven with circumspection, it had power to spare and a comfortable ride. Only if it was regarded as a modern sports car did serious flaws appear. The ride was only good at moderate speeds on well-surfaced roads, but there was not sufficient spring travel at the back to give the compliant ride of a modern car. The tiny fuel tank was an unfortunate feature.

Right: author surveys the RV8 beside his Heritage twin cam MGB.

1995- MGF 1.8i

MG went back into production with a thoroughly modern car. The RV8 gave notice that MG was making a comeback, the MGF showed that it had arrived. The new arrival made no concessions to tradition. It was mid-engined and up to date, making its own way in the world just as the first MGs did over 70 years before. It did hold good to one of MG's founding principles however; it used major components from a volume series to keep production costs down and ensure service and maintenance remained within reach of a large number of owners. MG would still represent spicy sporty motoring, but not at any price.

Project Phoenix to return MG to the market began in the late 1980s, gaining momentum in 1989, when Mazda launched the MX-5 Miata. This indicated to supporters of MG's revival that sports cars were commercially viable, even attractive. Work was put in hand on a number of two-seaters, some based on Maestro components with a transverse twin overhead camshaft development of the O-series used in the Rover 800, and front-wheel drive. Among

BODY roadster, 2 doors, 2 seats; weight 2337lb (1060kg).
ENGINE 4 cylinders, in-line; mid transverse; 80mm x 89.3mm, 1796cc; compr 10.5:1; 118bhp (88kW) @ 5500rpm; 65.7bhp/L (49kW/L); 122lbft (165Nm) @ 3000rpm.
ENGINE STRUCTURE twin belt-driven ohc; 16-valves; aluminium cam cover, cam carrier, cyl head & block, bearing ladder, sump, damp cylinder liners; MEMS electronic ign multipoint fuel injection; 5-bearing crank.

TRANSMISSION rwd; sdp clutch; 5-speed manual synchromesh gearbox; final drive 3.938:1.
CHASSIS steel monocoque structure; ifs by double wishbones, interconnected Hydragas springs, anti-roll bars; servo ventilated front disc brakes, 9.5in (24cm), solid at rear; ABS optional; rack and pinion, electric PAS optional; 11 Imp gal (13.2 US gal, 50L) fuel tank; 6-spoke alloy wheels; 185/55 VR15 tyres front, 205/50 VR15 rear; 6J rims.
DIMENSIONS wheelbase 93.7in (238cm); track 55.1in (140cm) front, 55.5in (141cm) rear; turning circle 34.45ft (10.5m); ground clearance 47.2in (120cm); length 154.1in (391.4cm); width 64.1in (162.8cm); height with hood 49.6in (126cm).
PERFORMANCE maximum speed 120mph (193kph); 22.1mph (35.5kph) @ 1000rpm; 0-60mph (96kph) 8.7sec; 9kg/bhp (12kg/kW); fuel con 26.4mpg (10.7L/100km).
PRICE £15,995 PAS £550, ABS £650, hardtop £995: 1996 £16,395.
PRODUCTION 67,000 all MGF.

1995- MGF 1.8i (2)

the rear-drive contenders were two front-engined V8s, one with steel, one with plastic body panels. The code names were prefixed PR for Phoenix Route and the initiative was helped along by internal changes at Rover Group.

The Rover board and John Towers, director of engineering, harboured no illusions about the commercial realities. Marketing director Kevin Morley shared the view that the old days of badge engineering were gone, although it would be impossible to spend huge sums of money on a unique car. Shortage of cash for new model development was one reason Rover Group had a co-operative arrangement with Honda. If a new strain of MG could be done relatively cheaply however, then it would be. A partnership would be helpful so

another vital development was the creation of Mayflower Vehicle Systems to take a stake with Rover in the manufacture of the MGF body. In 1991 Mayflower bought the Coventry body-building company Motor Panels, which dated back to 1920 and

had old associations with MG, Tickford, and the Coventry Hood and Sidescreen Company. The other main elements that brought the car about were Roy Axe's Design Research Associates team at Warwick working on sports car design, Rover Group Special Products department under Don Wyatt looking at niche market cars, and the enthusiasm of Nick Stephenson head of engineering and design. At Canley, a former Triumph plant, Gordon Sked had yet another design group including the MGF's style guru Gerry McGovern awaiting instructions.

The development that proved most crucial to the MGF was the replacement of the long-serving A-series engine with the K-series. It was important to the morale at Rover, and to the new small

**Right: MGFs lined up at press launch.
Far right: mid-mounted K-series 1.8-litre engine.**

group that regarded themselves as MG people, that MG would emerge as a free-standing make in its own right. It would not do, they felt, for it to be a sub-Honda or even a sub-Rover brand. The 16-valve K-series engine gave the group confidence that the engineering capacity existed to carry this through. Its unique aluminium sandwich structure held together by ten through-bolts, began as a study into the practicality of plastic engine components. It went on to research aluminium components and emerged as one of the most innovative engine designs of the 1990s.

The MGF emerged the clear winner of the design competition. In contrast with the days when Cecil Kimber would produce a prototype at the motor show and await firm orders before committing himself to production, now MG made experimental cars, some testing certain aspects of the design and not looking like MGFs at all. These simulators included Toyota MR2s with the K-series engine to

try out installation details, 15 being Metro vans with the engine behind the driver. Following the first hand-made cars came prototypes looking like MGFs, with sufficient real production-ready components to be used for road tests. About 26 were made and the number of production parts was gradually increased as tooling became available. 34 of those were made. By the time all the tooling was in place a further 65 Quality Proving (QP) cars were made to ensure the design was ready for production. Then a further 100 were made to ensure the quality was repeatable and the car ready for sale. In all 239 cars were made before production began in July 1995.

1995- MGF 1.8i VVC

The reception accorded the MGF was little short of ecstatic, and it was oversubscribed as soon as it went on sale. It even commanded premium prices at auction. Critics praised the ride quality, the stiff body construction, refinement, brakes, grip, trim, and appearance.

The more expensive version with Variable Valve Control (VVC) provided an additional 25bhp (18.6kW) and took the engine up to over 7000rpm. It would be an exaggeration to say this transformed the performance, but it certainly put the car among the leading performers in an increasingly competitive class. Reservations about anti-lock brakes and power steering being optional at extra cost did not apply to the VVC model where they were included in the price.

The handling was excellent for a touring car, a shade too compliant for a sports car, but with a bias towards understeer it was strictly in accordance with the well-established Safety Fast slogan, and demonstrated how precisely the designers understood the MG market. The image of the make may have altered radically during the Leyland era, but now that it was back in independent hands and run by car people rather than accountants, they were able more or less to restart MG where it had left off in 1980.

BODY roadster, 2 doors, 2 seats; weight 2359lb (1070kg).

ENGINE 4 cylinders, in-line; mid transverse; 80mm x 89mm, 1796cc; compr 10.5:1; 145bhp (108.1kW) @ 7000rpm; 80.7bhp/L (60.2kW/L); 130lbft (174 Nm) @ 4500rpm.

ENGINE STRUCTURE twin belt-driven ohc; 16-valves, multicam with VVC; aluminium cam cover, cam carrier, cylinder head, block, bearing ladder, sump, damp cylinder liners; MEMS electronic ignition, multi-point fuel injection; 5-bearing crankshaft.

TRANSMISSION rwd; sdp clutch; 5-speed manual synchromesh gearbox; final drive 4.2:1.

CHASSIS steel monocoque structure; independent suspension by double wishbones, interconnected Hydragas springs, anti-roll bars; servo ventilated front disc brakes, 9.5in (24cm), solid at rear; ABS; rack and pinion, electric PAS; 11 Imp gal (13.2 US gal, 50L) fuel tank; 5-spoke alloy wheels; 185/55 VR15 tyres front, 205/50 VR15 rear; 6J rims.

DIMENSIONS wheelbase 93.7in (238cm); track 55.1in (140cm) front, 55.5in (141cm) rear; turning circle 34.45ft (10.5m); ground clearance 47.2in (120cm); length 154.1in (391.4cm); width 64.1in (162.8cm); height with hood 49.6in (126cm).

PERFORMANCE maximum speed 130mph (209kph); 20.7mph (33.3kph) @ 1000rpm; 0-60mph (96kph) 7.0sec; 7.4kg/bhp (9.9kg/kW); fuel consumption 26.4mpg (10.7L/100km).

PRICE £18,875.

PRODUCTION 67,000 all MGF (March 2001).

In September 1997 Californian Land Rover technician Terry Kilbourne brought MG back into the record books at Bonneville by driving EX253, a specially prepared MGF, at 217mph (348.35kph) on the Bonneville salt flats. The car kept most of its standard features with the addition of a 40cm tapered tail, a flat-deck tonneau cover, a tear-drop canopy with a roll hoop, and a lightning flash echoing the Gardner MG. The 1.8-litre K-series engine was exchanged for a turbocharged 1.4-litre producing 329bhp, 333PS (245.338kW) on super unleaded fuel.

The following year's EX255 was a more formidable proposition. With a supercharged MG V8 in place of the customary MGF 4-cylinder its aim was to beat the 254.91mph (409.207kph) set by Phil Hill in EX181 in 1959. Supercharging failed to deliver the required power, so it was turbocharged instead by Janspeed, to be driven in a record attempt by Andy Green, who had broken the sound barrier in Thrust SSC. Recognisably an MGF with wheel spats, tail fins, smooth undertray, and a bubble canopy over the driving seat the car was resplendent in light metallic green. Failure of a clutch withdrawal bearing led to abandonment of the attempt at the 50th Bonneville Speed Week.

EX255:
BODY lhd single-seat record breaker; weight 3086.4lb (1400kg).
ENGINE 8 cylinders, 90 deg V; mid; 94mm x 86.4mm, 4797cc; 942bhp (702.458kW) @ 8000rpm; 196.4bhp/L (146.4kW/L); 590lbft (800Nm) @ 16psi supercharger boost.
ENGINE STRUCTURE pushrod ohv; hydraulic tappets; reinforced, cross bolted version of production aluminium cyl block; cyl heads specially engineered with large valves and improved porting; Omega forged pistons; valves inlet 1.9in diameter, exhaust 1.6in; forged H-section steel connecting rods; cam-driven mechanical centrifugal compressors feeding into two water cooled heat exchangers; charge air temperatures not exceeding 30°C; exhaust 4 into one large bore manifolds and open twin exhausts; sequential fuel inj system with self learning fuelling strategy; no radiator, recirculating large capacity tank with heat exchanger; dry sump with twin scavenge pumps; 5-bg crank machined from solid steel billet with 2.1in big end journals and 2.25in main bearings.
TRANSMISSION rwd; 5.5" triple plate sintered AP racing clutch; modified Hewland type NMT 6-speed sequential transaxle installed upside down with a step up gear between engine and gearbox; GKN race specification drive shafts, Lobro inboard and CV outboard joints.
CHASSIS Font body structure to rear bulkhead standard MGF steel construction; space frame in 2in seamless steel tubing rear of bulkhead to house new power unit; standard MGF steel panels for wings, bonnet and doors; remaining demountable body panels in carbon fibre epoxy attached with Dzus fasteners; ifs, MGF double wishbone based with increased castor angle; Hyragas units non-interconnected with adjustable stiffened spring rates; lowered and restricted suspension travel as MGF Cup spec; front subframe retained solidly mounted using MGF Cup suspension mounts;

irs, MGF double wishbone based, raised in body structure to improve aero drag; MGF Hyragas units non-interconnected with adjustable stiffened spring rates; MGF Cup Eibach dampers; geometry and travel modified to improve anti-squat, give clearance to underbody profile, and accommodate rear track. Rear space frame of standard MGF. Hubs and bearings, front standard MGF; rear Range Rover. Brakes un-servoed 4 wheel ventil cast iron discs as MGF Cup spec, discs increased from 260mm to 310mm; uprated competition callipers with high temp pads to 800°C; Mooneyes steel wheels with flush fitting disc covers; front 4.5Jx16, rear 7Jx18; Mickey Thompson tyres rated to 375+mph front tyres 24.5 x 7.5 x 16; rear tyres 26.5 x 9 x 18. Underfloor modifications for aerodynamics: 3-stage step diffuser; fuel tank 30L (6.6 Imp gal, 7.9 US Gal). Chrome Moly safety / roll cage; two carbon fibre AFFF 4000R fire extinguisher systems, front bay and cockpit, and engine bay; 6 point seat belts with leg and arm restraints; twin braking parachute system stored in 8in dia tubes, 12ft dia high speed, 15ft dia low speed. Aerodynamics: Cd 0.180-0.195 dependent on additional aero aids used. Frontal area 1.48M², Cda 0.266-0.289M².

DIMENSIONS wheelbase 263cm (103.5in); track 140cm (55.1in) front, 125cm (49.2in) rear; length 456cm (179.5in). Body extended by 400mm at rear with twin F18-style fins either side of bootlid extension. Width 163cm (64.2in); height 117cm (46.1in).

PERFORMANCE maximum speed 255mph (409.351kph); 3.27kg/bhp (4.39kg/kW).

PRODUCTION 1.

Top right: Andy Green with MG EX255 and EX181.
Right: MG's Project EX253. On 20 August, 40 years after Stirling Moss took EX181 to a 1500cc class speed record of 245.64mph (395.41kph), MG returned to the salt flats at Bonneville, USA, with a largely standard MGF (except for a longer tail and windscreen removed) to record 217.400mph (349.87kph), the fastest production MGF ever.

1998 MGF Super Sports Concept

Geneva Motor Show surprises included the MGF's sequential gearchange, its supercharger – and the K3 Magnette, chassis K 3001 raced in the 1933 Mille Miglia by Lord Howe.

The MGF Concept looked like a regular MGF with a composite plastic cockpit cover, racing tyres and aluminium wheels, aerodynamic guide vane strips on the lower sills, and a huge air intake for the mid-engine like one of the marine ventilators sported by MGs in the 1920s.

Turbocharging was rejected on the grounds that the supercharger kept the engine within more manageable rev limits, suitable for the sequential automatic gearshift that was a variation on the continuously variable transmission (CVT) steel belt transmission first seen on the Rover 200.

Flared side panels in the aluminium body accommodated a wider track, with large, rather dramatic wheels and low-profile tyres. Bumpers were carbon-fibre composites. The show car had deep red bodywork and full length white tonneau, with chrome embellishments in the style of a modern racing MG. The cockpit had a raked low drag racing windscreen and the seats, fully trimmed in white leather with red stitching, reflected the white and chrome interior theme.

BODY roadster, 2 doors, 2 seats; weight approx 2337lb (1060kg).
ENGINE 4 cylinders, in-line; mid transverse; 80mm x 89mm, 1796cc; compr 10.5:1; 197.3bhp (147.1kW); 109.9bhp/L (81.9kW/L).
ENGINE STRUCTURE twin belt-driven ohc; 16-valves; aluminium cam cover, cam carrier, cylinder head, block, bearing ladder, sump, damp cylinder liners; MEMS electronic ignition, multi-point fuel injection; supercharger and intercooler; 5-bearing crankshaft.
TRANSMISSION rear wheel drive; sdp clutch; 5-speed manual synchromesh gearbox; final drive 3.938:1.
CHASSIS steel and aluminium bonded structure; independent suspension by double wishbones, interconnected Hydragas springs, anti-roll bars uprated to racing specification; servo ventilated 29.5cm (11.6in) AP Racing disc brakes; ABS; rack and pinion, electric PAS; 11 Imp gal (13.2 US gal, 50L) fuel tank; eight-spoke alloy road wheels; 210/605 R16 race tyres front; 220/640 R17 race tyres rear.
DIMENSIONS wheelbase 93.7in (237.5cm); track 56.7in (143.9cm) front, 58.6in (148.9cm) rear; turning circle 34.45ft (10.5m); length 154.1in (391.4cm); width 64.1in (162.8cm).
PERFORMANCE maximum speed approx 140mph (225kph); 0-60mph (96kph) 6.1sec; 5.4kg/bhp (7.2kg/kW).
PRODUCTION 1.

A realistic representation of a modern weekend racer, its supercharger could also be regarded as a complete-combustion solution to California's clean-air legislation, particularly with the VVC engine.

The MGF was not radically altered for 2000. A makeover of the interior brought new materials including some convincing timber look-alikes. Curiously, trompe d'oeil walnut or ash for the facia was not disdained on MGs. When the walnut veneer-on-plywood facia of the T-series gave way to Rexine, it was regarded as a workmanlike and having weather-resistant practicality. Open cars in the ordinary course of things were subject to the vagaries of weather. So it was with the plastic wood of the MGF. Instrument faces reverted from cream to silver, there were new tyre and wheel options, but the most radical departure was the option of a Steptronic gearbox. There had been fully automatic MGBs and MGCs, the K3 and R-type had the novel Wilson preselector, ZB Magnettes briefly had the lacklustre semi-automatic Manumatic, but the MGF's Belgian-made ZF VT1 Ecotronic with wet clutch was entirely new. Its origins lay in the 1960s Daf belt-drive transmission, but with steel-segment pusher belts instead of rubber and fabric puller ones, its evolution was substantial. Most important the engine did not whine up to high steady rpm and wait until the transmission caught up with it. Steptronic was a slick manual shift with a flick of the lever, or if the driver chose a reliable automatic that did not soak up power.

VVC specs:
BODY roadster, 2,doors, 2,seats; weight 2359lb (1070kg).
ENGINE 4 cylinders, in line; mid transverse; 80mm x 89mm, 1796cc; compr 10.5:1; 145bhp (108kW) @ 7000rpm; 80.7bhp/L (60.1kW/L); 128lb ft (174 Nm) @ 3000rpm.
ENGINE STRUCTURE twin belt-driven ohc; 16-valves, multicam with VVC; aluminium cam cover, cam carrier, cylinder head, block, bearing ladder, sump, damp cylinder liners; MEMS electronic ign, multi-point fuel injection; 5-bearing crankshaft.

TRANSMISSION rear wheel drive; sdp clutch; 5-speed manual synchromesh gearbox; optional Steptronic; final drive 4.2:1.
CHASSIS steel monocoque structure; ifs by double wishbones, interconnected Hydragas springs, anti-roll bars; servo ventilated front disc brakes, 9.5in (24cm), solid at rear; ABS; rack and pinion, electric PAS; 11 Imp gal (13.2US gal, 50L) fuel tank; 5-spoke alloy wheels; 185/55 VR15 tyres front, 205/50 VR15 rear; 6J rims.
DIMENSIONS wheelbase 93.7in (238cm); track 55.1in (140cm) front, 55.5in (141cm) rear; turning circle 34.45ft (10.5m); ground clearance 304.8in (120cm); length 154.1in (391.4cm); width 64.1in (162.8cm); height with hood 49.6in (126cm).
PERFORMANCE maximum speed 130mph (209kph); 20.7mph (33.3kph) @ 1000rpm; 0-60mph (96kph) 7.0sec; 7.4kg/bhp (9.9kg/kW); fuel consumption 26.4mpg (10.7L/100km).

Top: the Steptronic
gear selector.

Right: the MGF range;
1.8i, 1.8i Steptronic
and 1.8i VVC.

2000 MGF Super Sports

The 1998 concept MGF Super Sports was a bold initiative but it did not have the unqualified blessing of MG's owners, BMW. Conceived in what came to be known as the Gaydon skunk works operating, as Rob Oldaker famously described, "under the Munich radar," it had been unveiled somewhat peremptorily at Geneva by the usually self-composed Bernd Pischestsreider. Press and MG devotees applauded and, although it did not have the crucial backing of the management for production in 1999, it gained a second wind. A great deal had been learned (as MG had been learning since the 1920s) from racing, namely the MGF Cup. When the Super Sports reappeared at Geneva in 1999 as a road car with windscreen and road equipment, improvements were included as a result of racing experience. Designer David Woodhouse left to join General Motors, and his successors eradicated his racier aspects, equipping it with Recaro seats and Grenadine leather like the 75th anniversary MGF. The air intake was enlarged, the sequential gearbox dropped, and same-size tyres used front and back. All that was wrong was the timing. Rover was exhausted with the launch of the important 75, and by the time attention could be diverted to MG, so much had altered on the political landscape that it never had any real chance of going into production.

BODY roadster, 2 doors, 2 seats; weight approx 2337lb (1060kg).
ENGINE 4 cylinders, in-line; mid transverse; 80mm x 89mm, 1796cc; compr 10.5:1; 197.3bhp (147.1kW); 109.9bhp/L (81.9kW/L).
ENGINE STRUCTURE twin belt-driven ohc; 16-valves; aluminium cam cover, cam carrier, cylinder head, block, bearing ladder, sump, damp cylinder liners; MEMS electronic ignition, multi-point fuel injection; supercharger and intercooler; 5-bearing crankshaft.
TRANSMISSION rear wheel drive; sdp clutch; 5-speed manual gearbox; final drive 3.938:1.

CHASSIS DETAILS steel and aluminium bonded structure; ifs by double wishbones, interconnected Hydragas springs, anti-roll bars uprated to racing specification; servo ventilated 29.5cm (11.6in) AP Racing disc brakes; ABS; rack and pinion, electric PAS; 11 Imp gal (13.2 US gal, 50L) fuel tank; seam-welded 17in KN alloy wheels; 225/45-17 Goodyear Eagle F1 tyres.
DIMENSIONS wheelbase 93.7in (238cm); track 56.7in (143.9cm) front, 58.62in (148.9cm) rear; turning circle 34.45ft (10.5m); ground clearance 304.8in (120cm); length 154.1in (391.4cm); width 64.1in (162.8cm).
PERFORMANCE maximum speed approx 140mph (225kph); 0-60mph (96kph) 6.1sec; 5.4kg/bhp (7.2kg/kW).

The ink was scarcely dry on the agreement devolving control of Rover from BMW, before MG Rover was formally created and the first new MGFs introduced. Left to itself the new management immediately extended the model's market coverage at both ends. At the top, as a further acknowledgment to MG's racing heritage, the MGF Trophy 160 Special Edition was equipped with a tuned version of the K-series 1.8-litre VVC engine. This had a wide-bore exhaust, developed 10 per cent more power than standard, and promised new levels of performance still well within the MGF's well-balanced ride and handling envelope. Competition spring and damper rates were applied to the interconnected Hydragas suspension, which also had a 20mm lower ride height, and the brakes were AP racing units with red MG-branded callipers. Lightweight forged and spun alloy wheels were an option and the aerodynamic qualities were enhanced by spoilers front and rear. At the lower end of the price scale the 1.6i had a shorter-stroke version of the K-series engine, losing scarcely any of the 1.8's vigour, yet keeping the features that made the MGF so popular. Electric power steering, driver's airbag, rake-adjustable steering wheel, anti-theft alarm, electric windows, and alloy wheels were all retained at an effective price reduction of £1,500 on the 1.8i.

[1.6 in brackets]
BODY roadster; 2 doors, 2 seats; weight 2370lb (1075kg).
ENGINE 4 cylinders, in-line; mid, transverse; 80mm x 89.3mm [80mm x 79mm]; 1796cc [1589cc]; cr 10.5:1; 159bhp (118kW, 160PS) @ 7000rpm [111bhp (82kW, 112PS) @ 6250rpm]; 88.5bhp/L (65.7kW/L) [69.9bhp/L (51.6kW/L)]; 128 lb ft (174 Nm) @ 4500rpm [107lbft (145Nm) @ 4700rpm].
ENGINE STRUCTURE Trophy belt-driven multi-cam 4 inlet, 1 exhaust, Variable Valve Control (VVC); 4 valves per cyl; aluminium cyl head and block; MEMS 3 engine management; 5-bearing crankshaft; [belt driven twin overhead camshaft, 4 valves per cylinder].
TRANSMISSION rwd; sdp clutch; 5-spd synchromesh manual gearbox; final drive 4.200:1 [3.938:1].
CHASSIS steel monocoque; ifs by double wishbones, interconnected Hydragas springs, telescopic dampers, anti-roll bars; servo ventilated front disc brakes 11.9in (30.4cm) [9.5in (24cm)], solid at rear; ABS, dual circuit; rack and pinion, electric PAS; 11 Imp gal (13.2 US gal, 50L); 195/45 R16 tyres 7J rims front, 215/40 R16 7Jrims rear, [185/55 front & 205/50VR15 tyres 6.0J rims rear]; multi-spoke alloy wheels.
DIMENSIONS wheelbase 93.7in (238cm); track 55.5in (141cm) front, 140cm (55.1in) rear; turning circle 34.65ft (10.6m); ground clearance 4.72in (12cm); length 153.9in (391cm); width 64.2in (163cm); height 49.2in (125cm) [49.9in (127cm)] with hood.
PERFORMANCE max 137mph (220.5kph) [116mph (187kph)]; 20.7mph (33.3kph) @ 1000rpm [22.1mph (35.5kph)]; 0-60mph (96kph) less than 7.0sec [9.6sec]; 6.8kg/bhp (9.1kg/kW) [9.7kg/bhp (13.1kg/kW)]; fuel consumption 36.3mpg (7.8L/100km), Euro III emission standard, declared CO_2 190g/km [38.4mpg (7.4L/100km), declared CO_2 177g/km].
PRICE Trophy 160 £20,995; 1.6i £15,500.

Above and right: the MGF Trophy 160SE was something of a fashion statement, with Trophy Yellow and Trophy Blue specially created for it, augmenting the popular Solar Red and Anthracite Black. Bright mesh grilles, body-colour inserts in the door casings, and leather and fabric seats were among the features designed to secure its appeal.

Far right: MGF 1.6i.

2001 ZR 1.4 litre; ZR 1.6 litre

Cecil Kimber tailored volume-production cars in the 1920s with a distinctive approach that emerged as Morris Garages', later MG's, style. He added speed subtly so as not to alarm insurance companies or wary customers, and his recipe was just as effective in the 2000s as it had been in the 1920s. Kevin Howe, Rob Oldaker, and Peter Stevens created a new generation of MGs in much the same way. It was no stroke of inspiration; plenty of car couturiers had been copying Kimber for years. This time the odds were if anything longer than in Kimber's day, with a world market full of high quality competition not least from a company that had adopted the Kimber-principle in 1927. The Bavarian Motor Works manufactured an enhanced Austin Seven by first light of the 1930s and now set a standard everybody else endeavoured to match. Rover had rubbed shoulders with BMW for five years or more and, taking the 25 as a basis, newly renamed MG. Rover evolved a car code-named X30 with a choice of 1.4-litre or 1.6-litre engines. Forty per cent stiffer springs and a 20mm lower ride height not only gave it better roll stiffness and body control, but also gave the impression of being more in tune with its target audience. Once again Kimber's legacy of Safety Fast had held good.

[1.6 in brackets]
BODY hatchback; 3 or 5 doors, 5 seats; weight 2249lb (1020kg).
ENGINE 4 cylinders, in-line; front, transverse; 75mm x 79mm [80mm x 79mm]; 1396cc [1589cc]; cr 10.5:1; 102bhp (76kW, 103PS) [108bhp (80kW, 109PS] @ 6000rpm; 73.1bhp/L (54.4kW/L) [68bhp/L (50.3kW/L)]; 91lbft (123Nm) [102lbft (138Nm)] @ 4500rpm.
ENGINE STRUCTURE twin belt-driven overhead camshaft; 4 valves per cyl; aluminium cylinder head and block; MEMS3 engine management; 5-bearing crankshaft.
TRANSMISSION front wheel drive; sdp clutch; 5-speed manual synchromesh gearbox; final drive 3.765:1.
CHASSIS steel monocoque; ifs by MacPherson strut with coil springs, telescopic dampers and anti-roll bars; rear suspension H-frame with coil springs, telescopic dampers, anti-roll bars; disc brakes front, drum rear, dual circuit; rack and pinion PAS; 11 Imp gal (13.2 US gal, 50L) fuel tank; 205/50 R16 tyres, 6.5J rims.
DIMENSIONS wheelbase 98.4in (250cm); track 57.9in (147cm); turning circle 33.1ft (10.1m); ground clearance 5.3in (13.5cm); length 157.1in (399cm); width 66.5in (169cm); height 55.1in (140cm) approx.
PERFORMANCE maximum speed 111mph (178.2kph) [115mph (184.6kph)]; 50.5mph (31.4kph) approx @ 1000rpm; 0-60mph (96kph) 10.2sec [9.5sec]; 10kg/bhp (13.4kg/kW) [9.4kg/bhp (12.8kg/kW)].

2001 ZR 2.0 litre diesel; ZR 160 1.8 litre

MG record-breaking driver George Eyston tackled diesel records , in 1933 at Brooklands, attaining 104.86mph (168.331kph) in his streamlined Safety Saloon. Its 8.9-litre AEC made the L-series engine in the MG ZR look like watchmakers' work, a testament to the transformation in power and flexibility of modern turbocharged compression ignition units. The Rover version of the L-Series gained a new high-pressure injection pump late in 1999, one of a number of improvements that enhanced torque by a towering 14 per cent and gave much improved top-gear performance. Its 50-70mph time of 7.0sec was only 0.1sec behind the petrol 1.8-litre Rover 25 GTi. Improvements extended to more responsive steering, as a result of a 12 per cent higher-geared rack, and sportier spring and damper rates. At the back the twist-beam suspension's H-frame was stiffened, and instead of equal bump-and-rebound damping, the ratio was changed to provide less on bump and more on rebound. There were extra rebound springs at the front and a 20mm reduction in ride height as in the 25 GTi. Anti-roll bars were stiffened, and tyres were half an inch wider and lower profile. Brake discs were increased from 284mm to 325mm in front and 276 to 280mm at the back. Bigger pads of improved materials were introduced to match the car's speed.

[1.8 in brackets]
BODY hatchback, 3/5 doors, 5 seats; weight 2491lb (1130kg).
ENGINE 4 cylinders, in-line; front transverse; 84.5mm x 89mm [80mm x 89.3mm], 1994cc [1796cc]; compr 19.5:1 [10.5:1]; 99bhp (74kW, 100PS) @ 4200rpm [159hp (118kW, 160PS) @ 7000rpm]; 49.6bhp/L (37.1kW/L) [88.5bhp/L (65.7kW/L)]; 177lbft (240Nm) @ 2000rpm [128lbft (174Nm) @ 4500rpm].
ENGINE STRUCTURE belt-driven single overhead camshaft; 2 valves per cylinder; aluminium cylinder head, cast iron block; DFI engine management; turbocharger and intercooler; 5-bearing crankshaft. [belt-driven multi-overhead camshafts (4 inlet and one exhaust); 4 valves per cylinder; aluminium head and block; MEMS3 engine management].
TRANSMISSION front wheel drive; sdp clutch; 5-speed manual synchromesh gearbox; final drive 3.938:1 [4.2:1].
CHASSIS steel monocoque; ifs by

MacPherson strut with coil springs, telescopic dampers and anti-roll bars; rear suspension H-frame with coil springs, telescopic dampers, anti-roll bars; disc brakes front, drum rear, dual circuit; ABS; rack and pinion PAS; 10.99 Imp gal (13.2 US gal, 50L) fuel tank; 205/50 R16 tyres, 6.5J rims. (205/45 R17 tyres, 7J rims)
DIMENSIONS wheelbase 98.4in (250cm); track 57.9in (147cm); turning circle 33.1ft (10.1m); ground clearance 5.3in (13.5cm); length 157.1in (399cm); width 66.5in (169cm); height 55.1in (140cm) approx.
PERFORMANCE maximum speed 113mph (181.4kph) [125mph (200.6kph)]; 26.5mph (42.5kph) @ 1000rpm approx; 0-60mph (96kph) 9.9sec [7.8sec]; 11.4kg/bhp (15.3kg/kW) [7.1kg/bhp (9.6kg/kW); fuel con (combined) 55.4mpg [37.8mpg].

In modular terms the ZS was one stage up from the ZR with an additional 12cm (4.7in) on the wheelbase, and most of the extra 50cm (19.7in) accounted for by the 4-door saloon's 470dm³ boot. The 5-door was 16cm (6.3in) shorter, offering 720dm³ of luggage space with the seats flat. In both cases the good proportions of the Rover 45 were unimpaired and the spring-stiffening process continued at the front and rear. The steering rack ratio changed from 18.1:1 to 16.4:1 to give faster response, further improved by fine-tuning the power assistance. The K-series engine lived up to all the promises of 1985.

A restatement of the MG identity was necessary from the launch of the new range at the end of January 2001. It was achieved by the classic speed cues of aerodynamic aids, wings and spoilers, low-profile tyres, and chunky aluminium wheels. Decorative chrome was reduced to a minimum and body-colour was used for the MG grille and air intakes. Peter Stevens stripped out all the wood-and-leather that made Rovers perilously older-generation, replacing it with practical modern new-age textures like that of carbon-fibre or shiny metallics to secure the cars' appeal to younger buyers. Supportive upholstery was necessary to give drivers what Rob Oldaker was fond of calling outrageous fun.

[1.8 in brackets]
BODY hatchback, saloon; 5 doors, 4 doors, 5 seats; weight 2447lb (1110kg), [2546.3lb (1155kg)].
ENGINE 4 cylinders, in-line; front transverse; 80mm x 79mm [80mm x 89.3mm], 1589cc [1796cc]; compr 10.5:1; 108bhp (80kW, 109PS) @ 6000rpm [116bhp (86.5kW, 117PS] @ 5500rpm; 68bhp/L (50.3kW/L) [64.6bhp/L (48.2kW/L)]; 102lbft (138Nm) @ 4500rpm [118lbft (160Nm) @ 2750rpm].
ENGINE STRUCTURE 2 belt-driven overhead camshafts; 4 valves per cylinder; aluminium block and head; MEMS3 engine management; 5-bearing crankshaft.
TRANSMISSION front wheel drive; sdp clutch; 5-speed manual synchromesh gearbox; final drive 3.765:1 [3.938:1].
CHASSIS steel monocoque structure; ifs by double wishbone and coil springs; irs multi-link with coil springs; telescopic dampers and anti roll bars front and rear; disc front, drum rear dual circuit brakes;

ABS; rack and pinion PAS; 12.1 Imp gal (14.5 US gal, 55L) fuel tank; 205/50 R16 tyres, 6.5J rims.
DIMENSIONS wheelbase 103.1in (262 cm); track 58.3in (148cm) front, 57.9in (147cm) rear; turning circle 33.9ft (10.36m); ground clearance 5.3in (13.5cm) saloon; length h/b 171.7in (436cm), saloon 180in (452cm); width 66.9in (170cm); height 53.9in (137cm).
PERFORMANCE maximum speed 118.3mph (189.9kph) [121.5mph (195kph)]; 19.9mph (32kph) [35kph (21.801mph)] approx @ 1000rpm; 0-60mph (96kph) 10.3sec [9.3sec]; 10.3kg/bhp (13.9kg/kW) [9.6kg/bhp (12.8kg/kW)]; fuel consumption 39mpg (7.23L/100km) [30.7mpg (9.2L/100km)].

MG Rover by-passed the 2.0-litre KV6 for the 2.5-litre in what it regarded as the foundation ZS that formed the basis of MG's official re-entry into the British TOCA Tour race series. MG had been out of saloon car racing since the Y-type 1˘-litre cars of the 1950s, and the ZS with the full-house racing version of the 175bhp (130kW) 6-cylinder was looking for outright country-wide wins, rather than the entirely worthy but ultimately less satisfactory class victories in the clubby confines of Silverstone. The performance of the lusty 4-cylinder diesel would have seen it among the leaders in 1951, when Dick Jacobs and Ted Lund were struggling round the old Silverstone circuit in 2min 18sec at about 75mph (120.4kph). Stirling Moss's 3.4 Jaguar was only just breaking 2min, 86.7mph (139.2kph).

The road ZS enjoyed the new MG chassis engineering, with 17in wheels, firmer suspension, improved brakes, and steering designed for keen drivers. Wind-tunnel testing was used to confirm the aerodynamic package of skirts and spoilers that had been designed to minimise drag and lift. Sports exhaust tailpipes were housed within a heat shield to fit into the rear bumper leaving satisfactory ground clearance. The interior also came in for the MG generic treatment, with specially contoured sports seats to hold the occupants in place during fast cornering.

[2.5 KV6 in brackets]

BODY 5-door hatchback, 4-door saloon; weight 2712lb (1230kg), 2789lb (1265kg).

ENGINE 4 [6] cylinders, in-line [90deg V]; front transverse; 84.5mm x 89mm [80mm x 82.8], 1994cc [2497cc]; compr 19.5:1 [10.5:1]; 99bhp (74kW, 100PS) @ 4200rpm [175bhp (130kW, 177PS) @ 6500rpm]; 49.6bhp/L (37.1kW/L) [70.1bhp/L (52.1kW/L)]; 177lbft (240Nm) @ 2000rpm [177lbft 240Nm @ 4000rpm].

ENGINE STRUCTURE belt-driven single overhead camshaft [4 belt-driven overhead camshafts]; 2 [4] valves per cylinder; turbocharger and intercooler; aluminium cylinder head, cast iron [aluminium] block; DFI engine management; 5-bearing [4-bearing] crankshaft.

TRANSMISSION front wheel drive; sdp clutch; 5-speed manual synchromesh gearbox; final drive 3.938:1 [3.89].

CHASSIS steel monocoque structure; ifs by double wishbone and coil springs; irs multi-link with coil springs; telescopic dampers and anti roll bars front and rear; disc front, drum rear dual circuit brakes; ABS; rack and pinion PAS; 12.1 Imp gal (14.5 US gal, 55L) fuel tank; 205/50 R16 tyres, 6.5J rims [205/45 R17, 7J rims].

DIMENSIONS wheelbase 103.1in (262 cm); track 58.3in (148cm) front, 57.9in (147cm) rear; turning circle 33.9ft (10.36m); ground clearance 5.3in (13.5cm) saloon; length h/back 171.7in (436cm), saloon 178in (452cm); width 66.9in (170cm); height 53.9in (137cm).

PERFORMANCE maximum speed 115.2mph (185kph); 25.8mph (41.4kph) @ 1000rpm; 0-60mph (96kph) 10.6sec; 12.4kg/bhp (16.6kg/kW) [7kg/bhp (9.5kg/kW)] fuel consumption 50.5mpg (5.6L/100km).

2001 ZT 2.5 litre KV6 160PS, ZT 2.5 litre KV6 190PS

There was a choice in the up-range MG versions of the Rover 75 module. Customers were offered two front-drive cars with different versions of the KV6, and right at the summit of the new order was a rear-drive car with an extremely powerful V8. The engineering of the 75 was almost beyond reproach. It had been evolved with the utmost care in co-operation with BMW and was made to the highest standards. It was more than three quarters of a century since the somewhat hit and miss nature of MG engineering at Oxford and to a lesser degree Abingdon prevailed. It was not unsuccessful and produced some remarkable cars, but it depended heavily on the skill, talent, and experience of a handful of people. Syd Enever, H N Charles, Gerald Palmer, Reg Jackson, and Cec Cousins had the necessary qualities and produced great cars that were commercially successful. Quite a lot of their contemporaries did not. By the 1990s international safety, environmental, and sometimes seemingly fatuous regulations made such demands on car manufacturers that the old laissez-faire approach was no longer appropriate. Huge teams of designers and engineers were deployed on new cars, with the result that almost all were satisfactory, and quite a lot were exemplary. Among the best was the Rover 75 on which the ZT was based.

[190PS in brackets]
BODY saloon; 4 doors, 5 seats; weight 3186lb (1445kg).
ENGINE 6 cylinders, 90deg V; front transverse; 80mm x 82.8mm, 2497cc; compr 10.5:1; 159bhp (118.6kW, 160PS) @ 6500rpm [198bhp (147.7kW, 190PS) @ 6500rpm]; 63.7bhp/L (47.5kW/L) [79.3bhp/L (59.2kW/L)]; 177lbft (240Nm) @ 4000rpm.
ENGINE STRUCTURE 4 belt-driven overhead camshafts; 4 valves per cyl; aluminium cyl head and block; Siemens engine management; 4-bearing crankshaft.
TRANSMISSION front wheel drive; sdp clutch; 5-speed manual synchromesh gearbox; final drive 3.944:1.
CHASSIS steel monocoque structure; ifs by MacPherson strut with coil springs; irs Z-axle with coil springs; anti roll bars front and rear; telescopic gas-filled dampers; front disc, rear drum dual circuit brakes; ABS; rack and pinion PAS; 14.25 Imp gal (17.1 US gal, 64.8L) fuel tank; 225/ 45 R18 tyres, 7.5J rims.
DIMENSIONS wheelbase 108.1in (274.6cm); track 59.25in (150.5cm); turning circle 37.3ft (11.4m); ground clearance 6.1in (15.5cm); length 186.9in (474.7cm); width 70in (178cm); height 55.3in (140.4cm).

2001 ZT V8 260PS V8

Revealing the V8 ZT at Longbridge early in 2001 meant that work on the car was under way but not much more. Rob Oldaker vouchsafed no details beyond the bare essentials. The car displayed at the press conference might as well not have had an engine; the bonnet was firmly locked. All Oldaker would reveal was that the exceptional torsional stiffness of the Rover 75 body shell enabled the development of a rear wheel drive edition capable of dealing with 256.4bhp (191.23kW 260PS) from a substantial V8. While there were few practical limits to the power that could be transmitted through front wheel drive (electronics could more or less eliminate torque steer and wheelspin) where large amounts of power were going to be employed in an all-weather road car, rear wheel drive or, as Jaguar found with the X-type, four wheel drive may be desirable or even necessary.

The prognosis was that production was probably a year or more away, but when the car did make its appearance it would be a fine flagship for a new range that would be augmented by a number of sub-species along the way. Out went the Rover's whimsical oval instruments and wood veneer. In came an aircraft-style facia panel appropriate for a 21st century sports saloon.

BODY saloon; 4 doors, 5 seats.
ENGINE 8 cylinders, V; front; 256.4bhp (191.23kW, 260PS).
TRANSMISSION rwd; manual synchromesh gearbox; automatic.
CHASSIS steel monocoque structure; ifs by MacPherson strut with coil springs; irs with coil springs; anti roll bars front and rear; telescopic gas-filled dampers; front disc, rear drum dual circuit brakes; ABS; rack and pinion PAS; 14.2 Imp gal (17 US gal, 64.6L) fuel tank; 225/45 R18 tyres, 7.5J rims.
DIMENSIONS wheelbase 108.1in (274.6cm); track 59.25in (150.5cm); turning circle 37.3ft (11.4m); ground clearance 6.1in (15.5cm); length 186.9in (474.7cm); width 70in (178cm); height 55.3in (140.4cm).

2001 MGF 1.8i 120PS; sequential CVT, 1.8VVC

MG sports cars always tried to be like frontline racing cars in appearance, handling, and character. When superchargers were in, MGs had them. When all-enveloping bodywork arrived, MGs had that too (although it took a little time from the TF to the MGA). When the engine moved behind the driver in grand prix racing it moved behind the driver in MGs too. So when racing drivers began to change gear with buttons on the steering wheel it was only natural MG drivers should as well. The Constant Velocity Transmission (CVT) of the Belgian ZF Getriebe NV Sint-Truiden was an integrated engine and transmission unit that introduced electronic steps in the continuous (and stepless) performance of the CVT. The reception accorded the 1999 introduction of sequential gear shifting was less than enthusiastic however, *Autocar* finding too many decisions taken out of the driver's hands and a loss of performance over the car tested in 1995. Fuel consumption also suffered, testers blaming the frequency with which the sequential car's engine revved up to the 6,000rpm limit. It rose from an average of 26.4mpg (10.7L/100km) and a best of 33.6mpg (8.4L/100km) to 22.7mpg (12.4L/100km) and 32.6mpg (8.7L/100km), reducing the range from the contents of the 50-litre tank to under 300miles (482.8km).

[VVC in brackets]
BODY roadster; 2-doors, 2-seats; weight 2370lb (1075kg).
ENGINE 4-cylinders, in-line; mid, transverse; 80mm x 89.3mm, 1796cc; compr 10.5:1; 119bhp (88kW, 120PS) @ 5500rpm [143bhp (107kW, 145PS]; 66.3bhp/L (50kW/L) [79.6bhp/L (59.6kW/L)]; 121lbft (165Nm) @ 3000rpm [128lbft (174Nm) @ 4500rpm].
ENGINE STRUCTURE twin belt-driven overhead camshafts; [multi overhead cams four inlet, one exhaust] 4 valves per cyl; aluminium cyl head, block; MEMS3 engine management; 5-bearing crankshaft.
TRANSMISSION rwd; sdp clutch; 5-speed manual synchromesh gearbox; final drive 3.938:1. Optional ZF CFT23 Electronic 6-speed sequential, final drive 4.05:1.
CHASSIS steel monocoque; ifs by double wishbones, interconnected Hydragas springs, telescopic dampers, anti-roll bars; servo ventilated front disc brakes 30.4cm (11.9in), 9.5in (24cm), solid at rear;

ABS, dual circuit; rack and pinion, electric PAS; 11 Imp gal (13.2 US gal, 50L) fuel tank; VR18 tyres 7J rims, multi-spoke alloy wheels.
DIMENSIONS wheelbase 93.7in (238cm); track 55.5in (141cm) front, 55.1in (140cm) rear; turning circle 34.6ft (10.6m); ground clearance 4.7in (12cm); length 153.9in (391cm); width 64.2in (163cm); height 1.6i 50in (127cm) with hood.
PERFORMANCE maximum speed (manufacturer's figure) 120mph (198kph) [130mph (209kph)]; 26.1mph (42.1kph) manual, 22.3mph (35.9kph) sequential @ 1000rpm in top (6th speed position) manual selection; 0-60mph (96kph) 10.4sec [7.0sec]; 9kg/bhp (12.2kg/kW) [7.5kg/bhp (10kg/kW)]; fuel consumption combined 38.4mpg (7.4L/100km [36.3mpg (7.8L/100km)].

Sports cars had long been expected to make compromises for speed. In the days of feeble engines weight was ruthlessly pared, seats sacrificed, quietness, comfort, weather protection, and even in the early years safety was neglected. MG opposed such concessions, as Kimber's Safety Fast slogan showed, and as engines grew stronger so shortcomings were overcome. Comfort improved, better hoods kept out rain, and you could have more seats. Lancia, Volvo, and Reliant pioneered the sports estate car in the 1960s with three doors, and at the 2001 Geneva motor show MG Rover showed the first-ever MG sports estate with five. Code-named X11, it appeared together with four new products including the long-awaited Rover 75 Tourer and ZR ZS and ZT saloons. The MG brand now extended to five models with 22 engine variations. Deliveries of the X11 were planned for the autumn, starting with the 2.5-litre KV6 quad-cam aluminium engine, followed in 2002 by 260PS and 375PS V8s in radically re-engineered cars with rear wheel drive. A basic requirement for sporting handling was a stiff bodyshell, and the well-engineered Rover's enabled the redesign to proceed with confidence.

Components that could influence handling were tuned to create sports cornering abilities similar to the rest of the new range, with MG-style alloy wheels and lowered suspension. The front brake discs were a generous 325mm in diameter and a high-geared steering rack with revised valving was expected to sharpen steering response and feel. A deep front air-dam enhanced the aerodynamics, reduced lift and increased the size of the air intake. Outside there was a body-colour MG grille, with bright stone-guard mesh.

Specially developed front sports seats were shaped to give good support appropriate for the X11's expected cornering ability. The interior had new MG instrumentation, a 'technical' finish for the main fascia and console. The MG X11 estate version had an outstanding body rigidity of around 20,000Nm per degree. Stiffness of this calibre provided a firm foundation for suspension tuning.

BODY estate; 5 doors, 5 seats.
DIMENSIONS wheelbase 108.1in (274.6cm); track 59.1in (150.5cm); turning circle 37.3ft (11.36m); ground clearance 6.1in (15.5cm); length 188.7in (479.2cm); width 70in (177.8cm); height 56.1in (142.4cm).

A load-carrying capacity
of over 1200 litres contributed
to the practicality of the estate,
providing good access and
functionality. The 1.1m
aperture lift-up tailgate
incorporated an opening
rear window and, by lowering
the 60:40 split-folding rear seat
backrest, the flat loadspace
area extended to 2.06m. Boot
space was 400 litres, 680 litres
filled to the roof. Maximum
capacity with seats folded
was 1222 litres.

1893 William Morris sets up in James Street, Cowley St John.

1902 Morris opens bicycle dealership 48 High Street Oxford, and 100 Holywell Street, known as Longwall.

1903 Morris enters partnership, The Oxford Automobile and Cycle Agency, at 16 George Street, George Street Mews and New Road. Business fails, Morris borrows money to buy back tools. Never enters a partnership again. Resumes repair business at 48 High Street and motor trade at Longwall.

1907 Expands garage business at Longwall.

1908 Sells 48 High Street to Edward Armstead.

1912 Oct: WRM Motors established. £4000 capital from Earl of Macclesfield.
Nov: Morris shows designs of Morris Oxford at Olympia. Gordon Stewart of Stewart & Ardern buys 400.

1913 The Morris Garages (W R Morris, proprietor) established in Longwall, Queen Street and St Cross Road.
29 Mar: First Morris Oxford: body by Raworth, engine and gearbox White & Poppe, axles E G Wrigley, bull-nose radiator by Doherty Motor Components.

Built at Temple Cowley.

1914 Jan: WRM Motors lists six Morris Oxfords. Standard £180. De Luxe coupe £255. Sports £220.
Apr: Morris sails to USA with Hans Landstad of White & Poppe, meets Continental Motor Manufacturing Company in Detroit, Michigan. Landstad joins WRM Motors.

1915 Apr: Morris Cowley two-seater with American engine and gearbox.

Below: Morris Garages petrol pumps. Injunction on back wall behind Bullnose Morris Oxford encourages Morris's Buy British policy.

Sep: Chancellor of the Exchequer, Reginald McKenna, imposes 33-and-a-third per cent import duty on cars.
Sep: First engines for Morris Cowley delivered from Continental. Supplies erratic due to war.

1916 Mar: Engine imports now badly affected by wartime shipping restrictions.

1918 Nov: Last Morris Cowleys with Continental engines.

1919 Mar: Morris Garages manager, F G Barton, resigns due to ill health. Replaced by Edward Armstead.
July: WRM Motors liquidated. Morris forms Morris Motors. WRM Motors tied to unacceptable distribution agreement. First Hotchkiss engine.
Aug: Morris sets up Osberton Radiators at Cowley, helping H A Ryder and A L Davies (from Doherty Motor Components) to buy it.

1920 Jan: Cecil Cousins joins Morris Garages at Clarendon Yard.
Syd Enever, aged 15, joins Morris Garages in Queen Street.

1921 Cecil Kimber joins Morris Garages as sales manager. Enever moves to

MG the company

Clarendon Yard.

1922 Mar: Kimber becomes general manager, following departure of Edward Armstead, who commits suicide.
Autumn: First Morris Garages Chummy based on Morris Oxford with lowered springs, special paint and leather trim.

1923 1 Jan: William Morris buys Hollick & Pratt coachbuilders for £100,000 after a fire. Sold to Morris Motors in 1926. Morris also buys Osberton Radiators.
Feb: Chummy production goes from Longwall to Alfred Lane under Cecil Cousins.
Mar: Cecil Kimber takes Chummy on Land's End Trial with Russell Chiesman.
May: Hotchkiss factory in Gosford Road Coventry bought by Morris for £349,423. F G Woollard becomes works manager.
16 July: The Morris Company formed.
Nov: First appearance of octagonal MG logo in Morris Garages advertisement in *The Isis*.
Dec: Morris buys E G Wrigley.

1924 Jan: Miles Thomas joins W R Morris to launch *Morris Owner*.
May: *Morris Owner* carries advertisement

Top: Last big vintage MG, the magnificent 18/100 Tigress proved a disappointment at Brooklands.

for Morris Garages with MG octagon.

1925 13 Mar: Carbodies begins building 'Old Number One'. FC 7900 registered 27 March, 1925.
10-11 Apr: Land's End Trial. Kimber and Wilfred Matthews enter in FC 7900.
Sep: MG production starts Bainton Road alongside Osberton Radiators.

1926 28 Apr: The Pressed Steel Company registered at Cowley.
29 Jun: W R Morris sells personal businesses to Morris Motors; Osberton

Radiators becomes Morris Radiators Branch, Hotchkiss becomes Morris Engines Branch, and Hollick & Pratt becomes Morris Bodies Branch. Morris Motors established 1919 becomes Morris Motors (1926).
Sep: Flat-rad Morris Oxfords replace bull-nosed.
Dec: William Morris buys SU (Skinners' Union named after brothers who founded it) for £100,000. Renamed The SU Company.

1927 23 Feb: William Morris buys bankrupt Wolseley Motors for £730,000.
27 Jun: Morris Industries registered and takes over SU. Morris Industries supersedes The Morris Company.
2 July: The Morris Garages formed as limited company.
Apr-Sep: New £16,000 factory built for MG at Edmund Road Cowley.
29 Dec: MG takes Morris Light Six to build prototype 18/80 with MG radiator, designed with Ron Goddard of Radiators Branch, made by tinsmith named Cudd.

1928 Spring: The MG Car Company

(Proprietors: the Morris Garages) formed to make MG cars.

17 Aug: 18/80 Mark 1 announced in *The Autocar* with chassis drawn by Cecil Cousins.

31 Aug: *The Motor* announces Morris Minor at Austin Seven prices.

14 Sep: *The Motor* announces new Minor sports model as 'The Morris Midget … produced by the MG Car Company Ltd Oxford.'

11 Oct: Stand 150 at Olympia taken by MG showing Midget, 14/40 Mark IV, and 18/80.

1929 Mar: M-type Midget production begins at Edmund Road, Cowley.

Aug: Morris Motors (1926) becomes Morris Motors.

Sep: MG begins move to former Pavlova Leather factory at Abingdon-on-Thames Berks. H N Charles chief designer.

17 Oct: Olympia Motor Show: MG Midget Sportsmans Coupe.

1930 20 Jan: Inaugural luncheon at Abingdon.

11 Feb: MG shows plans for 18/100 Mark III Tigress.

21 July: MG Car Company takes over car manufacturing business from The Morris Garages. Cecil Kimber managing director. 19,000 £1 shares, of which 18,995 bought by Morris Industries. Remaining five held by William Morris, Cecil Kimber, Morris's secretary, solicitor, and accountant. Morris buys 51 Aldates and builds new Morris Garages garage with head office for £80,000.

Autumn: 'Safety Fast' becomes MG slogan.

5 Sep: Letter in The *Light Car* suggests an MG club.

Oct: Morris Garages assigns lease of Pavlova Leather Works to MG Car Company.

12 Oct: MG Car Club formed. John Thornley honorary secretary.

1931 3 Mar: Cecil Kimber announces 750cc Montlhéry Midget. Mock-up shown at Abingdon.

16 Mar: 750cc Montlhéry Midget Mark II, C-type announced.

4 Sep: F-type Magna 12/70 Six and four-scater Midget D-type introduced.

15 Oct: Olympia Motor Show. M-type Midget with all-metal body.

3 Nov: John Thornley starts at Abingdon as interviewer in service department.

1932 7 Jun: Mark III Montlhéry Midget

5 Aug: J2 Midget announced.

13 Oct: Olympia. Magnette on Stand 24.

26 Oct: First prototype K3 chassis K3751.

1933 Mar: L-type Magna. J4 in production.

Apr: Wolseley engineer Leonard Lord becomes MD of Morris Motors, aged 36.

May: First issue of The MG Magazine, price 6d (2°p).

July: Last 18/80.

5 Sep: Bigger engine for Magnette; J2 revised.

1934 Jan: Magic Magnette EX135 created for Eyston.

2 Mar: P-type Midget announced.

30 Mar: N-type Magnette announced.

19 Sep: KN Magnette pillarless saloon.

1935 15 Feb: Cresta Magnette; N-type with special body produced by E Bertelli of Feltham.

Apr: R-type.

Apr: *The Sports Car* replaces The MG Magazine.

1 July: William Morris sells MG Car Co

and Wolseley Motors (1927) to Morris Motors. Cecil Kimber becomes director of Morris Motors, but only general manager at MG, his place taken by Leonard Lord. Abingdon designers go to Cowley. Syd Enever remains head of experimental department.

5 July: *The Autocar* dismayed to hear MG will cease racing.

10 July: Formal transfer of MG shares from Morris Industries to Morris Motors.

21 Sep: Jaguar launches SS 2.6litre.

17 Oct: MG 2.0litre SA described 4 Oct in *The Autocar* appears at Olympia.

1936   24 Apr: MG SA Tickford Foursome drophead coupe launched.

19 Jun: MG Midget TA replaces PB.

Jul: Charlesworth-bodied SA 2.0-litre Tourer.

27 Aug: L P Lord resigns as MD after Morris refuses request for shareholding. His place taken by Oliver Boden.

2 Oct: MG VA 1°litre advertised 'For space for grace for pace...'

1937   Oct: Charlesworth SA 2.0-litre tourer modified.

1938   Feb: Receiver appointed for Riley.

Summer: MG WA launched.

19 Aug: MG TA Tickford launched.

8 Sep: Riley (Coventry) registered by William Morris and sold to Morris Motors.

1939   May: TB Midget replaces TA.

Mar: Oliver Boden dies, replaced as vice chairman by Miles Thomas

1940   May: Morris Motors renamed the Nuffield Organization.

1941   Nov: Cecil Kimber sacked by Miles Thomas.

1944   2 Oct: Morris Garages acquires Charles Raworth.

1945   4 Feb: Cecil Kimber killed in railway accident.

Apr: Cowley prepared for MG TC Midget, under direction of H A Ryder.

Sep: Nuffield Metal Products formed, incorporating Morris Pressings Branch, set up in 1939.

17 Sep: First production MG TC (Nr 0252, engine Nr 1163) .

Oct: MG TC Midget launched.

1947   1 Jan: RAC horsepower tax changes to annual tax based on engine size. Replaced a year later by flat annual fee of £10.

Above: artist's licence. Sales brochure flattery of TD Midget in Trafalgar Square.

May: MG Y-series saloon launched.

Aug: Reginald Hanks and Sydney Smith become directors of Morris Motors.

19 Nov: Sir Miles Thomas resigns as chairman of Nuffield Group. Reginald Hanks becomes vice chairman and restructures board. Sydney Smith takes charge of MG at Cowley, 'Pop' Propert at Abingdon.

Feb: Minister of Supply, George Strauss, announces steel allocated only to manufacturers that export over 75% of output.

27 Oct: Earls Court Motor Show. MG YT open four-seater tourer. Morris Minor MM launched. Austin and Nuffield Organization in exploratory talks, which cease by July 1949.

Dec: US-spec MG TC Midget still right-hand drive.

1949 Jan: Wolseley moves from Ward End in Birmingham to Cowley.

1 May: Riley production transferred from Foleshill to Abingdon. Riley factory becomes part of Morris Engines. Wolseley turns to machining and tractors as Tractor & Transmissions Branch.

20 July: Jack Tallow (ex-Riley) takes over from Propert as MG's general manager at Abingdon.

10 Nov: first production MG TD (chassis 0252); last TC (Serial Nr 10,001, chassis 10,251).

1950 18 Jan: MG TD Midget launched.

15 Apr: EX 135 shown at New York Motor Show.

May: production MG TD Midget Mk II.

Jun: petrol rationing ends.

Above: author's cherished MGA, 1960.

1951 Dec: 10,000th Abingdon car:Riley 2°L.

17 Oct: MG YB at Earls Court Motor Show.

1952 31 Mar: Nuffield Motors and Austin form British Motor Corporation (BMC); Leonard Lord deputy chairman and MD Lord Nuffield chairman.

21 Oct: Leonard Lord agrees to Austin-Healey 100. EX 175 rejected.

3 Nov: John Thornley, assistant general manager, takes over as general manager at Abingdon.

Dec: TD Mark II, produced since May

1950 alongside standard TD, gets enamel badges and black and white MG logos instead of brown and cream. On introduction of TF in 1953 all MG badges are black and white.

17 Dec: Lord Nuffield resigns; L P Lord to be chairman.

1953 8 Jan: TF prototype EX 177 presented to BMC's joint board of management.

Mar: Gerald Palmer's twin-cam engine approved for development at Morris Engines.

4 Apr: MG TD-based open and coupe Arnolt Family-and-Sports Car at New York International Motor Sports Show.

17 Aug: Last TD, chassis no TD/29,915.

Sep: First TF; chassis no TF/501.

21 Oct: MG ZA Magnette and TF Midget at Earls Court show.

Dec: A V Oak, technical director at Cowley since January 1943, retires.

1954 6 Jun: First drawing for DO1062 (MGA).

Jun: Drawing office set up at Abingdon. Staff transferred from Cowley.

July: MG TF 1500, Midget name dropped.

Terry Mitchell starts work on DO1062.

MG the company

Aug: Syd Enever starts to develop EX 175.

Sep: Last MG TF 1250.

1 Dec: BMC Competitions Department opens at Abingdon under Marcus Chambers.

1955 Apr: MGA launch postponed to June, then September.

Last MG TF 1500 chassis no TF/10,100.

16 May: First production MGA made.

16 Jul: First production MGA leaves factory.

22 Sep: MGA at Frankfurt Motor show.

19 Oct: MGA at Earls Court show.

Nov: Alec Issigonis returns to BMC Longbridge.

1956 1 Feb: Don Hayter joins MG design Abingdon as senior layout draughtsman.

16 May: 100,000th MG, left-hand drive MGA 1500 tourer, built at Abingdon.

Sep: ZB Magnette launched.

Sep: MGA coupe announced.

12 Oct: Production version of MGA Vanden Plas alloy hardtop.

17 Oct: Earls Court. MGA Coupe and ZB Magnette Manumatic and Varitone.

1957 31 Jan: Donald Healey shows George

Harriman Q1 prototype Austin-Healey Sprite; production begins at Abingdon in 1958.

11 July: EX181 leaves Southampton on Queen Mary for the USA.

Nov: production of Austin-Healey 100/6 BN4 transferred from Longbridge to Abingdon. Donald and Geoffrey Healey become consultants.

1958 20 May: Austin-Healey Sprite Mark 1 launched.

Below: Abingdon assembly. Varied production including MGAs, ZA Magnettes and (far left) Riley Pathfinders.

19 Jun: EX214/1 MGB prototype drawing completed by Don Hayter.

15 July: MGA Twin Cam launched; 100 journalists drive four at the Fighting Vehicles R&D establishment at Chobham, Surrey. One crashes, one breaks down.

12 Nov: Pininfarina Magnette Mark III launched, built at Cowley.

Dec: MG ZB Magnette discontinued.

1959 Mar: Austin-Healey 3000 launched. Built at Abingdon.

Apr: First issue of *Safety Fast.*

May: production starts of MGA 1600 with 1588cc B-series engine.

1 July: Austin-Healey 3000 replaces 100-Six.

31 July: MGA 1600 launched. MGA 1500 earned $60 million from the USA.

26 Aug: Morris Mini Minor (ADO15) launched.

1960 Spring: MGA Twin Cam discontinued.

May: Pressed Steel begins first MGB prototype.

Nov: Innocenti of Italy launches 998cc Spyder based on Austin-Healey Sprite.

Dec: production of Sprite Mk I ends.

MG the company

Above: MGA as a club rally car. Irish competitor sets off downhill on Rest-and-Be-Thankful on the RSAC Scottish Rally.

1961   May: Austin-Healey Sprite Mark II launched.
Jun: Midget Mark I (GAN 1) launched. First use of plastic, red-backed, chrome octagon on black shield for grille badge. Later adopted for MGB and 1100.
Jun: MGA 1600 Mark II launched.
July: Mini Cooper with 997cc A-series engine introduced.
26 Jul: MGB design abandons radical rear suspension.
Sep: Roy Brocklehurst becomes MG project engineer.

18 Sep: introduction of MG Magnette Mark IV.
30 Sep: Marcus Chambers' place taken by Stuart Turner.

1962   Mar: New York Motor Show. 100,000th MGA from Abingdon displayed in metallic gold with cream leather trim and gold painted wire wheels.
24 Mar: First production MGB, left-hand-drive, Iris Blue, GHN3-102. 12 production cars built by May, including right-hand-drive GHN3-101.
Jul: MGA 1600 Mk II discontinued; final chassis no GHN2-109071.
20 Sep: AD023 MGB launched.
2 Oct: MG 1100 (ADO16) announced.
17 Oct: Earls Court. MG 1100 and MGB shown. MG Midget Mk I and Austin-Healey Sprite Mk II appear with 1098cc engine. Midget GAN2. Debut of Triumph Spitfire.

1963   4 Apr: MGB assembled at BMC Australia Zetland New South Wales.

1964   Jan: John Thornley awarded OBE for services to Air Training Corps.
Jan: Jacques Coune's MGB Berlinette at Brussels Motor Show.

11 Feb: Design work starts on MGB replacement, EX234.
9 Mar: MG Midget Mark II (GAN3).
Oct: 5-bearing B-series engine supersedes 3-bearing in MGB.

1965   July: BMC makes offer for Pressed Steel effective September 1965.
22 Jul: Rover buys Alvis.
20 Oct: MGB GT at Earls Court.

1966   Jun: Leonard Lord, now Lord Lambury, retires from BMC board. George Harriman becomes chairman, Joe Edwards managing director.
11 Jul: BMC and Jaguar agree merger, finalised in December.
19 Oct: MG Midget Mark III (GAN4) launched at Earls Court with 1275cc A-series engine. Also Austin-Healey Sprite Mark IV.
3 Nov: Assembly of pre-production MGC begins at Abingdon, two months after Healeys reject BMC's proposed Austin-Healey 3000 Mark IV. 13 pre-production MGCs built for development.
11 Dec: Leyland agrees merger with Rover, effective March 1967.
14 Dec: BMC and Jaguar announce new

1967   joint holding company: British Motor Holdings. Joe Edwards becomes BMH chief executive under Sir George Harriman.

Feb: Industry Minister Anthony Wedgwood Benn announces exploratory talks between Leyland and BMH to House of Commons.

Mar: BMC Comps Stuart Turner replaced by Peter Browning.

18 Oct: MGC, MGC GT and MGB Mark II at Earls Court. MG 1100 Mark II launched.

Oct: Merger discussions between BMH and Leyland follow meeting at Chequers between George Harriman (BMH), and Donald Stokes (Leyland), at invitation of prime minister Harold Wilson.

6 Nov: Design centre established at Cowley under Roy Haynes. Dick Burzi keeps small studio at Longbridge.

Nov: first cars to meet new US safety and emissions requirements built with 'Abingdon Pillow' padded dashboards and dual-circuit brakes. Austin-Healey 3000 Mark III discontinued. Single car built for UK in May 1968.

1968   Jan: Harris Mann joins Austin-Morris styling studio.

17 Jan: £320 million merger of Leyland Motor Corporation with BMH forms British Leyland Motor Corporation. Cars divided into Austin-Morris (including MG) and Specialist Cars (with separate Rover, Triumph and Jaguar boards).

Apr: MG 1300 replaces 1100 Mark II. Joe Edwards resigns from BMH prior to formation of BLMC. Harry Webster and

Below: MG might-have-beens. Roger Stanbury's 18/80 and Eric Dymock's 2-litre Twin Cam fuel-injected 5-speed Heritage shell MGB.

George Turnbull, ex Triumph, in charge of Austin-Morris.

8 Apr: end of production of Magnette Mark IV.

14 May: British Leyland Motor Corporation created.

22 May: Roy Haynes proposes MG ADO28 (Morris Marina).

Aug: Harry Webster announces advanced engineering and conservative styling for Austin, more style and conservative engineering for Morris.

5 Aug: BLMC board views three AD028 prototypes by Pininfarina, Michelotti, and Roy Haynes. Haynes's proposals accepted.

Sep: Sir George Harriman retires.

15 Oct: Earls Court show. Sir Donald Stokes instructs comps department to go for outright wins.

16 Oct: MG 1300 Mark II launched at Motor Show; two-door only.

1969   Apr: Austin-Morris design transferred from Cowley to studio formerly occupied by Dick Burzi. Interior design remains at Cowley until October.

27 June: John Thornley retires, replaced

by Les Lambourne, assistant general manager.

July: Riley 1300 production discontinued; Riley 4/72 carries on until October.

4 Aug: MGC production stops.

18 Sep: last MGC leaves Abingdon.

19 Sep: BLMC board approves ADO67, the Austin Allegro of 1973.

11 Oct: British Leyland facelift MG Midget and MGB with recessed matt black grilles.

15 Oct: Mini Clubman and 1275GT at Earls Court. Austin and Morris 1300 GT effectively replaces MG 1300. Austin-Morris interior design moves from Cowley to Longbridge.

5 Nov: Abingdon starts work on mid-engined AD021.

1970 Jan: Roy Haynes leaves BLMC.

Autumn: Engineers Spen King and Mike Carver visit USA to research market for new TR sports car. Competition between Austin-Morris styling Longbridge, Triumph Canley, and Michelotti. MG Abingdon not invited to put forward mid-engined AD021.

14 Oct: Austin Maxi 1750 introduced at Earls Court, with longer-stroke E4 engine planned for AD0 21.

31 Oct: Abingdon Comps Department closes. Special Tuning continues as low-cost unit.

4 Nov: MG ADO21 full-size clay viewed by British Leyland management.

29 Dec: Work on ADO21 ceases.

1971 Jan: Austin-Healey Sprite rebadged Austin. Healey royalties stop.

27 May: 250,000th MGB, left-hand-drive Blaze MGB GT, completed at Abingdon.

May: Enever retires as chief engineer. Roy Brockleburst takes over.

July: Austin-Morris styling studio MG Magna proposal for new BLMC corporate sports car approved and becomes Triumph TR7. Last Mini Cooper, last Austin Sprite.

4 Aug: Abingdon instructed to build MGB GT V8, following assessment of Costello car.

31 Aug: MG 1300 Mark II discontinued.

1972 Mar: Rover-Triumph created under Sir George Farmer. Board has seven Rover and five Triumph members.

Spring: MG SSV1 experimental safety vehicle shown at Washington road safety exhibition.

4 May: MG Midget with round rear wheel arches.

Aug: MGB range facelifted for 1973 MY.

Sep: O-series engine emerges as overhead-cam B-series. Soft bumpers approved for MGB.

6 Nov: Last MGB produced in Australia.

12 Dec: Production of MGB GT V8 starts.

1973 Feb: British Leyland plans MGB in case TR7 is late; O-series engine due April 1974.

July: Roy Brockleburst transferred to BL Advanced Engineering. Don Hayter becomes chief engineer at Abingdon.

15 Aug: MGB GT V8 launched.

Sep: Bumper overriders for MG Midget, MGB and MGB GTs in the USA

1974 Jan: Work starts on ADO88.

Summer: O-series engine decided on for MGB and Marina by 1977 model year, autumn 1976. Delayed to 1978 MY.

Jul: British Leyland cash crisis. Banks discuss £150 million loan.

16 Oct: Soft bumpers in production for

MG the company

Midget, MGB, MGB GT and MGB GT V8. Midget adopts Triumph Spitfire 1493cc engine.
27 Nov: Banks and government discuss BLMC's finances.
3 Dec: Triumph Spitfire 1500 launched in UK with same engine as Midget 1500.
6 Dec: Tony Benn tells Parliament government guarantees BLMC's capital.
18 Dec: Sir Don Ryder, governmental industrial advisor, appointed to investigate BLMC.

1975 1 Jan: MGB GT withdrawn from USA.
Jan: Triumph TR7 two-door sports coupe announced for sale only in USA.
26 Mar: Ryder Report recommends government contribution of £2.8 billion over seven years; company split into four divisions: cars, trucks and buses, international, and special products.
May: David Bache appointed design director.
Jun: Overdrive made standard on UK-market MGBs.
27 Jun: British Leyland Motor Corporation renamed British Leyland; government 99.8% shareholder.

11 Aug: British Leyland formally nationalised.
Sep: Endurance testing of prototype O-series engines in MGB, Princess and Marina.
13 Sep: Austin-Morris 18-22 series is renamed Princess as first post-Ryder marque realignment.
16 Dec: Government secures Chrysler UK with £162.5 million.

1976 19 May: Triumph TR7 introduced in UK and Europe.
Jun: MGB withdrawn from Continental Europe.
Jun: Rover SD1 3500 launched with aluminium 3528cc V8.
July: last two MGB GT V8s made at Abingdon after production ends in June.

1977 Jan: Work restarts on 'federalising' O-series engine for MGB, aiming for introduction in 1980.
Feb: pilot-build of Triumph TR7 Sprint and TR7 V8 begins at Speke.
1 Nov: Michael Edwardes joins British Leyland.

1978 Jan: ADO88 replaced by slightly larger LC8 project.

Feb: Edwardes reveals plan to reorganise Austin-Morris including MG, and Jaguar-Rover-Triumph.
15 Feb: Proposal for Speke factory to close and move TR7 production to Canley.
1 Apr: BL Motorsport Abingdon homologates TR7 V8 rally car.
3 Apr: government provides £450 million equity in British Leyland.
26 May: Triumph TR7 production ends at Speke. TR7 Sprint and Lynx cancelled. TR7 V8 – the TR8 – delayed two years.
1 July: British Leyland renamed BL. Leyland name stays on commercial vehicles. Austin-Morris is under Ray Horrocks, and Jaguar-Rover-Triumph under William Pratt-Thompson.
July: Development MGB with O-series engine presented to BL management. Approval of £275 million for LC8 Metro.
July: 1.7- and 2-litre O-series engines introduced in Princess 2 range.
8 Aug: John Z DeLorean builds factory in Belfast Northern Ireland for making sports cars with government grants.
Aug: BL exploratory talks with Honda.

Sep: 1.7-L O-series engine for Marina 2.

Sep: MG becomes part of Jaguar-Rover-Triumph.

Oct: Triumph TR7 production restarts at Canley after five-month gap. US dealers unhappy with deliveries.

1979 1 Apr: Peter Mitchell joins BL Heritage, later British Motor Heritage.

Apr: US-market MGB Limited Edition (LE) model introduced at New York Motor Show.

15 May: Memorandum of understanding between BL and Honda. New Triumph saloon to be built at Canley based on Honda Ballade/Civic. Introduction planned October 1981.

Jun: Sharp rise in strength of sterling affects BL, in particular US exports. BL forms CORE (Co-ordination of Resources) strategy. Edwardes Plan streamlines company.

9 July: BL meets industry minister Sir Keith Joseph to discuss funding of LC10.

Jul: Triumph TR7 convertible launched five years after TR7 coupe, for USA only.

Aug: Midget production runs down; among the last are 500 for Japan.

Assembly of Vanden Plas 1500 transferred to Abingdon. Golden Jubilee at Abingdon.

10 Sep: Announcement of closure of AEC Park Royal. BL plans to end production of MG sports cars at Abingdon and manufacturing at Canley.

13 Sep: John Thornley invites 445 US Jaguar-Rover-Triumph-MG dealers to urge BL to continue MGB production.

26 Sep: BL claims loss of £900 on every MGB. Austin Allegro 3 launched.

30 Sep: MG clubs London protest rally

14 Oct: Alan Curtis of Aston Martin Lagonda and Peter Sprague in the USA

prepare bid for MG marque and MGB.

16 Oct: Curtis discusses bid with consortium.

17 Oct: Union leaders recommend BL workers accept Edwardes Plan.

18 Oct: Consortium led by Aston Martin Lagonda announces bid to take over MG name and factory.

1 Nov: BL workforce ballot: 80% vote, of which 87.2% accepts Edwardes Plan

6 Nov: Californian MG dealers and 416-strong US JRT dealer council threaten to sue BL for £100 million if MGB withdrawn. BL says MGBs will remain available until 1981, pledges to keep the MG marque.

12 Dec: last MG Midget down Abingdon production line, a black UK-specification car for the British Motor Heritage collection, brings total to 224,817.

Dec: BL discusses MG Boxer project, low-cost MG offshoot from Triumph TR7, to placate US JRT dealers. Idea abandoned early in 1980, and MG returned to Austin-Morris from JRT.

20 Dec: BL says government agrees to recovery plan and a further £205 million.

1980

Jan: 500,000th MGB, a black roadster, built at Abingdon.

14 Jan: Jaguar-Rover-Triumph issue press release: 'MGBs will be produced until late 1980 ... available into early 1981. The MG name will be retained and there are plans to build a successor to the MGB when production ends at Abingdon.'

31 Mar: Aston Martin consortium meets BL board, agreeing £30 million deal for exclusive world-wide license to MG name and Abingdon factory.

Apr 1980: Triumph TR7 production begins at Rover in Solihull, overlapping with production at Canley.

1 July: Aston Martin announces nearly half required £30m has been withdrawn. Last hope is that Japanese and Arab backers provide £12m. Aston Martin makes a quarter of workforce redundant.

2 July: William Pratt-Thompson, head of BL International, announces Abingdon factory to be sold.

4 July: Alan Curtis talks with Japanese in an effort to acquire funds for take-over.

9 July: BL car divisions reorganised again: JRT dissolved, Jaguar becomes separate once more. Volume cars (Austin-Morris) absorbs Rover and Triumph to form Light Medium Cars (LMC). Cars Commercial looks after marketing and product planning. Triumph Spitfire discontinued. LM10 approved by BL board for 1983 launch.

Aug: last production-specification MGB bodyshell produced at Pressed Steel, Stratton St Margaret, Swindon.

8 Oct: Austin Metro launched.

17 Oct: Austin Metro at NEC Motor Show, Birmingham.

23 Oct: last MGB goes down the line at Abingdon.

24 Oct: MG factory at Abingdon closes.

1981

Jan: £990 million further state funding of BL over next two years.

26 Jan: announcement by BL of last MGB derivative, the UK-only MGB and MGB GT LE.

Feb: Henry Ford II acquires one of the last US-specification MGB LEs for the Ford Museum.

18/24 Mar: Auction of MG factory contents: 434 buyers, 3600 lots, totalling £100,000 for BL.

10 May: BL claims Jaguar loses £2 million per month due to unfavourable dollar/sterling exchange.

13 May: Ray Horrocks of BL announces Solihull Rover factory to close for all but Land Rover.

16 May: final auction of Abingdon contents.

15 Jun: BL Motorsport moves to Cowley. Plans laid for MG Metro 6R4.

26 July: *Sunday Times* says BL plans MG-badged version of the Metro.

6 Aug: MG is among names considered for performance Metro.

Sep: Austin Allegro discontinued.

7 Oct: Triumph Acclaim launched.

12 Nov: Ray Horrocks and Honda sign co-operative agreement in Tokyo for new executive car, coded XX.

1982

Jan: Banks agree to lend BL £277 million over 8-10 years. David Bache resigns as design director following management disagreements, replaced by Roy Axe, formerly of Chrysler.

May: Austin Rover Group formed from Austin, Morris, MG, Rover and Triumph. Harold Musgrove chairman and chief executive.

5 May: MG Metro 1300 announced.

1 July: BL announces Morris name to be phased out.

22 Oct: MG Metro Turbo announced at Motor Show.

Nov: Sir Michael Edwardes leaves BL, publishes *Back From The Brink*.

1983 Feb: MG Metro 6R4 prototype handed over by Williams Engineering to Austin Rover Motorsport at Cowley.

1 Mar: Austin Maestro range includes MG1600.

Apr: new director of interior design is Richard Hamblin, reporting to Roy Axe. Gordon Sked is director of exterior design.

11 Jun: Interim facelift for Metro includes MG.

1984 31 Mar: MG Metro 6R4 has competition debut in a Yorkshire rally with Tony Pond.

25 Apr: Montego range includes 2-litre fuel-injected MG version with O-series engine. S-series replaces R-series in MG Maestro 1600. LC10 has cost £210 million. BL reports first operating profit,

£4.1 million, since 1978.

19 Jun: British Motor Industry Heritage Trust (BMIHT) appoints David Bishop, ex materials control manager at Austin-Morris Body Plant Cowley, assistant MD.

10 Aug: Jaguar privatised. Government keeps 'golden share' until end of 1990.

Sep: Austin Rover formed as LMC is integrated with Cars Commercial.

3 Oct: MG Maestro 2.0 EFi replaces 1.6-litre S-series-engined version.

1985 3 Apr: MG Montego Turbo.

8 May: Harold Musgrove announces Austin Rover Cars of North America (ARCONA) in partnership with Norman Braman to launch Austin Rover/Honda XX in the USA in 1987.

Jun: FISA bans four-wheel drive Group B cars for 1987, substituting Group S and limiting power to 300bhp (223.71kW).

19 Sep: MG EX-E concept car launched at Frankfurt Motor Show.

1 Nov: MG Metro 6R4 homologated for international debut on RAC Rally.

1986 2 Feb: Roy Hattersley tells Parliament General Motors wants to buy Leyland Trucks and Land Rover.

Apr: MG Maestro introduced in Japan. Design studios at Canley reorganised: Gordon Sked director of production design studio; Richard Hamblin director of concept design studio.

1 May: Graham Day appointed chairman of BL.

2 May: Henri Toivonen and Sergio Cresto killed in Lancia Delta S4 Group B rally car.

3 May: Jean-Marie Balestre of FISA announces Group B rally cars banned from Jan 1987; Group S abandoned.

Jul: BL renamed Rover Group

15 July: Honda/Rover joint project XX launched as Rover 800 series.

Sep: Harold Musgrove leaves Rover Group.

Dec: David Bishop starts British Motor Heritage MGB bodyshell project.

1987 18 Apr: US-market Sterling (Rover 800) launched at New York Motor Show.

May: Austin Rover Motorsport Division at Cowley closed down.

Nov: Sterling 800 range on sale in the USA.

1988 29 Feb: First MGB bodyshell produced

at Faringdon.

1 Mar: British Aerospace (BAe) talks with government about acquisition of Rover.

30 Mar: British Aerospace buys Rover Group for £150 million, the government writing off £800 million debt. £2.98 billion in state aid received since 1975.

13 Apr: British Motor Heritage launches MGB bodyshell.

22 Oct: MG Maestro Turbo announced at Birmingham Motor Show, to be built by Tickford.

19 Dec: MG-badged coupe based on planned cabriolet derivative of the Rover 200 (R8) photographed for the archives.

1989 Jan: Rover board restructured. Graham Day hands over to George Simpson, board members reduced from 36 to 11. John Towers becomes production engineering director and Graham Morris takes over as Sterling president from Chris Woodwark.

14 July 1989: Honda announces £300 million first European assembly plant at Swindon, and 20% equity stake in Rover. Rover takes 20% stake in HUM (Honda UK Manufacturing).

18 Sep: Graham Day suggests sports car. Project Phoenix to investigate three MG concepts, with different engine/drive train configurations: PR1, PR2 and PR3. 'PR' stands for Phoenix Route, nicknamed 'Pocket Rocket'.

11 Oct: New Rover 200 range launched at London Motorfair. First production application of K-series engine.

Oct: Roy Axe takes charge of Rover's advanced design studio. Richard Hamblin works on Project Phoenix, and places contracts for running prototypes.

1 Dec: Shareholders accept Ford's cash offer for Jaguar.

1990 28 Mar: Executive committee approves activities leading to Rover Special Products (RSP) running prototypes.

Mar: Work starts on Heritage MGB V8 project; Mark Gamble builds prototype at Snitterfield, to be completed by May.

2 May: Launch of revamped Metro with 1.1- and 1.4-litre K-series engines. Top of range GTi not an MG.

Jun: Rover board reviews PR1, PR2, PR3 and PR4 (similar to PR2, but with a steel body). PR3 increased in size.

19 Sep: Graham Day tells press at Motor Show, 'We are going to do a proper MG.'

1991 Jan: Rover commissions consultants MGA and ADC to develop styling clays based on PR3 mid-engined layout. John Towers becomes MD in charge of product supply.

Apr: Rover Special Products researches significance of MG badge to potential customers.

May: Two styling models for PR3 presented. Rover approves PR3 from development to 'D Zero'.

Jun: Customer clinic tests of sports car concepts; leads to rejection of pop-up headlamps and abandonment of PR5, seen as a Jaguar/Aston Martin style, not MG. Rover management approves RV8.

July: proposal of PR3 1.6-litre K-series engine with optional supercharger.

9 Aug: Rover Group drops US Sterling marque; servicing back-up for Sterling models maintained.

Sep: Gerry McGovern begins work on styling clay for PR3 at Canley.

Autumn: MG-badged saloons discontinued after MG Maestro and

Montego 2.0i.

Dec: Roy Axe forms independent consultancy. Gordon Sked now in charge of Rover design.

1992 Jan: MG RV8 prototype presented at Rover dealer conference.

22 Jan: Styling of PR3 clay model approved.

3 Mar: Geneva show. Rover 200 Cabriolet launched (Project Tracer nearly became an MG). Rover 800 coupe also launched.

Mar: Styling of PR3 approved. Rover staff invited to give opinions on elements of an MG.

Jun: Teaser brochure for RV8 issued with studio photograph of DEV1 prototype, 'The Shape of Things to Come'.

18 Sep: MG Car Club, MG Owners' Club and others invited to preview of MG RV8 at Canley.

20 Oct: RV8 launched by John Towers at Birmingham Motor Show, together with Rover 200 coupe.

Nov: Rover board approves 1.8-litre K-series with optional VVC.

Dec: PR3 design signed off. Mayflower and Rover agree Mayflower to raise £24

Above: MG 75th anniversary limited edition MGF, 1999.

million for design, engineering and production of bodyshells.

1993 Mar: Rover board approves PR3. Launch planned for 1995.

31 Mar: Mayflower investment includes rights issue to raise £34.6 million. Production of over 10,000 a year expected, with sales of £20 million for a 6-year contract.

31 Mar: First production MG RV8 at Cowley for BMH museum (chassis Nr 251, British Racing Green metallic). First six customer cars completed on 19 April.

Apl: Rover 620 launched.

Oct: Woodcote Green MG RV8 at Tokyo Motor Show.

1994 13 Jan: First 46 RV8s leave Southampton for Japan.

31 Jan: Sale of Rover Group to BMW AG for £800 million.

21 Feb: Honda relinquishes 20% shareholding in Rover, which releases its 20% in Honda's UK manufacturing subsidiary.

18 Mar: Title and ownership of Rover Group officially transferred to BMW AG. Rover Group comprises two sub-groups: Rover Group Holdings plc, Birmingham (with 89 subsidiaries) and Rover Group USA Inc, Lanham, Maryland (with four subsidiaries).

July: Pre-production examples of MGF completed, using final tooling.

Sep: Pilot production of MGF.

1995 6 Feb: Preview of MGF for MG Car Club, MG Owners' Club, Octagon Car Club at Gaydon.

20/24 Feb: Dealer MGF launch.

7 Mar: MGF launched at Geneva.

May: Rover 416 and 420 launched.

MG the company

4 Aug: First volume-production MGF built at Longbridge CAB2.

23 Sep: First customer MGF deliveries.

Oct: MGF makes its UK and Japanese Motor Show debuts.

Nov: Rover 214 and 216 launched.

22 Nov: Last MG RV8, Woodcote Green bound for Japan.

1996 1 Feb: MGF awarded 'Japanese Import Car of The Year'. 300 MGFs sold in Japan, and a further 1200 ordered.

21 Feb: Test session at Castle Combe for Japanese journalists to drive MGF development car.

1 Jun: John Towers leaves Rover BMW.

1 Sep: Walter Hasselkus becomes chief executive of Rover Group.

Oct: Rover 200vi launched.

1997 4 July: Unions and Rover BMW management agree 3 year deal for jobs and investment.

1998 20 May: Rover Oxford plan inaugurated

July: Rover reduces workforce by 3000.

Aug: Unions and BMW agree changes in working practices.

Sep: Rover BRM Limited Edition 200

21 Oct: Rover 75 replaces 400 and 600;

sales and productivity warning.

Dec: Hasselkus retires, replaced by Bernard Sämann.

1999 5 Feb: Bernd Pischetsreider and Wolfgang Reitzle resign from BMW board.

Aug: MGF designer Gerry McGovern leaves.

Oct: Rover 25 replaces 200 series. Rover 45 replaces 400 series.

Oct: BMW and Alchemy engage in talks about Rover's disposal.

2000 Mar 16: Alchemy Partners led by Jon Moulton makes unsuccessful bid for Rover.

May: Phoenix consortium buys Rover from BMW. Phoenix consists of John Towers, Nick Stephenson and David Bowes (Lola Engineering), Terry Whitmore (Mayflower), John Edwards (Rover dealers), Brian Parker (non-executive) and Peter Beale. Parker and Whitmore later resign.

May: Kevin Howe appointed CEO Longbridge.

June: Chris Bowen operations director, Bob Beddow human resources, John

Parkinson sales and marketing, John Millett finance and strategy, Rob Oldaker product development join management board.

July 7: Peter Stephens, former McLaren, Lamborghini, Jaguar, and Lotus designer joins MG Rover.

Aug: Plan announced for Le Mans joint venture with Lola.

2001 30 Jan: New MG range on show at Longbridge.

Rover production line moved to Longbridge.

1923 Land's End Trial: Cecil Kimber drives Morris Oxford Chummy with Russell Chiesman.

1925 Land's End Trial: Kimber drives 'Old Number One' FC7900 with Wilfred Matthews, wins one of three 1st class awards.
MCC High Speed trial, Brooklands: two 1st class awards.

1926 MCC High Speed trial, Brooklands: 1st class award.

1927 San Martin Circuit Race near Buenos Aires: first MG race victory. A 14/40 wins 100km (62-mile) race outright.

1929 JCC High Speed Trial Brooklands: Five 1st class awards.
MCC High Speed Trial Brooklands: five 1st class awards MCC High Speed Trial Brooklands.
Mont des Mules hill climb, Monte Carlo: 3rd fastest.

1930 Double Twelve Race, Brooklands: Team Prize; Randall/Montgomery (M-type) 3rd in class, 14th overall; Townend/Jackson 5th; Roberts/Pollard 6th. Stisted/Black 4th in class. Worseley/Foster 7th in class. MG 18/100 Tigress fails after two hours.

Land's End Trial: 18 1st class awards.
Le Mans 24-hour race: first MG entries by Huskinson and Fane (28) and Captain FHB Samuelson (29). Huskinson/Fane entry driven by Murton-Neale/Hicks crashes with damaged steering and retires after 82 laps with broken crankshaft. Samuelson/Kindell retire after 28 laps with bearing failure.
Monte des Mules hill climb Monte Carlo: class win.
RAC Trial. Kenneth Marsh (standard MG Midget): 100 consecutive ascents of Beggars Roost without stopping engine.
Zbrazlav-Jiloviste, Czechoslavakia: hill climb, class win.

1931 Brooklands 500-mile (805km) handicap race. Eddie Hall (s/seater C-type) 3rd overall, class win; winning team.
Double Twelve race, Brooklands: 14 Montlhéry C-types entered and take first 5 places. Four teams entered by the Earl of March, Cecil Randall, ATG Gardner and the Hon. Mrs Chetwynd. Earl of March/Staniland finish 1st, Gibson/Fell 2nd, Hamilton 3rd; Parker/Cox 4th, Black/Fiennes 5th.
Irish Grand prix: 1st and 3rd.
Le Mans 24-hour race: two u/s C-types, Samuelson/Kindell (31) and Mrs Chetwynd/Mrs Stisted (32). Samuelson disqualified for slow final lap. Chetwynd retires with sheared timing gear key.
Monte Carlo Rally: Sir Francis Samuelson

Left: Earl of March Brooklands Double 12 1931.

Right: Norman Black winner of 1931 Ulster TT. Earl of March (left), MG mechanic Frankie Tayler (right) died in the Kaye Don Isle of Man accident in 1934.

enters M-type Sportsmans Coupe.

Saorstat Cup race, Dublin: 1st, 2nd, 3rd and team prize.

Ulster Tourist Trophy race: Black (C-type Midget 42) 1st 67.9mph (109.27kph), 0.9mph (1.45kph) faster than lap record; Crabtree 3rd.

1932   Le Mans 24-hour race: Samuelson/Black (s/c C-type 32) retire with punctured fuel tank after 53 laps.

Ulster Tourist Trophy: Eddie Hall (C-type) 3rd; Hamilton crashes in practice.

1933   Australian Grand Prix: 3rd.

Avusrennen: class win.

British Empire Trophy Brooklands: 3rd.

Brooklands 500mile handicap race: Eddie Hall (single-seater K3 chassis K3006) 1st.

Coppa Acerbo Junior race, Pescara, Italy: Whitney Straight beats Maseratis in K3.

Craigantlet hill climb, Belfast: FTD.

Eifelrennen: class win.

Freiburg and Riesenberg hill climbs: Class wins.

International trophy, Brooklands: 2nd, 3rd, 4th; 1st, 2nd and 3rd in class.

Le Mans 24-hour race: Ford/Baumer (s/c C-type Midget 41) achieve first finish in

6th overall, 1482.15 miles (2385.22km) at 61.7mph (99.29kph). MG 1st 750cc, 2nd in Index of Performance.

Mille Miglia, Brescia, Italy: three MG K3 Magnettes entered by Earl Howe, managed by Hugh McConnell. George Eyston and Count Giovanni 'Johnny' Lurani (39) 1st in class; Earl Howe/Hamilton (42) 2nd in class; Birkin/Rubin (41) do not finish but set new record for Brescia section.

Mont des Mules hillclimb, Monte Carlo: G W J H Wright (K3) wins class and breaks class record.

Monte Carlo rally: K3 2nd in braking and acceleration tests, 64th out of 69 overall.

Phoenix Park, Dublin: 1st.

RAC Mannin Beg race Isle of Man: Mansell's Midget one of two finishers of 14 starters.

Relay Race Brooklands: 1st.

Southport 100 Miles Race: 1st.

Ulster Tourist Trophy race: Tazio Nuvolari in K3 (17, chassis K3003 – the Eyston/Lurani Mille Miglia car) wins 40sec ahead of Hamilton in a J4 (25). Nuvolari breaks lap record.

1934   Mille Miglia, Brescia, Italy: three K3 Magnettes with Roots superchargers entered by Earl Howe, managed by Hugh McConnell. Howe/Thomas crash; Eddie Hall/Joan Hall retire; Penn-Hughes/Lurani 2nd in class.

RAC Mannin Beg race, Isle of Man: Norman Black (K3 Magnette 22) 1st; Dodson (K3 Magnette) 2nd; Eyston (offset single-seater Magnette 8) 3rd; Martin (K3 Magnette 12) 4th; Eccles (K3 Magnette) 5th; Ronnie Horton (offset single-seater K3 Magnette) 7th; Everitt (Q-type Midget 15) 8th. Handley (K3 9) and Hamilton (s/seater K3 4), crash. Kaye Don injured and MG mechanic Frankie

MG Racing and Rallying

Tayler killed testing Don's Magnette.

Le Mans 24-hour race: Eccles/ Martin (K3 Magnette 34) 4th on distance, 1st in 1100cc class; Ford/Baumer (K3 Magnette 33) 2nd overall before retiring; Maillard-Brune/Druck (Midget 53) retire after 30 laps; Anne Itier/Druck (P-type Midget 52) 17th on distance, 2nd in 100cc class.

RAC TT race at Dundrod: racing debut of NE Magnette. Winner Dodson (27) 465-mile (748.32km) on handicap at 74.65mph (120.13kph), beating Eddie Hall's 3669cc Bentley. Other NEs driven by Eyston (25), Handley (26) and Norman Black (28).

1935 500 Miles Race, Brooklands: 5th, 1st in class.

Albi Grand Prix, France: 4th.

Australian Grand Prix: 1st, 2nd, 3rd, 4th.

Bol d'Or 24 Hours Race, Montlhéry: 1st.

British Empire Trophy, Brooklands: 4th overall, 1st in class.

Centenary Grand Prix, Australia: 1st.

County Down Trophy Race, Ireland: 1st.

Coupe de l'Argent Race, Montlhéry: 2nd, 1st in class.

Craigantlet Hillclimb, Belfast: FTD.

Eifelrennen, Germany: 1st 2nd and 3rd in class.

GP des Frontières, Belgium: class win.

GPs de France, Montlhéry: class win.

Grand Prix d'Orléans: 2nd and 3rd.

Hill climbs: Feldberg, Grossglockner, La Turbie, Stelvio, Shelsley Walsh: class wins.

International Trophy Race, Brooklands: 3rd (1st in class), Team prize.

Junior Car Club International Trophy, Brooklands: four of the six R-types entered. Everitt/Malcolm Campbell 1st in class, 6th overall; Evans (38) 2nd in class, 7th overall; Black/Handley do not finish. Hall, Manby/Colegrove, and Lens (K3 Magnettes) 3rd, 8th and 11th.

Le Mans 24-hour race: 7 MGs entered, Eyston's 'Dancing Daughters' – six women in three P-type Midgets. Doreen Evans/Barbara Skinner (55) 25th, Joan Richmond/Mrs Simpson (56) 24th, Margaret Allan/Colleen Eaton (57) 26th. Baumer/Ford (39) and Hertzberger (41) in K3 Magnettes retire; Maillard-Brune/Druck (K3 Magnette 42) finish 9th and win class; Viale/Debille (Midget 58) retire at 98 laps with s/c problems.

Leinster Trophy Race, Ireland: 2nd and Team prize.

Nuffield Trophy Race, Donington: 3rd.

Phoenix Park 200 Miles Race, Ireland: 1st, 3rd and Team prize.

RAC Mannin Beg race: Eyston, Handley, Black, and Baird (R-types) fail to finish.

Southport 100 Miles Race: 2nd.

Welsh Rally: Premier award, Team prize.

1936 1500cc race, Circuit of Ceskobrodsky, Czechoslovakia: 1st. Circuit of Lochotin, Czechoslovakia: 1st.

500 Miles, Brooklands: two class wins.

Australian Tourist Trophy Race: 1st.

Bol d'Or 24 Hours Race, Montlhéry: 2nd, 1st in class.

Centenary 100 Miles Race, Australia: 1st.

County Down Trophy Race, Ireland: 2nd.

GP des Frontières, Belgium: 1st.

Hill climbs: class wins at Bussaco, Craigantlet, Feldberg, La Turbie, Mount Washington, Ratisbona, Santarem.

Kimberley 100 Miles, S Africa: 1st.

Limerick Race, Ireland: 1st.

MCC Trials Championship: 1st.

Phoenix Park 200 Miles Race: 1st and 3rd.

Southport 100 Miles Race: 1st.

MG Racing and Rallying

1937   Australian Grand Prix: 1st and 2nd.
Cork Grand Prix, Ireland: 1st.
Donington Park 12 Hours Race: Team prize.
GPs de France, Montlhéry: class win.
International Trophy Race, Brooklands: 3rd, 1st in class.
Kimberley 100 Miles Race, S Africa: 1st.
Le Mans 24-hour race: Dorothy Stanley-Turner/Enid Riddell (P-type Midget 54) finish 16th 1294.08 miles (2082.56km).
Leinster Trophy Race, Ireland: 2nd.
MCC Trials Championship: 1st.
Phillip Island Race, Australia: 1st.
Phoenix Park 200 Miles Race, Dublin: 3rd.
Rand 120 Miles Race, S Africa: 2nd; Rand 170 Miles Race: 3rd.
Ulster Trophy Race, Northern Ireland: 2nd and 3rd.

1938   200 Miles Race, Brooklands: class win.
Alexandria Bay Race, USA: 1st and 2nd.
Australian Grand Prix: 3rd.
Bol d'Or 24 Hours Race, Montlhéry: 2nd, 1st in class.
British Empire Trophy Race, Brooklands: class win.
Brooklands International Trophy: 4th.

Circuit of Ireland Trial: 1st.
Derbyshire Trial: 1st and Team award.
Le Mans 24-hour race: Itier/Bonneau (streamlined P-type 49) 12th, 4th in class.
Elsie Wisdom/Dobson (Midget 50) retire after 48 laps.
Limerick Race: 1st.
New South Wales 300 Miles Trial: 1st 2nd 3rd and 4th.
Paris/St Raphael Rally, France: 1st.
Phoenix Park Handicap Race: 2nd.
Scottish Rally: 1st 2nd and 3rd in class.
South Australia 50 Miles Race: 1st and 3rd.
South Australia Grand Prix: 2nd and 3rd.
Southport President's Cup Race: 1st.

1939   Australian Grand Prix: 1st.
Bol d'Or 24 Hours Race: Class win.
GP des Frontières, Belgium: 3rd.
Le Mans 24-hour race: Collier brothers (P-type Midget 36) 'Leonides' built from one of the 1935 Le Mans cars. Miles Collier/Lewis Welch retire after 63 laps, 528 miles (849.71km); Bonneau/Mathieu (Itier's rebodied Midget 47) retire after 40 laps.
Leinster Trophy Race, Ireland: 2nd.
Phoenix Park Handicap: 2nd and 3rd.

1945   Coupe de la Libération Race, Paris: 2nd.

1946   Argentine 100 Hours Trial: 1st.
Coupe du Salon Race, Paris: 2nd.
New South Wales GP: 1st 2nd and 3rd.

1947   Australian Grand Prix: 1st 2nd and 3rd.
Chappell Cup, Keller Cup and Colmore Trophy Trials: 1st.
Circuit of Ireland Trial: 1st and 2nd.
Highland Three Days Rally: class win.
Hill climbs: Ballinascorney and Sierre/Montana Hillclimbs: FTD.
Lyons Cup Race, France: 5th.
O'Boyle Trophy Race, Curragh, Ireland: 1st 2nd and 3rd.
Prix de la Blècherette Race, Lausanne, Switzerland: 1st 2nd and 3rd.
Rheims Cup Race, France: 6th, 7th and fastest lap.
Ulster Trophy Handicap Race, Ballyclare, N Ireland: 1st and 2nd.
Watkins Glen, New York: 11 MGs take part in first race, two driven by Sam and Miles Collier.

1948   Australian Grand Prix: 2nd.
Berne Sports Car GP, Switzerland: 1st.
Hill climbs: Enniskerry, Killakee: FTD.
Leinster Trophy Race: 2nd and 3rd.
O'Boyle Trophy Race, Curragh, Ireland:

1st and 2nd.
Vue des Alpes hillclimb, Switzerland: 1st 2nd and 3rd in class.
Watkins Glen GP, USA: 3rd.

1949 Alpine Trial: 1st and 2nd in class and Coupe des Dames.
Berne Sports Car GP, Switzerland: 2nd.
Circuit of Ireland Trial: Team prize.
Fairfield Memorial Trophy Race, S Africa: 2nd.
Le Mans 24-hour race. George Phillips/ 'Curly' Dryden (TC Midget) disqualified after giving mechanic illegal lift to pits.
Leinster Trophy Race, Ireland: 1st.
Lisbon Rally, Portugal: 3rd in class.
O'Boyle Trophy Race, Curragh, Ireland: 1st 2nd and 3rd.
Spa/Francorchamps 24 Hours Race, Belgium: 2nd in class.

1950 Alpine Trial: class win and Team award.
Blandford Camp: prototype TD Mark II (EX 171) driven by Dick Jacobs beats HRGs.
Champion Trophy Race, Dundrod, N Ireland: 3rd.
Dundrod TF three-hour race: 3 'FRX' TD.
Mark IIs beat HRG opposition, finishing

1st 2nd and 3rd in class.
Fairfield Memorial Trophy Race, S Africa: 1st and 3rd.
Le Mans 24-hour race: Phillips/ Winterbottom (MG TC) 18th overall at 72.82mph (1 17.19kph), 2nd in class.
Leinster Trophy Race: 2nd and 3rd.
O'Boyle Trophy Race: 1st and 3rd.
Palm Beach 1300 Rally: 1st and 3rd.
Palm Beach Races: 1st and 2nd in class.
Palm Springs Sports Car Race: 2nd and 3rd.
Production Car Race, Silverstone: 2nd 3rd and 4th in class.
RAC Tourist Trophy Race, N Ireland: 1st 2nd and 3rd in class.
Sebring: first race at Hendrick Field, Sebring, Florida. Six hours. Van Driel (TC 1) 1st in class, 5th overall; O'Hare/ Milliken (TC 3) 2nd in class, 6th overall; Keith/ Wilder (TC 25) 2nd in class G, 9th overall; Viall/Charlwood (TD 22) 4th in class, 13th overall; Brundage/Cook (TD 32) do not finish.
Silverstone production car race: TD Mark IIs driven by Dick Jacobs, George Phillips and Ted Lund, 2nd 3rd and 4th in class.

Van Riebeck Trophy Race, S Africa: 1st and 3rd.
Westhampton Races, USA: 1st and 3rd.

1951 Alpine Trial: 3rd in class.
Australian Jubilee Grand Prix: 3rd.
British Empire Trophy Race, Isle of Man: 2nd and 3rd in class.
Champion Trophy Race, Dundrod: 3rd.
Circuit of Ireland Trial: 1st.
Daily Express Rally: 1st.
Interlaken Rally, Switzerland: 1st.
Isle of Wight Rally: 1st 2nd and 3rd in class, Team prize and Coupe des Dames.
Lakeland '300' Rally, USA: 1st.
Le Mans 24-hour race: Phillips/Rippon (TD Midget 43) 116mph (186.68kph) on Mulsanne Straight but retire with engine problems.
Leinster Trophy Handicap Race, Ireland: 3rd and Team prize; Leinster Trophy Scratch Race: 3rd.
Morecambe Rally: 2nd and 2 class wins.
Paris/St Raphael Rally: 3rd (1st in class).
Production Car Race, Silverstone: class win.
RAC Rally of Great Britain: 1st and 3rd in class.

MG Racing and Rallying

Rallye des Neiges, France: 2nd.
San Diego Road Race, USA: class win.
Scottish Rally: 2 class wins, Team prize.
Sebring 12-hour race: Ash/Van Driel (1390cc MG MkII Special 4) 2nd in class, 6th overall; Thompson/Kinchloe, Hansgen/Pearsall, O'Hare/Allen (TD Midgets 2, 52 and 5) 3rd 4th and 6th in class (8th 10th and 12th overall), Team prize.

1952 Circuit of Ireland Trial: 1st, Team award.
Circuit of Munster Rally, Ireland: 1st.
Daily Express Rally: 1st 2nd and 3rd in class, Team award.
Edenvale Sports Car Race, Canada: 1st 2nd and 3rd.
Falkirk Rally, Scotland: 1st.
Helsingland Sports Car Race, Sweden: 1st.
Johore Production Car Race, Malaya: 1st 2nd 3rd and 4th.
Leinster Trophy Handicap Race, Ireland: 2nd and 3rd.
O'Boyle Trophy Race, Curragh: 3rd.
Production Car Race, Silverstone: class win.
Sebring 12 Hours Race, USA: Team prize.
Tulip Rally, Holland: 3rd, 1st in class.

Ulster Trophy 1300cc Race, Dundrod: 1st.
1953 Australian Grand Prix: 2nd and 3rd.
British Empire Trophy Pace, Isle of Man: 3rd in class.
Canyon Rally, Canada: 1st.
Daily Express Rally: 1st 2nd and 3rd in two classes, Team award.
Delaware Valley Trophy Race, USA: 2nd and 3rd.
Evian/Mont Blanc Rally: 3rd in class.
Falkirk Rally, Scotland: 1st.
Great American Mountain Rally, USA: 1st, two class wins.
Johore Production Car Race, Malaya: 1st 2nd and 3rd in class.
Morecambe Rally: class win, Team award.
Omaha National Sports Car Race, USA: 2nd and 3rd.
Production Car Race, Silverstone: 1st and 3rd in class.
RAC Coronation Rally: YB saloons (149, 150 and 151). Geoff Holt 2nd in class, 15th overall; Len Shaw 1st in class, 6th overall; G Holt unplaced.
RAC Rally of Great Britain: 1st 2nd and 3rd in class.
RAC Tourist Trophy Race, N Ireland:

class win.
Rally to the Midnight Sun, Sweden: class win.
Sam Collier Memorial Trophy Race, USA: Class win.
Sebring 12-hour race: 1389cc MG special (4) of Ash/Ahrens 2nd in class, 13th overall; Shields/McKinsley (TD Midget 53) 3rd in class, 15th overall; Wellenburg/Wonder (TD 42) 4th in class, 16th overall; MG specials Allen/Longworth (44) 5th in class, 19th overall; Paterson/Brundage (14) 7th in class, 28th overall; Leibensperger /Class (61) 36th overall.
Circuit of Ireland Trial: 3rd in class, Team Award and Ladies award.
Tulip Rally, Holland: Class win.
Winter Handicap Race, S Africa: 1st and 2nd.
1954 Australian Grand Prix: 2nd.
Bogota Sports Car Race, Colombia: 1st 2nd and 3rd in class.
British Redex Rally: 1st and 2nd in class.
Circuit of Ireland Trial: 2nd and 3rd and Team award.
False Bay Production Car Race, S Africa: 1st.

MG Racing and Rallying

Leinster Trophy Handicap Race: 1st.
Mount Druitt 24 Hours Race, Australia: class win.
Production Car Race, Silverstone: class win.
RAC Rally of Great Britain: class win.
Sebring 12-hour race: Ehrman/Allen 5th in class, 11th overall in MG 'Motto' special (54). MG specials driven by Herzog/Lansing (99), Derujinsky/Underwood (100), and Franklin Curtis (59) dnf.
Westhampton Production Car: class win.

1955   Daily Express Production Touring Car Race, Silverstone: Jacobs, Foster and Waller (ZA Magnettes) 1st 2nd and 3rd.
Dundrod TT: Flockhart/Lockett (prototype twin-cam EX182 34) retire with ignition trouble; Lund/Stoop (1500 36) retire; Fairman/Wilson (1500 35) 4th in class.
Le Mans 24-hour race: three EX 182 prototypes. Miles/Lockett (41) 12th, Lund/Waefflerand (64) 17th, Jacobs/Flynn (42) crashes near Maison Blanche at 6.39pm, 2° hours into the race, minutes after Mercedes crash of Pierre Levegh.
MCC Hastings Rally: 1st and Team award.

Monte Carlo Rally: 4 ZA Magnette. Holt/Asbury/Brookes (49 'Aramis') 178th; Holt/Collinson/Cave (58 'Athos') 237th; Len Shaw/Brown/ Finnemore (36 'Porthos') 202nd; D'Artagnan' driven by Chambers.
Montlhéry publicity endurance runs: Ken Wharton (MGA) 102.54 miles (165.02km) in an hour; John Gott (racing MGA) 112.36mph (180.82kph), tyre bursting at three quarters distance requiring a re-start.
RAC Rally of Great Britain: Pat Moss/Pat Faichney (TF 193) drive through heavy snow, 3rd in ladies' competition. Holt/Brookes (Magnette 198) 1st in class.
Scottish Rally: 1st 2nd and 3rd in class, Team prize.
Sebring 12-hour race: TF debut. Ash/Black (76) 8th in class, 38th overall; Ryan/Kinne (77) 9th in class, 39th overall.
Settlers' Handicap Race, S Africa: 2nd and 3rd.
Van Riebeck Trophy Race, S Africa: 2nd.
Alpine Trial: 3rd in class, Coupe des Dames.

1956   Autosport Production Sports Car Championship: winner.

Cape Grand Prix, S Africa: 1st.
Circuit of Ireland Trial: Team award.
Ladies' European Rally Championship: winner.
Liège-Rome-Liège Rally: 4 MGAs (1489cc B-series) entered. Milne/Bensted-Smith (15) 7th in class, 14th overall; Burgess/Croft-Pearson (24) retire with sump damage; Mitchell/Anne Hall (38) 26th overall, 2nd in Ladies' class; Gott/Tooley (75) 6th in class, 13th overall.
Lyons/Charbonnières Rally, France: Coupe des Dames .
Mille Miglia, Brescia: Nancy Mitchell/Pat Faichney (MGA 227) 3rd in class, 74th overall, Mitchell highest placed female 1624km (1009.13 miles) in 15hr 7min 28sec. Scott-Russell/Haig in (MGA 229) 2nd in class.
Monte Carlo Rally: two alloy-panelled MG Magnette ZAs. Grant/ Norman Davis/ Cliff Davis (34) retire with electrical problems; Susan Hindermarsh/Nancy Mitchell/Doreen Reece (327) finish 59th overall, 3rd in Ladies' class.
RAC Rally of Great Britain: 1st 2nd 3rd in class.

MG Racing and Rallying

Rallye des Alpes: Mitchell/ Faichney (MGA 227) 3rd in class, 15th overall, win Ladies' prize; Milne/Johns (MGA 314) 4th in class; Shephard/Williamson (MGA 308) 5th in class.

Scottish Rally: 2nd in class, Ladies Award.

Sebring 12-hour race: three-car team of white MGAs prepared by BMC Competitions Department at Abingdon. Driven by Americans, win Team prize. Kinchloe/Spittler (50) 4th in class, and 19th; Ash/Ehrman (49) 5th in class, 20th overall; Allen/Van Driel (51) 22nd overall.

Tulip Rally: Mitchell/Reece Magnette (147) excluded for non-standard alloy panels.

1957   Ladies' European Rally Championship: winner.

Leinster Trophy Handicap Race: 2nd.

Liège-Rome-Liège Rally: Mitchell/Johns (MGA 5) 9th in class, 16th, win Ladies' prize; Milne/Shepherd (24) retire due to accident; Gott/Tooley (MGA 48) 8th in class, 14th overall.

Lyons/Charbonnières Rally, France: Coupe des Dames.

Mille Miglia, Italy: 2nd and 3rd in class.

Production Car Race, Silverstone: 1st and 2nd in class.

Sebring 12 Hours Race, USA: 1st and 2nd in class and Team prize.

Settlers' Handicap Race, S Africa: 3rd.

1958   Autosport Three Hours, Snetterton: 3rd.

BRSCC Saloon Car Championship: class win.

Liège-Rome-Liège: Gott/Brookes (MGA Twin Cam 78) 9th overall (first factory Twin Cam entry in international rallying).

RAC Tourist Trophy Race, Goodwood: 3rd in class.

1959   Acropolis Rally: 2nd and 3rd in class.

Autosport Production Sports Car Championship: class win.

Circuit of Ireland Trial: 3rd in class.

Grand Touring Race, Silverstone: 1st 2nd and 3rd in class.

Le Mans 24-hour race: Lund/Escott (MGA Twin Cam 33) retire in 21st hour.

Pietermaritzburg Six Hours Race: 2nd and 3rd on index.

Rand Nine Hours Race, S Africa: 3rd.

Sebring 12-hour race: four Twin Cams entered by Hambro with BMC Canada, Ehrman/Saidel (28) 2nd in class, 27th

overall; Parkinson/Dalton (29) 3rd in class, 34th overall; Flaherty/Pickering/ Decker (30) 4th in class, 45th overall.

1960   Autosport Production Sports Car Championship: class win.

Autosport Three Hours, Snetterton: 3rd.

Circuit of Ireland Trial: 2nd in class.

Le Mans 24-hour race: Lund/Escott (32) 1st in class, 12th on distance at 91.12mph (146.64kph).

Phoenix Park Handicap Race: 2nd, 3rd.

RAC Tourist Trophy Race, Goodwood: 3rd in class.

Rallye Deutschland: 2nd in class.

Sebring 12 Hours Race, USA: 3rd in class.

1961   Le Mans 24-hour race: Lund/Olthoff (58) retire after 15 laps.

Monte Carlo Rally: Donald and Erle Morley (MGA 1600 Coupe 314) 1st in class, 28th overall; Riley/Hughes (Midget (44) 1st in class, 33rd overall.

RAC Rally: 1st and 2nd in class.

Sebring 12-hour race: Parkinson/Flaherty (MGA 1600 De Luxe coupe 44) 1st in class, 14th overall; Riley/Whitmore (43) 2nd in class, 16th overall.

1962   Bad Homburg Rally, Germany: class win.

MG Racing and Rallying

Brands Hatch Six Hours Race: class win.
Dunlop Hillclimb, Singapore: class win.
Liège-Rome-Liège Rally: Gott/Shepherd (MGA 1600 Mark II Coupe 49) retire.
Monte Carlo Rally: two class wins.
RAC Rally: Rev Rupert Jones/David Seigle-Morris (1100 11) the only MG entry, retire with broken piston.
Sebring 12-hour race: Ecurie Safety Fast MGA 1600 Mk II De Luxe Coupes. Sears/Hedges (51) 4th in class, 16th overall; Olthoff/Whitmore (52) 6th in class, 20th overall; Flaherty/Parkinson (63) 5th in class, 17th overall.
Tulip Rally: Aaltonen/Palm (MGA 1600 Coupe 11) 1st in class, 15th overall; Gold/Hughes (Midget 59) 3rd in class, 38th overall.

1963 Autosport Production Sports Car Championship: 3rd, 1st in class.
Grand Touring Race, Silverstone: 1st and 2nd in class.
Le Mans 24-hour race: Alan Hutcheson/Paddy Hopkirk (MGB 31) crash at Mulsanne but finish 12th overall at 91.96mph (147.99kph).
Leinster Trophy Race, Ireland: 3rd.

Monte Carlo Rally: Rev Rupert Jones/Phillip Morgan (Midget 158) 1st in class; Raymond Baxter/McMillen (1100 268) 4th in class.
Nürburgring 1000 Km: 2nd and 3rd in class.
Riverside Sports Car Races, USA: six class wins.
Sebring 12-hour race: Jim Parkinson/Jack Flaherty (MGB 47), Christabel Carlisle/Denise McCluggage (MGB 48) retire.
Tour de France Automobile: Hedges/Sprinzel (MGB 155) retire after accident.

1964 Austrian Alpine Rally: 1st and 2nd in class.
Grand Touring Race, Silverstone: class win.
Le Mans 24-hour race. Hopkirk/Hedges (MGB 37, BMO 541B) 19th overall, 99.95mph (160.85kph).
Monte Carlo Rally: Don and Erle Morley (MGB 83) win GT class, 17th overall.
Nürburgring 1000 Kilometres Race, Germany: 1st and 2nd in class.
RAC Rally: Fitzpatrick/Handley (MGB 177) retire after accident; Mayman/Domleo (MGB 39) retire with clutch problems.

Sebring 12-hour race: Leslie/Dalton (MGB 47) 3rd in class, 17th overall; Adams/Brennan 4th in class, 22nd overall.
Spa-Sofia-Liège Rally: no MGBs finish.
Tour de France Automobile: Hedges/Sprinzel (MGB 153) retire with head gasket failure.
Warwick Farm Sports Car Race, NSW, Australia: 1st.

1965 Austrian Gold Cup Rally: 1st.
Brands Hatch 1000 Miles Race: 1st, and 1st 2nd and 3rd in class.
Bridgehampton 500 Miles Race, USA: 4th, 1st in class.
GT Constructors' Championship: Midget 2nd in class; MGB 3rd in class.
Kingsway Trophy Race, Phoenix Park, Dublin: 1st 2nd 3rd 4th and 5th.
Le Mans 24-hour race: Hopkirk/Hedges (MGB 39) 11th out of 14 finishers, at 98.25mph (158.11 kph), 2nd GT 2-litre.
Sebring 12-hour race: Brennan/Morrell (MGB 49) 2nd in class, 10th prototype, 25th overall; Pricard/Pease (MGB 48) 6th in class, 10th GT, 32nd overall. Mac/Hedges (Midget 68) 1st in class, 12th GT, 26th overall.

MG Racing and Rallying

Targa Florio: Hopkirk/Hedges (Midget GT 'Jacobs' coupe 44) 2nd in class, 11th overall.

1966 Austrian Alpine Rally: 2nd in class.
Brands Hatch 500 Miles Race: 3rd, two class wins.
Circuit of Ireland Trial: class win.
Circuit of Mugello Race, Italy: 3rd GT.
Class G Championship, USA: 1st.
Marathon de la Route 84-hour race at the Nürburgring: Vernaeve/Hedges ('Old Faithful' 47) outright winners after 5260 miles (8464.92km); Roger Enever/Alec Poole (MGB 46) retire.
Montlhéry 1000 Km Race: 2nd and 3rd in class.
Scottish National Speed Championship: 1st.
Sebring 12-hour race: Manton/Mac/Brown (MGB 59) 1st in class, 3rd GT, 17th overall.
Spa 1000 Km Race, Belgium: 1st GT, 1st in class.
Surfers Paradise 12 Hours Race, Queensland, Australia: class win.
Targa Florio race. Makinen/Rhodes ('Old Faithful' 64) 1st GT, 9th overall. Hedges/

Handley (MGB 66) 2nd 2-litre GT, 3rd in GT class.

1967 Amasco Racing Championship: 1st.
Berglandfahrt Rally, Austria: 1st.
London Rally: class win.
Monza 1000 Km Race: class win.
Rallye de Styrie Orientale, Austria: 1st.
Sebring 12-hour race: first MGB GT entry. Makinen/Rhodes in 'Old Faithful' (48) with 1824cc 8-series engine 3rd GT, 12th overall; Hopkirk/ Hedges (MGB GT 30) with 2004cc B-series engine 1st in class, 3rd prototype, 11th overall.
Spa Sports Car GP, Belgium: class win.
Targa Florio, Sicily: Hopkirk/ Makinen (lightweight MGB GT) 3rd in class, 9th overall.

1968 Sebring 12-hour race: Hopkirk/Hedges in 'Mabel' (MGC GTS 44) 1st in class, 3rd prototype, 10th overall; Rodriguez/McDaniel/Bill Brack (MGB GT 66) 5th in class, 18th overall; Truitt/Canfield (Midget actually Austin-Healey Sprite) 1st in class, 1st sports car, 15th overall; Waldron/Gammon/Scott (MGB 67) 7th in class, 31st overall.
Marathon de la Route: Fall/Fledges/

Vernaeve (MGC GTS 4) 6th overall.
Targa Florio, Sicily: 2nd Sports.
84 Hours Marathon, Nürburgring, Germany: class win.

1969 Sebring 12-hour race: Hopkirk/Hedges (MGC GTS 35) 9th prototype, 15th overall; Hill/Brack (MGC GTS 36) 15th prototype, 34th overall; Truitt/Blackburn (MGB GT 62) 8th GT, 28th overall; Colgate/Parks (MGB 99) 5th in class, 32nd overall; Waldron/Scott/Donley (MGB 64) 6th in class, 38th overall

1970 Sebring 12-hour race: Belperche/Gammon/Mummery (MGB 57) 25th overall, Scott/Lanier/Houser (MGB 58) next.

1971 Sebring 12-hour race. Neither MGB (51 and 52) finishes.

1978 Sebring 12-hour race. Kleinschmidt/Culpepper/Koch (MGB 52) 14th in class, 30th overall.

1984 MG Metro 6R4 competition debut in a rally in Yorkshire, driven by Tony Pond.

1985 MG Metro 6R4 homologated for its international rally debut on the RAC Rally.

1987 Group B rally cars banned from January, and planned Group S abandoned.

MG Speed Records

Year	Month	Driver(s)	Car	Place	Class	Records
1930	December	Eyston	EX 120 u/s	Montlhéry	750cc	3 at max 87.3mph (140.49kph)
1931	February	Eyston	EX 120 s/c	Montlhéry	750cc	5 at max 97.07mph (156.21kph)
	February	Eyston	EX 120 s/c	Montlhéry	750cc	4 at max 103.13mph (165.97kph)
	March	Eyston	EX 120 s/c	Brooklands	750cc	2 at max 97.09mph (156.25kph)
	September	Eyston	EX 120 s/c	Montlhéry	750cc	101.1mph (162.7kph)
	September	Eldridge	EX 127 s/c	Montlhéry	750cc	110.28mph (177.47kph)
1932	February	Eyston	EX 127 s/c	Pendine	750cc	118.39mph (190.52kph)
	November	Hall	Midget s/c	Brooklands	750cc	2 at max 74.74 mph (120.28kph)
	December	Eyston	EX 127 s/c	Montlhéry	750cc	2 at max 120.56mph (194.02kph)
	December	Eyston, Denly, Wisdom	J3 s/c & EX127 s/c	Montlhéry	750cc	All remaining Class H records
1933	September	Eyston	EX 127 s/c	Brooklands	750cc	3 at max 106.72mph (171.74kph)
	October	Eyston, Wisdom, Denly, Yallop	L2 Magna u/s	Montlhéry	1100cc	Various max 80.49mph (129.53kph)
	Oct/Nov	Denly	EX 127 s/c	Montlhéry	750cc	11 at max 128.63mph (207kph)
1934	March	Horton	K3 s/c s/seater	Brooklands	1100cc	6 inc 117.03 miles (188.34km) in 1 hour
	May	Horton	C-type s/c s/seater	Brooklands	750cc	6 at max 111.74mph (179.82kph)
	July	Horton	K3 s/c s/seater	Brooklands	1100cc	83.2 mph (133.89kph)
	August	Everitt	Q-type s/c	Brooklands	750cc	2 at max 79.88mph (128.55kph)
	October	Everitt	Q-type s/c	Brooklands	750cc	2 at max 85.59mph (137.74kph)
	October	Eyston	EX 135 s/c	Montlhéry	(s/c) 1100cc	12 at max 128.69mph (207.1kph)
	December	Maillard-Brune, Druck	Q-type s/c	Montlhéry	750cc	Various at max 76.30mph (122.79kph)
1935	May	Kohlrausch	EX 127 s/c	Gyon	750cc	4 at max 130.51mph (210.03kph)

MG Speed Records

1936	October	Kohlrausch	EX 127 s/c	Frankfurt	750cc	3 at max 140.6mph (226.27kph)
	December	Hertzberger	K3 s/c	Montlhéry	1100cc	3 at max 109.74mph (176.60kph)
1937	June	Gardner	ex-Horton s/c K3 s/seater	Frankfurt	1100cc	2 at max 142.63mph (229.54kph)
	June	Gardner	ex-Horton s/c K3 s/seater	Montlhéry	1100cc	5 at max 130.52mph (210.05kph)
	October	Gardner	ex-Horton s/c K3 s/seater	Frankfurt	1100cc	4 at max 148.8mph (239.46kph)
1938	November	Gardner	Gardner-MG s/c	Frankfurt	1100cc	2 at max 187.62mph (301.94kph)
1939	May	Gardner	Gardner-MG s/c	Dessau	1100cc	3 at max 203.5mph (327.5kph)
	June	Gardner	Gardner-MG s/c	Dessau	1500cc	3 at max 204.2mph (328.62kph)
1946	October	Gardner	Gardner-MG s/c	Jabbeke	750cc	3 at max 159.151mph (256.12kph)
1947	July	Gardner	Gardner-MG s/c	Jabbeke	500cc	4 at max 118.061mph (190.00kph)
1949	September	Gardner	Gardner-MG s/c	Jabbeke	500cc	3 at max 154.86mph (249.22kph)
1950	July	Gardner	Gardner-MG s/c	Jabbeke	350cc	3 at max 121.09mph (194.87kph)
1951	August	Gardner	Gardner-MG s/c TD	Utah	1500cc	6 at max 137.4mph (221.12kph)
1952	August	Gardner	Gardner-MG s/c TD	Utah	1500cc	2 at max 189.5mph (304.96kph)
1954	August	Eyston, Miles	EX179 u/s TF	Utah	1500cc	8 at max 153.69mph (247.33kph)
1956	August	Miles, Lockett	EX179 u/s Twin Cam	Utah	1500cc	16 at max 170.15mph (273.82kph)
1957	August	Ash, Wisdom	EX179 u/s A-series	Utah	1100cc	3 at max 118.13mph (190.11kph)
	August	Ash, P Hill	EX179 s/c A-series	Utah	1100cc	6 at max 143.47mph (230.89kph)
	August	Moss	EX181 s/c Twin Cam	Utah	1500cc	5 at max 245.64mph (395.31kph)
1959	September	Wisdom, Ehrman, Leavens	EX219 s/c A-series	Utah	1100cc	15 at max 146.95mph (236.49kph)
	September	P Hill	EX181 big s/c Twin Cam	Utah	2000cc	6 at max 254.91mph (410.23kph)
1997	August	Kilbourne	MG EXF 1433cc	Utah	1100-1500cc	217.4mph (349.8/kph)

Picture Credits

Illustrating every MG has depended on the generosity of individuals and MG clubs as well as commercial archives. Our thanks go to all those who have loaned in some cases quite valuable material, including the following:

Aston Martin p229 both.

F Body p39.

D Cocup / Enever personal album pp11, 14, 15, 17, 19, 52, 53, 55 both, 71 both, 83 top, 88, 89, 90, 105, 106, 107 both, 111 top, 137, 300, 301.

E S Dymock pp1, 10, 30, 34 top, 36 left, 37 right, 41 top, 47 bottom, 50, 95 top, 116, 144, 145, 159 left, 194, 195 all, 248, 251 both, 288, 291, 299.

G Harris pp2, 44, 45 both.

Magna Press Photographic Library pp16, 31, 41, 47 bottom, 61, 79 both, 80, 81 left, 91 top, 97, 101, 103, 121 right, 123 left, 125 top, 133, 141, 155, 157 right, 162, 165, 169, 175, 191, 202, 284, 285, 289.

National Motor Museum, Beaulieu p8.

R W Stanbury pp9, 13, 18, 40, 41 middle & bottom, 43 both, 49 both, 62, 63, 64, 67, 69, 73 bottom, 75 all, 77, 84, 85 bottom, 110, 113 top left, 114, 115 middle and right, 124, 131 right, 142, 143 right, 148, 149 both, 160, 161 top and bottom, 187 left and bottom, 231 left, 287.

R Monk (MG Owners Club) pp57, 59, 73 top, 83 bottom, 85 top, 87, 91 right, 110, 113 left, 115 left, 121 left, 125 right, 127, 143 left, 151, 163, 177 both, 181 left, 185, 187 top, 189, 193, 201 right, 203 top, 207 right, 209, 211, 213, 215, 217, 221, 223 right, 225, 227 left and right.

A Roberts pp95 left, 99, 139 both, 196, 237 both, 247 both.

Commissioned photography was by Peter Burn.

Acknowledgments

The publishers thank Kevin Howe, chief executive officer of MG Rover, and his staff; in particular Gordon Poynter, Greg Allport, and Kevin Jones for their help in making this book possible. Nothing contributes to knowledge of any make so much as driving the cars, and for that the author has generations of public relations officials of MG, BMC, and their successors to thank for making available test cars of every MG since the 1950s. His thanks also go to those MG owners who have enabled him to take the wheel of cars made in the thirty years before that.

MG cars are so well documented that the publishers' quest for accuracy has been challenging. We have consulted widely to try and get things right, and we are grateful to all the MG clubs, in particular to Roche Bentley, Richard Monk, and Richard Ladds of the MG Owners' Club for their encouragement and help, especially in our quest for photographs. Rob Gammage and Peter Browning of the MG Car Club, Geoff Radford, Harry Crutchley of the MG Octagon Car Club, and members of the Early MG Society were equally supportive of yet another MG book to add to the wealth of material available.

Roger Stanbury, who is not only an early MG owner and Vintage Register chairman but also Dove Publishing's solicitor, has been of immense help and support, providing critical comment at every stage of production. He has shared his invaluable contacts with many MG authorities on whose experience we have drawn, including Darrell Cocup with his memorabilia concerning John Thornley and Syd Enever.

Authors Phil Jennings and Robin Barraclough, whose 'Oxford to Abingdon' is the definitive work, Mike Hawke whose 'K3 Dossier' has been invaluable, and Malcolm Green, with his patient advice and endless selection of Magna Press photographic archives, have been freely consulted, and we are also indebted to Michael Bowler. Among other MG historians whose work has been invaluable are David Knowles, the post-1945 equivalent of Jennings and Barraclough, and Andrew Roberts, who kindly read the finished manuscript with the benefit of his long experience of MG.

Included in the photographic sources we used, credited separately, was the National Motor Museum at Beaulieu. As with all Dove Publishing books, our thanks are due to our production consultant David Bann of Landmark and Andrew Barron of Cloth Hall Studios for the jacket design. Administration and book design were by Ruth Dymock.

Bibliography

Combat, Barré Lyndon, William Heinemann London, 1933 Circuit Dust, Barré Lyndon, John Miles, 1934 Grand Prix, Barré Lyndon, John Miles 1935; Wheelspin, More Wheelspin, Wheelspin Abroad, CAN May; Racing Round the World, Count Giovani Lurani; Motor Racing and Record-Breaking, George Eyston and Barré Lyndon; Safety Last, George Eyston; Fastest on Earth, George Eyston; Magic MPH, Lt Col ATG Gardner, Motor Racing Publications, 1951; The Life of Lord Nuffield, PWS Andrews, E Brunner, Basil Blackwell Oxford, 1955; Maintaining the Breed, John Thornley, Motor Racing Publications London, 1950-1956; The MG Companion, Kenneth Ullyett, Stanley Paul, 1960; Out on a Wing, Sir Miles Thomas, Michael Joseph London, 1964; The Bullnose and Flatnose Morris, L Jarman & R Barraclough, David & Charles 1965; MG Magnette K3, Wilson McComb, Profile Publications, Leatherhead, Surrey, 1966; MG 18/80, Wilson McComb, Profile Publications, 1966; MG M-type, Wilson McComb, Profile Publications, 1967; The Bullnose Morris Cowley, L Jarman RI Barraclough, Profile Publications 1967; The MG Story, JN Wherry, Chilton Books, 1967; The Magic of MG, Mike Allison, Dalton Watson 1972; MG The T Series, Richard Knudson (ed) Motorcars Unlimited, Savannah, Ga, USA, 1973; MG The Sports Car America Loved First, and MG: The Sports Car. Richard L Knudson, Motorcars Unlimited Oneonta NY, 1975; The Bullnose and Flatnose Morris, Lytton Jarman & Robin Barraclough, 1976; An MG Experience, Dick Jacobs, Transport Bookman Publications London, 1976; The MGA, MGB, and MGC, Graham Robson, Motor Racing Publications London, 1977; MG and Austin Healey Spridgets, Chris Harvey; The MG A, B, & C, Chris Harvey; The Immortal T Series, Chris Harvey, Oxford Illustrated Press, 1977; MG, Wilson McComb, Osprey London 1978 (Story of MG Sports Car, Dent, 1972 revised); British Leyland, The truth about the cars, Jeff Daniels, Osprey, 1980; The T-Series MGs, Graham Robson, Motor Racing Publications London, 1980. The Sprites and Midgets, Eric Dymock, Motor Racing Publications London, 1981; MG Past and Present, AF Rivers Fletcher, Gentry Books, 1981; MGB, Wilson McComb, Osprey London, 1982; MGA, Wilson McComb, Osprey London, 1983 MG File, Martin Buckley (Ed), Classic and Sportscar Bay View Books, Bideford, 1987; The Cars of BMC, Graham Robson, Motor Racing Publications, 1987; The MG Log, Peter Haining (Ed), Souvenir Press London 1988; The Kimber Centenary Book, Richard L Knudson (Ed) The New England MG T Register Oneonta NY, 1988; The Magic of the Marque, Mike Allison, Dalton Watson London 1989, (pb 1972, revised); Early MG, PL Jennings, PL Jennings, Llanbister, 1989; MG Sports Cars, Autocar archive, various publishers incl Hamlyn, Bay View, 1980s; Original MG T Series, Anders Ditlev Clausager, Bay View Books Bideford, 1989; Original MGB, Anders

Bibliography

Ditlev Clausager, Bay View Books; Original MGA, Anders Ditlev Clausager, Bay View Books; Original Sprite & Midget, Terry Horler, Bay View Books; Essential MG T-series Anders Ditlev Clausager, Bay View Books, 1989; MG Midget 1961-1979 and other Brooklands Books' compliations; MGB The Complete Story, Brian Laban, Crowood, 1990; MGB, Lindsay Porter, Haynes, 1992; MGB restoration and maintenance, Jim Tyler Osprey 1992; MG Midget and Austin-Healey Sprite restoration and maintenance, Jim Tyler Osprey 1993; K3 Dossier, Mike Hawke, Magna Press, Leatherhead, 1992; MGB Illustrated History, Jonathan Wood, Lionel Burrell, G T Foulis, Haynes, 1993; MG Gold Portfolio, Brooklands Books Ltd, Cobham, Surrey; Spriteley Years, John Sprinzel, Patrick Stephens, 1994 MG Road Cars Vol 1, 4 cylinder ohc 1929-1936, Malcolm Green, Magna 1994; The MG Collection, Richard Monk, Vol 1 pre-war models, Patrick Stephens 1994; The MG Collection, Richard Monk, Vol 2 post war models Patrick Stephens 1995; MG Trials cars, Roger F Thomas, Magna, 1995; MG V8 21 Years On: from launch to RV8, David A Knowles, Windrow and Greene 1995; Project Phoenix, The Birth of the MGF, Ian Adcock, Bloomsbury, 1996; MG Road Cars, Vol 2, 6 cylinder ohc 1931-1936, Malcolm Green, Magna 1997; MG Sports Cars, Malcolm Green, Bramley Books, 1997; Rallying in a works MG, Len Shaw, Magna, 1997; MG The Untold Story, David Knowles, Windrow & Green, 1997; MG Collectibles, Michael Ellman-Brown, Bay View Books, 1997; MG Photo-Archive 1945-1960, David A Knowles, Iconografix 1997; MG Photo-Archive 1961-1980, David A Knowles, Iconografix 1997; MG The Untold Story, David A Knowles, Windrow and Greene 1997; MG Britain's Favourite Sports Car, Malcolm Green, Haynes, 1998; Auto Architect, Gerald Palmer, Magna, 1998; MG from A to Z, Jonathan Wood, Motor Racing Publications, Croydon CR0 3RY 1998; Oxford to Abingdon, RL Barraclough and PL Jennings, Myrtle Publishing, Cwmfrain, 1998; MGs on Patrol, Andrea Green, Magna, Leatherhead, 1999; The Works MGs, Mike Allison & Peter Browning, Haynes, 2000; MG Saloon Cars, Anders Ditlev Clausager; MBG including MGC and MGB GT V8, David A Knowles, MBI 2000; MGF, David A Knowles, Haynes 2000.

Among the sources used in research were the author's archive collections of the Swiss annual Automobil Revue/Revue Automobile published by Hallwag, Automobile Year published by Editions J-R Piccard, Autocourse published by Hazleton, and also of The Motor, The Autocar, Autosport, Motor Sport, Classic Car, Classic & Sportscar, The Automobile, Safety Fast and Enjoying MG, Automobile Quarterly, and Veteran & Vintage, to all of whose proprietors motoring historians owe continuing thanks.

Index